The Godfathers of Horror Films

The Godfathers of Horror Films

Boris Karloff, Peter Cushing and Christopher Lee

Jennifer Selway

WHITE OWL
AN IMPRINT OF PEN & SWORD BOOKS LTD.
YORKSHIRE - PHILADELPHIA

First published in Great Britain in 2025 by
White Owl
An imprint of Pen & Sword Books Limited
Yorkshire – Philadelphia

Copyright © Jennifer Selway 2025

ISBN 978 1 39905 513 0

The right of Jennifer Selway to be identified as
Author of this Work has been asserted by her in accordance
with the Copyright, Designs and Patents Act 1988.

A CIP catalogue record for this book is
available from the British Library.

All rights reserved. No part of this book may be reproduced,
transmitted, downloaded, decompiled or reverse engineered in
any form or by any means, electronic or mechanical including
photocopying, recording or by any information storage and retrieval
system, without permission from the Publisher in writing. No part of
this book may be used or reproduced in any manner for the purpose
of training artificial intelligence technologies or systems.

Typeset by Mac Style
Printed in the UK by CPI Group (UK) Ltd, Croydon, CR0 4YY.

The Publisher's authorised representative in the EU for product
safety is Authorised Rep Compliance Ltd., Ground Floor,
71 Lower Baggot Street, Dublin D02 P593, Ireland.
www.arccompliance.com

For a complete list of Pen & Sword titles please contact

PEN & SWORD BOOKS LIMITED
47 Church Street, Barnsley, South Yorkshire, S70 2AS, England
E-mail: enquiries@pen-and-sword.co.uk
Website: www.pen-and-sword.co.uk
or
PEN AND SWORD BOOKS
1950 Lawrence Road, Havertown, PA 19083, USA
E-mail: uspen-and-sword@casematepublishers.com
Website: www.penandswordbooks.com

For Luke, Henry and Amelia

Contents

Introduction	viii
Timeline	x
Chapter 1 Youth	1
Chapter 2 Acting	19
Chapter 3 Hollywood	33
Chapter 4 Television	48
Chapter 5 Hammer	62
Chapter 6 Love	81
Chapter 7 Franchise	98
Chapter 8 War	114
Chapter 9 Monsters	134
Chapter 10 Downtime	154
Chapter 11 Afterlife	166
Chapter 12 The Films	175
Notes	200
Further Reading	201

Introduction

Boris Karloff – 1887–1969
Peter Cushing – 1913–1994
Christopher Lee – 1922–2015

This is a three-way biography – possibly a tri-biography. Boris Karloff, Peter Cushing and Christopher Lee have so much in common. They form a triumvirate of British stars who specialised in horror films, though their performances were often far superior to many of the films they made. Meanwhile, their attitude to the frequently derided horror genre was ambiguous to say the least. Their lives top and tail the twentieth century. What's more, these three actors embodied a kind of Englishness which was of its time and contributed to the success and texture of not only the horror films in which they appeared but also (in the case of Cushing and Lee) other movie franchises. They achieved fame at a time when celebrity culture – though it existed and had done since the golden days of Hollywood – was very different from what it is today. So there remain opaque and mysterious areas of their lives which are hard to fathom.

In this book I want to put the three men in context, set them against the background of what was going on at the time that they lived, enfold them in a social history. For as we move into the second quarter of the twenty-first century, the mindset of those who led creative lives in the twentieth century becomes ever more distant and foreign to us. The film industry was the most significant artistic endeavour of the twentieth century and one that has changed beyond all recognition in the twenty-first – though, thank goodness, we do all still go to the movies and catch an old film from time to time.

What sets horror apart from other cinema genres – westerns, musicals, gangster, noir etc – is the critical derision that until recently it routinely attracted. The films of Karloff, Cushing and Lee created a template for a kind of Gothic horror with literary roots which has since spun out into the many different sort of horror we recognise today – body horror, slasher, zombie, folk horror. They were the benign godfathers to a vast number of monstrous progeny.

Timeline

1887	William Pratt born in Camberwell, 23 November.
1897	Bram Stoker's novel *Dracula* is published.
1899	Start of the Boer War.
1909	William Pratt emigrates to Montreal, Canada.
1912	Universal Pictures is founded in Hollywood.
1913	William Pratt crosses the border into the United States and adopts the name Boris Karloff.
	Peter Cushing born in Kenley, Surrey, 26 May.
1914	Austria-Hungary declares war on Serbia on 28 July, heralding the start of the First World War.
1917	Karloff arrives in Los Angeles and the United States enters the war.
1922	Christopher Lee born in Belgravia, 27 May.
1930	Karloff marries Dorothy Stine.
1931	New York premiere of *Frankenstein*, 4 December – Karloff's eighty-first film.
1932	Karloff stars in *The Mummy*.
1933	The Screen Actors' Guild is set up in Hollywood with Karloff as a founder member.
1935	Karloff and Elsa Lanchester star in *The Bride of Frankenstein*.
1936	Cushing is offered the job of Assistant Stage Manager at the Connaught Theatre in Worthing.
1939	Cushing travels to Hollywood. Britain and Germany are at war.
1941	Lee's father dies and he volunteers for the RAF.
1942	Cushing returns to England, docking at Liverpool on 27 March and joins ENSA.
1943	Cushing marries Helen Beck on 10 April at Marylebone register office.

1946	Karloff marries Evie Helmore.
1947	Lee signs a seven-year contract with the Rank Charm School and James Carreras relaunches Hammer Films.
1948	Both Lee and Cushing have small roles in Laurence Olivier's film of *Hamlet*.
1951	Hammer sets up its base at Bray Studios in Berkshire.
1954	Cushing stars in the BBC's adaptation of George Orwell's *Nineteen Eighty-Four*. He buys his cottage in Whitstable.
1957	Hammer's first colour horror film *The Curse of Frankenstein* is released.
1958	Cushing and Lee star in Hammer's *Dracula*.
1959	Karloff moves back to England from Hollywood. Cushing and Lee star in *The Mummy*.
1961	Lee marries Gitte Kroencke, 17 March at St Michael's, Chester Square, Belgravia.
1969	Karloff dies on 2 February aged 81.
1971	Death of Helen Cushing.
1974	Lee plays Scaramanga in the Bond film *The Man with the Golden Gun*.
1977	Lee moves to Hollywood. Cushing appears in George Lucas's *Star Wars* as the Grand Moff Tarkin.
1989	Cushing awarded OBE
1994	Cushing dies on 11 August, aged 81.
2001	Lee plays Saruman in the first of the *Lord of The Rings* trilogy – *The Fellowship of the Ring*.
2009	Lee is knighted.
2015	Lee dies on 7 June, aged 93.

Chapter One

Youth

Boris Karloff was born on 3 November 1887, just a few months after Queen Victoria celebrated her Golden Jubilee and ten years before Bram Stoker's *Dracula* was published. Peter Cushing was born on 26 May 1913. In June, the suffragette Emily Wilding Davison threw herself in front of the King's horse, Anmer, at the Derby. Christopher Lee was born on 27 May 1922. Later that year the British Broadcasting Company (as the BBC was first called) began daily broadcasts in the Marconi company's London studio on the Strand.

Karloff, Cushing and Lee were all Londoners – born in Camberwell, Karloff's next address was 36 Forest Hill Road in Dulwich; Cushing lived in Kenley, Croydon, and Lee in Belgravia. They could all be said to be comfortably middle-class but perhaps it would be more accurate to say that in some respects they were *uncomfortably* middle-class. They did not quite meet the expectations of their families nor fit into the lives they seemed destined to pursue. They all struggled to find their feet as actors and none of them knew success at an early age. They were all good-looking Englishmen with cut-glass accents and a fondness for sport, but they never fitted into the mould of the romantic leading man. All three went to Hollywood and all three came back again.

In the late Victorian age, when Boris Karloff – or as he then was William 'Billy' Pratt – was born, youth was merely the period of education and preparation for your adult life. An appreciation of one's youth was something of a luxury because many children had neither education nor preparation for adult life. They were simply thrown into it.

Yet in the 1890s the demands of an increasingly industrialised society meant that there was a greater need for clerical workers of all kinds, equipped with literacy and numeracy and in need of being trained to meet the evolving demands of the working adult world. Consequently, the late nineteenth century saw a proliferation in the number of 'minor' public schools opening in response to the demands of the burgeoning middle-class. This was the changing world into which William Pratt was born.

William Pratt's path into adulthood would have seemed fairly assured. He came from an Anglo-Indian background, though the term would not be officially designated by the government until 1911. His mixed race mother Eliza Sarah Millward, born in 1848 in India, was the niece of Anna Leonowens, whose account of her experiences in Siam as governess of the King Mongkut was fictionalised in Margaret Landon's novel, which in turn was the inspiration for the Rogers and Hammerstein musical *The King and I*. Anna was also mixed race but, as was common practice at the time, she was vague about her origins, claiming that she had been born Anna Crawford in Caernarfon, Wales.

Eliza Millward married Edward John Pratt, who worked for the Indian Civil Service in the salt revenue department. He had already been married three times and fathered three children, who had all died. In 1879, still only in his 50s, he was forced to retire and returned to England with his family.

Billy, (and from now on we will all him Boris Karloff) was the youngest of the couple's nine children. His parents legally separated when he was only 2 years old. Edward, according to Boris Karloff's daughter Sara Jane, was 'a tough man, not very warm'. She says that following the break-up of her marriage Eliza had 'emotional issues', and because she was unable to care for her large family, Boris's elder sister (thirteen years his senior) took over the care of the little boy. Edward had gone to live in France and died in 1901.

'Boris didn't have much of a family life,' says Sara Jane. 'Being the youngest he was more like an only child.' The expectation was that the boys would follow their father into the Indian Civil Service. Edward and Frederick did just that while John and Richard went into the British diplomatic corps in China. All four enjoyed distinguished careers and expected that their little brother would too. But this chilly, rather proper family was rocked by tragedy when, in 1897, brother George, who had trained as a doctor but become an actor, accidentally shot dead his friend Frederick Lockyear. In 1904 George died of pneumonia. The loss of the brother who most resembled him was hard for Boris to bear.

While Edward, Frederick, John and Richard all attended Dulwich College, Boris went to Merchant Taylors' School in Middlesex, north London, in 1899 and was a boarder at Uppingham School in Rutland in the East Midlands from 1903.

The Jacobean playwrights Thomas Kyd and John Webster had attended Merchant Taylors', while Old Uppinghamians include Stephen Fry, Rick Stein and Hugh Jackman. Boris was not much of a scholar and said that he always felt regarded as 'the black sheep of the family, a nuisance who didn't have any brains and didn't do any work and was always getting into trouble of one sort or another'.

Sara Jane says that his older brothers 'would come home on leave and look over their younger brother's school reports very disapprovingly'. While grammar schools and the new private schools possibly provided a more rounded education suitable for the needs of the clerical classes, the sort of ancient public schools which Boris attended still focused almost exclusively on character-building, sport and the classics. At least Boris was fond of cricket but his earliest ambition was to go on stage and it seems unlikely that his schooldays were the happiest of his life.

Another great film star, Charlie Chaplin, born in 1889 – just two years after Karloff – was also a south London boy, but his poverty-stricken upbringing in nearby Walworth could not have been more different. At the age of 7 he was even sent to Lambeth workhouse and attended the Norwood School for destitute children.

In 1899, when both Chaplin and Karloff were approaching adolescence, the Boer War broke out. Britain wanted to unite the British South African territories of Cape Colony and Natal with the Boer republics of the Orange Free State and the Transvaal. The Afrikaans-speaking Boers wanted to maintain their independence. This bloody, cruel war ended on 31 May 1902 when the Treaty of Vereeniging was signed and the Boers accepted British sovereignty, but with limited self-government. 'I was vaguely aware of the war,' wrote the 10-year-old Chaplin in 1899, 'through patriotic songs, vaudeville sketches and cigarette cards of the generals.'

4 The Godfathers of Horror Films

Awareness and approval of empire, which had been fairly muted during most of the nineteenth century, certainly increased at the beginning of the twentieth – in part due to the Boer War and also because, increasingly, other land- and resource-hungry nation states were staking claims in territories around the globe. In 1900 the publisher Sir Cyril Arthur Pearson, a close friend of the Boer War hero and founder of the Scouting movement Robert Baden-Powell, founded the *Daily Express* (price one halfpenny) with the promise: 'Our policy is patriotic; our faith is the British empire.'

It's hard to imagine that as the Boer War ended the 12-year-old Boris was not aware of the celebrations marking the relief of Mafeking and Ladysmith which took place across the British Empire in February and May of 1900. A witness to the rejoicing in London after Mafeking observed:

> White-haired old ladies were to be seen carrying large union jacks in each hand. Young women had colours pinned across from shoulder to shoulder. Sober young men in spectacles stood at street corners blowing tin trumpets with all their might ... well-dressed young women of unusually proper demeanour traversed roadways arm-in-arm, six abreast, carrying flags and occasionally bursting into song. There was a singular absence of any official stimulus.[1]

Various organisations sprang up at the turn of the century devoted to burnishing the empire, among them the Imperial Federation League (1884), the British Empire League (1896), the League of the Empire (1901) and the Empire Day Movement (1903). Elgar composed his *Imperial March* in 1897 and *Land of Hope and Glory* in 1901.

The very beginnings of the film industry found inspiration in the Boer War. In 1897 Sagar Mitchell and James Kenyon founded Mitchell and Kenyon, a Blackburn-based commercial movie-making company. They specialised in documentary reportage but also made dramatised scenes of the Boer War, with the countryside around Blackburn standing in for South Africa – what today we would call 'fake news'. We see 'nurses' tending wounded soldiers who lie comfortably on a stretcher as though taking a nap. *The Dispatch Rider*, made in 1900, includes an 'explosion' which was etched by hand into the emulsion.

When Boris was very little, his reading matter (he was always a great reader) would most likely have been school and detective stories, which were extremely popular, with colonial subjects in the minority. But as the nineteenth century drew to a close a huge number of children's books with imperial themes were published. The most prolific authors were G.A. Henty and Gordon Stables, who wrote hundreds of boys' adventure stories. Their books were – to modern eyes – jingoistic and obnoxious with titles such as *With Clive in India: The Beginnings of an Empire* (1884) and *The Young Colonists: A Tale of the Zulu and Boer Wars* (1885). But they also looked West with stories set in North America, Australia and Canada.

These adventure stories were also the reality for thousands of Britons. In the century before the start of the First World War in 1914, ten million people emigrated from Britain to start a new life in the USA, Canada or Australia. Emigration was at its highest in 1910, by which time it had become a national talking point with many newspapers and magazines offering advice to those thinking of emigrating. The decision was a big one – much bigger than it would be today – because nobody seriously expected to return home, even for a visit. Emigrating meant waving farewell to your family with no real possibility of seeing them again.

The story goes that Boris Karloff, with a small legacy from his mother of £100, tossed a coin to decide whether he would go to Australia or Canada. He set sail from Liverpool on the *Empress of Britain* on 7 May, 1909. At 21 he already felt that he was a disappointment to his high-achieving brothers. 'I imagine,' he would say later, 'that when I got on the ship, brotherly sighs of relief could be heard in various far-flung British outposts. There was no weeping and no distress. I was on my way. To what I didn't exactly know.'[2]

The truth is that many other people were doing exactly the same thing. Both Australia and Canada were British colonies offering a better life. Australia had just about shaken off its reputation as a place where convicts were sent and was favoured by more affluent emigrants, while between 1896–1914 Canada was desperate to attract agricultural settlers from Britain. As such it seems a surprising choice for Boris Karloff, whose ambition was to be an actor and whose experience of farming must have been limited in south London. But perhaps he was aware that in the late 1800s there had been a boom in theatre construction in Canadian cities.

Between 1873 and 1892, forty theatres (each with more than a thousand seats) had opened. Appearing on the American version of *This is Your Life* on his 70th birthday in 1957, he says that his first employment in Canada was clearing land and shovelling coal. Before long he inveigled his way into a stock theatre company and took the stage name Boris Karloff, fearing (as he said on *This is Your Life*) that 'my own name Pratt might be unfortunate'. He claimed that Karloff came from his mother's side of the family though there is no evidence of this, while he plucked 'Boris' from 'the cold, Canadian air'. Billy Pratt was no more. Boris Karloff had arrived. From then on he was always known as Boris Karloff, though he never changed his name legally and never took American citizenship either.

* * *

One of the 'fancy-that' details of Peter Cushing's early life is that his mother dressed him in frocks and doted on his luxuriant hair. Aha, thinks the amateur developmental psychologist, that was a strange thing to do. What we forget is that while Edwardian society was decisively gendered in most areas, children did not count and were effectively genderless. Babies and toddlers wore dresses because they were easier to manage when it came to nappies and potty training. The handed-down christening gown worn by both baby boys and girls is the vestigial remains of this common practice.

Nellie Cushing, who had already had one baby boy, David, in 1910 may well have longed for a daughter but perhaps she was also conscious that she was not quite as posh as her husband's family and wanted to imitate the traditions of the upper classes by dressing Peter like a baby Edwardian toff. Husband George – a bit of a stuffed shirt by all accounts – was a quantity surveyor.

Peter was born on 26 May 1913. As an infant he suffered successive bouts of pneumonia, which was very often fatal in those days. The family lived in Kenley, Surrey, moving to 10 Druce Road in Dulwich during the First World War. Houses in this desirable street now change hands for around two million pounds.

It appears from the electoral register that the Cushings were lodgers as the main tenant was John W. Congden, a traveller in 'perfumery and chemist's sundries'. Along with the rest of Britain the pleasant south-east London suburb suffered from food shortages, rationing and the mandatory half-day closure of shops from 1917. The substantial German population of Dulwich came under scrutiny and suspicion. In the early hours of 6 December 1917 six bombs fell on Dulwich, killing a woman and a child. Resident John Greening wrote in his diary:

> It is no joke to be suddenly awakened before six in the morning by hearing guns firing around you but such was our awful experience at 4.45 am. As may be imagined we were out of bed and into our clothes in the twinkling of an eye. The din continued for upwards of one hour and three tremendous explosions made us tremble.

Cushing says that among his earliest memories was the sight of Zeppelins caught in the sweeping searchlights over Dulwich Village. His parents invented a game for the two little brothers to play during bombing raids. They would pretend to be 'Red Indians' (Native Americans) by hiding under the kitchen table with a large cloth draped over it like a wigwam.

Sensitive children listen to their parents, pick up on the mood music of the world around them. Later in life Cushing, with that air of pained gentleness, would always say that he disliked the term 'horror film' and preferred 'fantasy film'. In an interview with the BBC filmed in 1973 he said: 'Horror to me is a film like *The Godfather* [which had just been released] or anything to do with war, which is real and can happen and unfortunately will no doubt happen again sometime.'

Though the wigwam game makes it as though his parents were attuned to their sons' anxiety during bombing raids, they were also unkind in rather peculiar ways. If Peter did anything naughty his mother would punish him by singing the opening bars of a popular song called *Love Will Find a Way* before pretending to be dead. This, Cushing admits, had a disastrous effect on him psychologically, leaving him with a morbid fear of death. He received some consolation when older brother David suggested he should pinch Nellie when she pulled this trick.

George once punished his son in an equally horrendous manner, by locking him in the cellar leaving him in total blackness. The child – nearly 9 by now – suffered from terrible nightmares and begged his parents to allow him to sleep with them in their double bed. For years afterwards he would suffer from nyctophobia, an extreme fear of darkness. He tried to cure himself by taking solitary walks after midnight – a habit he eventually came to enjoy.

In 1925 the Cushings moved to 32 St James's Road in Purley, a striking art deco house on a steep hill which has an English Heritage blue plaque to his memory, put up in 2018. The architect is unknown, but the Cushings were the first residents and it stands out amid the mock-Tudor houses that dominated the inter-war period. The family lived here between 1925 and 1936.

Peter was not very academic, though he excelled at art and rugby. He was sent to board at Shoreham Grammar School in Sussex, a school whose client base was mostly well-to-do Londoners who wanted their sons to enjoy a bracing seaside environment. The prospectus explained:

> The premises, conveniently situated close to the railway station, sea and church are in every way adapted to accommodate the pupils and promote their health and comfort. There is an abundant supply of the purest water, and the drainage is excellent. Shoreham is drained into the sea. Shoreham has an excellent service of trains both from London Bridge and Victoria.

He dreaded becoming a boarder and only lasted one term, crying incessantly until his parents (his father thought he would 'get over it' given time) removed him.

His next school was Purley County Secondary School, also on St James's Road, where he was, by his own admission, a poor student but reasonably happy and good at sport. His infant frailty was overcome and by the time he left school he was more than six foot tall and weighed 12½ stone. He always imagined himself as an actor which was why most of the academic subjects passed him by, while his bother David – who called his little brother 'Brighteyes' – was on hand to help with his homework.

There were actors in the family. George Cushing's father, Henry William Cushing, had begun his career with Sir Henry Irving's company which toured the United States eight times between 1883 and 1904. He had previously worked as a civil engineer and brewer's architect but joined the company in 1892, appearing in Shakespeare's *King Henry VIII* at London's Lyceum Theatre. George's sister Maude Ashton had also acted professionally. A member of a troupe that toured in South Africa, she reprised the roles made popular by Gertie Millar (1879–1952), a glamorous star of the music hall and variety theatre from Bradford who had appeared on Broadway and in the West End. Cushing recalls seeing Maude (who thought her brother had married beneath him) appearing in a one-act play in the role of 'a lady of easy virtue'. She made Peter call her Maude ('for heaven's sake don't call me aunt'), and he thought her thrilling and glamorous.

His step-uncle, Wilton Heriot, appeared in the first production of *Charley's Aunt* in 1892. Heriot was also author (with Mark Ambient) of a popular comedy *A Little Ray of Sunshine*, which opened at the Royalty Theatre in London in 1898 and transferred to Broadway in 1899. The play also pops up in Orago in New Zealand, the production at the Princess Theatre receiving a favourable review in 1902. Heriot was in California when he was caught up in the tragic drowning of the beautiful vaudeville star Isadore Rush in 1904 in San Diego, where the company was on tour with the musical comedy *Glittering Gloria*. Heriot attempted to rescue her but was knocked unconscious by the waves and only just escaped drowning himself. Peter's middle name was Wilton, so obviously he was well thought of by the family.

Cushing was taken to see a Christmas production of *Peter Pan* and was totally enchanted by it. He longed for Peter Pan to come flying through his bedroom window and transport him to Never Never Land. The influence of the Boy Who Wouldn't Grow Up was not lost on Peter Cushing, nor on the people who knew and loved him.

In the years after the First World War, British public opinion became gripped by the fear that the nation had been 'brutalised' by the conflict and irrevocably scarred, a fear partially but not wholly soothed by the idea that typical British 'peaceableness' would triumph. Britain was a nervy, ragged place in the early 1920s, forging the narrative of the Great War that still pertains today – namely that it was a terrible and unnecessary tragedy that had decimated a generation of England's finest, and that the conflict was a calamitous act inflicted on the young by the old. Cushing always said that *Journey's End*, R.C. Sheriff's play set in the trenches, was one of his favourites. It opened in 1928 when Peter would have been 15, a very impressionable age.

The very idea of youth – its needs, its opinions, its potential – began to mean something in this period. Youth was not simply a period of preparation for the world of adult responsibilities. It was becoming a focal point for aspiration, idealism and organisation and a recognised biological stage. As early as 1904, for instance, *Adolescence*, a book by the American psychologist Granville Stanley Hall, had become a bestseller.

A third of British males born between 1901 and 1920 belonged to the Scout Movement, launched by Robert Baden-Powell in 1908. It was enormously popular, appealing both to parents – with its reassuring commitment to patriotism and empire – and to the scouts, who liked the uniforms and the open-air activities. It also burned with the spirit of the new mood of internationalism and a vague utopian idealism to counteract the disillusionment that had followed the war.

There were other organisations too – the Boys' Brigade and The Woodcraft Folk. In 1919 Frank Hornby launched the Meccano Guild to oversee the setting up of clubs while the *Meccano Magazine* kept the Guild informed of everyone's activities.

Cushing was a model maker all his life – model soldiers, model theatres and train sets all fascinated him. A Pathé newsreel from 1956 filmed him in his den in his Kensington home, painting models and setting up battle lines on the carpet. Appearing on *Desert Island Discs* on 23 February 1959, he chose painting materials and model soldiers as his luxury item.

We know he read comics, particularly *The Magnet* and *The Gem* and the adventures of schoolboy Tom Merry, the principal character in the St Jim's stories which appeared between 1907 and 1939. Most of the stories were by Charles Hamilton, also known as Frank Richards, the creator of Billy Bunter. Each day Cushing would turn to the *Pip, Squeak and Wilfred* strip cartoon in the *Daily Mirror* which ran from 1919 to 1956.

He also haunted his local cinema, the Electric Palace on the High Street in Thornton Heath, which opened with some fanfare in 1910. Its history followed the familiar route of so many picture houses in the twentieth century. In 1927 it became a Palais de Dance ballroom, then a launderette, then a furniture store. It has now been demolished.

Cushing was particularly fond of Tom Mix films. Mix (1880–1940) was an American actor who appeared in 291 films between 1909 and 1935 and was the first true Western star, ably assisted by his reliable white steed, Tony the Wonder Horse. In his memoirs Cushing recalls that in 1938 he finally met his idol. He was in a play at the Theatre Royal in Nottinghamshire, in the UK and Tom was appearing at the nearby House of Varieties with a version of Tony. Peter called him and was surprised when the great man asked for a favour. Would he look over Tom's contract and witness his signature. Astonishingly, Tom could neither read nor write.

By the late 1920s it was recognised in America and the UK that modern children's voracious appetite for cinemas presented both a threat to their moral wellbeing, but was also potentially beneficial. A report by British Instructional Films (a film production company) in 1928 found that more than 90 per cent of school children went to the cinema at least once a week. It seems an astonishing figure and admittedly the BIF had skin in the game. Yet an experimental introduction of the Saturday morning screening for children at the Kingsway cinema in central London had proved very successful and would become a mainstay of children's entertainment until the 1970s. Thus the children's film diet could be kept under scrutiny and their enthusiasm for movies encouraged. Tom Mix and his Wonder Horse were deemed suitable, along with Douglas Fairbanks, Mary Pickford, Harold Lloyd, Charlie Chaplin, Reginald Denny (a dashing English actor and aviator) and of course, newsreels.

The Cushing family tolerated the Punch and Judy shows that young Peter staged for their amusement, but there was no encouragement for the career in the theatre of which he dreamed. His elder brother David – having loathed an early job in the City working for an insurance broker – had been given money by their father to buy a farming smallhold near Reigate. Peter began his working life as a surveyor's assistant with the Coulsdon and Purley Urban District Council, but he bought a copy of *The Stage* (it cost fourpence) almost every week and applied to adverts for theatre jobs.

He welcomed any tasks which took him out of the surveyor's office. One of them was collecting pennies from the public lavatories and he was often sent out to stock up with tobacco and cigarettes for his fellow workers. Peter himself was an early convert to smoking, a habit he maintained throughout his life. Later he would wear white gloves when he smoked to avoid nicotine staining his fingers.

He had a Saturday off once a month (most weeks he had to work Saturday mornings) and would travel up to the West End, sneak into theatres via the stage door and simply revel in his surroundings. He continued to appear in school plays at this time and in his autobiography recalls a production of W.S. Gilbert's *Pygmalion and Galatea*. Playing the Athenian sculptor he decided that a Greek man should have hairless legs and borrowed his mother's Veet (a patent ladies' hair remover), with fairly disastrous results. It was an early indication of the attention to detail which would both impress – and occasionally infuriate – his colleagues throughout his long acting career.

* * *

May 1922 began with frost and rain. But then the temperatures rose to more than 30°C for four days in a row in London, with the hottest being 32.8°C on 22 May. There were reports of death by heatstroke and – as is customary in Britain – the newspapers began to give advice on how to cope. *The Times* told its readers that: 'The secret of keeping cool is to maintain a free circulation of air around the surface of the body. Every garment which is in any degree constricted interferes with air movement; loose open sleeves and thin fabrics, on the other hand, assist it.' The heat sparked flash floods and violent thunderstorms when several people were killed by lightning strikes. Hailstones the size of pigeon eggs battered Tunbridge Wells, breaking windows and destroying gardens.

The heat must have been particularly trying for Christopher Lee's heavily pregnant mother who gave birth to him at 51 Lower Belgrave Street on 27 May. Within days the temperature fell and a normal English summer resumed. The weather was not the only thing to get back to normal. In his autobiography *Tall, Dark and Gruesome*, Lee observes that 1922 was the first summer since the beginning of the First World War when the summer season returned in its full splendour – both parties, dresses and banquets reverted to pre-war opulence, though maybe the ladies' trains were not quite as long. But that was more a sign of emancipation than thrift.

The baby was named Christopher Frank Carandini Lee, a brother for Xandra who had been born in 1917. Theirs was an extraordinary family. His mother was the Contessa Estelle Marie Carandini (1889–1981), from an aristocratic Italian family that could trace its history back to Charlemagne or even Imperial Rome. She was a great beauty and her handsome husband Geoffrey Trollope Lee (1879–1941) was a dashing military man, a Lieutenant Colonel in the King's Royal Rifles who had served in the Boer War and during the First Word War. In 1915 he had trained Australian troops in Egypt and commanded them in 1916 at the Battle of the Somme. Geoffrey and Estelle married in 1910, a smart society wedding held at St George's Hanover Square.

Geoffrey, educated at Radley and Sandhurst, retired from the army at the age of 40 and thereafter 'confined himself to cricket and golf and blazing away at wildlife'. He was a very keen member of Sunningdale Golf Club in Berkshire. He also gambled heavily and left the marriage when Christopher was just 4 years old. Christopher remembers the marriage break-up as a complete shock, never adequately explained by either party.

The Contessa decamped to the picture-postcard mountain village of Wengen in Switzerland and Christopher attended Miss Fisher's Academy in Territet on Lake Geneva. Before long they all returned to London where Christopher went to Wagner School, a prep school for boys at 90 Queen's Gate, run by Orlando Henry Wagner and his wife Monica. He doesn't seem to have enjoyed life at either establishment.

In 1930, after the Lees divorced, the Contessa married Major Harcourt George St Croix Rose (1883–1955), nicknamed Ingle. He had already been married twice before and had two children of his own. His sister Evelyn (1885–1964) was the mother of James Bond writer Ian Fleming, and her husband Major Valentine Fleming had been killed in the First World War.

She became the mistress of the painter Augustus John with whom she had a daughter, the cellist Amaryllis Fleming (1925–1999) and later lived with the Marquess of Winchester. For reasons best known to herself Evelyn maintained that Amaryllis was adopted and that her father was untraceable. It wasn't until she was 24 that Amaryllis confronted her mother with the truth. Augustus John finally gave in. 'So you're my little girl, are you?' he growled. 'Don't tell your mother.'

Ingle's inclinations were as peripatetic as the Contessa's. The family first set up home in Chelsea in a five-storey townhouse in Elm Park Gardens with an orange front door. Ingle was extremely wealthy at the time, and the family duly engaged a butler, a cook, a housemaid and a scullery maid. There would be many moves after that.

For the Contessa with her new husband it was a time of diamonds and furs and fun. The novelist Evelyn Waugh mocked the excessive partying of the Bright Young Things in his bestselling novel *Vile Bodies* published in 1930. Lord Metroland, one of the characters in the book, observes: 'They had a chance after the war that no generation has ever had. There was a whole civilisation to be saved and remade. And all they seem to do is play the fool.'

Waugh observes so much in this novel that pinpoints that period. Two of his main characters are scions of ancient aristocratic families who have become gossip columnists. One is the 'fifteenth Marquess of Vanbrugh, Vanburgh de Brendon, Baron Brendon, Lord of the Five Isles and Hereditary Grand Falconer to the Kingdom of Connaught', while the other is the 'eighth Earl of Balcairn, Viscount Erdinge, Baron Cairn of Balcairn, Red Knight of Lancaster, Count of the Holy Roman Empire and Chenonceaux Herald to the Duchy of Aquitaine'.

Both the Contessa and Ingle were of this set whose web of connections reached across Europe to the Near East, linked by marriage, tradition, property, land ownership and a cast iron sense of entitlement. Lee was a little miffed that the laws of succession meant that he was – as the son of a contessa – never permitted to take the title of count. That would late be remedied, he observed dryly, by his close association with another European aristocrat – Count Dracula.

In a sense, this vast tribe of European aristocrats rose above political and national allegiances in the early years of the twentieth century. So much so that during the First World War the Titles Deprivation Act (1917) was passed to deprive German and Austrian relatives of the Royal Family of their English titles, many of which resulted from the network of marriages made by Queen Victoria's many children and grandchildren. It saved the Windsors from embarrassment, but was also controversial for that very reason.

The First World War had seen old ideas about the officer and upper classes challenged and had also been accompanied by a refugee crisis throughout Europe when hundreds of thousands were displaced. Those who had not lost all their money were able to travel but they often led rootless lives.

Christopher's mother with her many aristocratic connections throughout Europe must have been a magnet for these lost and flat-broke émigrés. Many of them were Russian, at least a million displaced by the Revolution of 1917 and the First World War. Many of those with money and connections ended up in Belgrade, Paris, Berlin or

London. Among them was Prince Felix Yusupov, a flamboyant member of one of the wealthiest families in Imperial Russia who had studied at University College Oxford between 1909 and 1913 before returning to Russia, where he would become one of Rasputin's assassins. He fled Russia after the assassination and spent the rest of his life in exile in France and London.

Christopher Lee remembers being woken up as a child in order to meet both the Prince and the Grand Duke Dmitri, a co-conspirator with Yusopov. Dmitri, a grandson of Tsar Alexander II, lived in exile in Britain and France and enjoyed a brief affair with Coco Chanel in the early 1920s.

For all his good looks and charm Dmitri was not made particularly welcome in London because George V and the British government did not want to alienate the new Bolshevik regime.

Ingle was an Old Etonian and the expectation was that Christopher would also attend the school. Summer Fields prep school in Oxford was a traditional feeder school for Eton so Christopher was sent there at the age of 9. Among his chums and contemporaries was Patrick Macnee, who is remembered by Lee in his autobiography as a far superior schoolboy actor. Macnee would find fame in *The Avengers* in the 1960s as the bowler-hatted, umbrella twirling hero John Steed. Born in 1922, both men would die within weeks of each other in June 2015.

Lee did reasonably well in the Eton exams and was interviewed by the celebrated ghost story writer M.R. James, who was then provost of Eton. Unfortunately, Lee was placed eleventh in the entrance exams and thus missed (by one place) the opportunity of being a full King's Scholar.

He would have been accepted as an Oppidan Scholar but this meant that Ingle would have had to pay higher fees. And like many during the Depression of the 1930s, Ingle was suffering financially.

Accordingly, Christopher was sent to Wellington College in 1936. The school had been founded in 1859 in honour of the Iron Duke to educate the orphaned sons of army officers. Lee found the martial culture was not to his taste. He was beaten frequently. 'It seems I had fallen among barbarians', he wrote in his autobiography. He was reasonably academic at Wellington but never took much interest in school plays. He must have been gratified when in 2011 the Christopher Lee Theatre opened at the Berkshire school in honour of their famous old boy.

As it turned out, he only had to put up with Wellington for three years because in 1939 Ingle was declared bankrupt with debts of £25,000 (equivalent to around £2 million today) and Christopher was told that he had to leave school and earn his own living. The days of diamonds and furs were well and truly over. The Contessa left Ingle and went to live at Ramblers Cottage, overlooking Wentworth Golf Course. Christopher's elder sister Xandra went to work as a typist. Before knuckling down to the life of a wage slave, Christopher was sent to Menton on the French Riviera for a holiday. Arriving first in Paris he was taken under the wing of the celebrated American war reporter Webb Miller (1891–1940).

Miller – a friend of Ingle's – was another of the interesting characters that Lee encountered in his youth. Miller had covered the air raids in London during the First World War and the Paris Peace Talks. He had interviewed Raymond Poincaré, Georges Clemenceau, David Lloyd George and Woodrow Wilson. In 1922 he witnessed the serial killer Henri Désiré Landru guillotined in Versailles. His gruesome and graphic report led to a Pulitzer Prize nomination.

Miller thought it would be instructive for the 17-year-old Christopher to witness another public execution in Versailles outside the Prison Saint-Pierre. It was that of another serial killer, Eugen Weidmann, which took place on 17 June 1939. His trial had been as sensational as that of Landru's and the two killers had shared the same defence lawyer, Vincent de Moro-Giafferi. It was the reaction of the spectators that Miller thought Lee should observe, their excitement and hysteria. It would be the last public execution in France and it was an experience that affected Lee for the rest of his life.

Miller – who had survived battlefields – would die mysteriously in 1940. His body was discovered on a railway track just outside Clapham Junction. It was believed he stepped off the train in the blackout thinking he was at a station.

After the unexpected diversion to Versailles, Lee continued to Menton. He stayed in the Pension Mazirov in the old port of Garavan, rather than in one of the many swanky hotels which he would have been accustomed to in the past. There were several trips to Monte Carlo just ten kilometres along the coast. The writer Somerset Maugham called Monte 'a sunny place for shady people'. Lee enjoyed seeing the beautiful people dance the rumba and the samba in the Sporting Club. There were Hollywood stars to gawp at too, such as Douglas Fairbanks dressed in blue sitting by the pool with his Great Dane on a lead.

Unfortunately the inevitability of war cut short his holiday and he had to return to England in a hurry. He found a job with a firm in the City, a transatlantic shipping company called United States Line. Like thousands of other clerical workers he travelled to Waterloo every day, departing from Virginia Water. Unlike many clerical workers he did not wear a bowler hat. He was already six foot four inches tall and did not feel the necessity to add to his height. He had also resigned himself to a lifetime of sleeping diagonally in bed. He moved jobs to Beecham's working as a messenger, then as a switchboard operator for £1 a week. He also joined the Home Guard.

In March 1941 his father Geoffrey Hill died suddenly of pneumonia and pleurisy. This death seems to have marked a turning point for his son. While not wishing to follow his father into the army, Lee wanted a more active part in the war and so he volunteered for the RAF. He was still a teenager but like so many of his generation, his youth had come to an abrupt end.

* * *

Chapter Two

Acting

Christopher Lee said that acting had been very good to him. One might have expected some portentous declamation about his art and his integrity. But on the contrary, he explained that the life of an international film star had enabled him to enjoy his other great passion – golf – on some of the world's greatest courses.

He, Karloff and Cushing shared a very British modesty about their talent, wearing it lightly at all times. In a radio interview in 1986 Cushing mused: 'I don't think that you can really be taught to be an actor ... it is a calling and you don't want to sound too pompous but it's a drive that you just can't brush under the carpet.' In 1962 in an interview in the *Illinois Herald and Review,* Karloff, then 76, poured scorn on the modern practice of 'method acting', describing it as an 'abomination'. He continued:

> The chief lesson young actors and actresses from these so-called modern schools learn is complete and unerring egoism. They are taught to relate everything to self. They care little for the words of the author, little of the dictates of the director, little for the efforts of other actors, and absolutely nothing for the audience.

Karloff seldom had a bad word to say about anyone, but in this interview he takes a swipe at Marlon Brando, a Hollywood actor forever linked to the more performative aspects of method acting. 'Take the case of Marlon Brando, who has been known to place rubber stoppers in his ears so he cannot hear the words spoken by other players ... Now I ask you, how can a player contribute to a play if he sets himself above it?'

Later in the interview he apologises for his outburst adding:

Actually I feel sorry for all young actors who really want a theatrical career. Whenever a youngster asks me what is the most important thing they must have to become a star, I tell them, 'You must have fire in your belly for there will seldom be anything else there'.

Passion tempered by a fear of being thought pompous, a contempt for new-fangled ways of learning to act and a nostalgia for the days when actors starved romantically for their art – the acting profession has always been regarded equivocally, and especially so in the first half of the twentieth century.

In 1895 Sir Henry Irving had become the first theatrical knight – an honour which has subsequently been bestowed on many actors, male and female. Actors can be national treasures and public figures, but they are also bohemian vagabonds, travelling players or plain luvvies. At the beginning of the twentieth century there were still itinerant players seeking work who advertised their services such as 'Gent for Heavies, or Lead', 'Man and Wife for Responsibles', and 'Painter to act'. On 18 October 1900, *The Stage* lists no fewer than 281 companies on the road.

There is something childlike about acting, the art of pretending to be someone else. How difficult can it really be? Laurence Olivier's famous putdown of the earnest method actor Dustin Hoffman on the set of *Marathon Man* – 'Why don't you just try acting, dear boy?' – amuses us because it confirms our suspicions that acting is just turning up and saying the lines.

The training of actors was a twentieth-century phenomenon. The great actor-managers of the nineteenth century gave way to a new dynamic whereby the director achieved greater prominence, which at the same time put the role of the actor under greater scrutiny.

The Royal Academy of Dramatic Art was founded in 1904 by Sir Herbert Beerbohm Tree. The Central School of Speech and Drama, founded by Elsie Fogerty, opened in 1906. The Guildhall School of Music opened in 1880 in the City of London and in 1935 the school added 'and Drama' to its title. Similarly the London Academy of Music was founded in 1861. Its speech examinations were available to the public in 1881 and – also in 1935 – it became the London Academy of Music and Drama (LAMDA).

Much of the teaching at these academies focused on the formal arts of oratory and rhetoric. But throughout Europe and the USA the art of acting was being anatomised and analysed at a time when there was a fascination with the new science of psychoanalysis and the unconscious.

Born in Russia, Konstantin Stanislavsky (1863–1938) developed what he called The System, which involved actors doing various relaxation and breathing exercises to achieve a state of what he called 'public solitude' on stage. Improvisation was key. The Actors Studio, founded by Elia Kazan in New York in 1947, based its work on Stanislavsky's principles and championed the Method style of acting. Among its celebrated members are Marlon Brando, Marilyn Monroe, James Dean, Paul Newman, Jack Nicholson and Harvey Keitel to name but a handful. 'What's my motivation?' is the well-known plea of every Method actor seeking to rationalise his performance.

Vsevolod Meyerhold (1874–1940) founded the Meyerhold Theatre school in 1923, one of countless schools and studios which took on the business of training actors before the Second World War. His own system of 'biomechanics' focused on movement and sought to exaggerate and celebrate the very theatricality of theatre. Michael Chekhov (1891–1955), nephew of the playwright Anton Chekhov, rejected Stanislavsky's insistence that the actor should draw on his or her own emotions, arguing that the emphasis should be on seeking out the character's feelings. Moving between Paris, Berlin, eastern Europe and the experimental community at Dartington Hall in Devon, he established the Chekhov Theatre Studio there in 1936. When war broke out he moved to America.

The German playwright Bertolt Brecht (1898–1956) went into theatre as a writer and became involved with all aspects of the craft, setting up the Berliner Ensemble in West Berlin in 1949. Rehearsals would go on for several months. Actors were required to observe, to question, to engage politically. Most of the exercises involved the cast working together. In the first stage of rehearsal actors got to know their characters; in the second phase they developed empathy and then, according to Brecht, 'there is a third phase in which you try to see the character from the outside, from the standpoint of society'.

This solemn navel gazing, which turned acting into an intellectual exercise, was in marked contrast to the kind of theatre world that Boris Karloff, Peter Cushing and Christopher Lee entered. Repertory theatres in Britain produced up to thirty-five plays a year. Even the top reps such as Birmingham and Liverpool would put on sixteen productions a year, changing plays every two or three weeks. Added to this pressure on the actors was that of performing twice nightly which was fairly common. Rather than drawing on emotions or wondering about your character's motivation, the most pressing business for a repertory actor was learning lines week in and week out, and then wiping their minds of them after the last performance on Saturday night, in preparation for the next production.

In the first two decades of the twentieth century British repertory theatre was booming. Known as stock theatre in America and Canada, this was where Boris Karloff's early ambitions lay. Initially he worked as a farm labourer for ten dollars a month, then moved on to Vancouver where he worked as a road digger. There was a spell as a real estate salesman, and an early marriage to a woman called Grace Harding. By telling some large fibs about his acting experience, he managed to persuade Walter Kelly, a theatrical agent in Seattle, to represent him. A couple of months later Karloff had a letter from Kelly telling him that he had been engaged by the Jeanne Russell Stock Company based in Kamloops in British Columbia.

Karloff's youthful bravado in Walter Kelly's office was tested to the limit when he found himself working in a professional theatre for the first time in his life. His first role was in Ferenc Molnar's 1908 play *The Devil*, as Hoffman, a 60-year-old banker. Said Karloff: 'I had finally become an actor but I mumbled, bumbled, missed cues, rammed into furniture and sent the director's blood pressure soaring. When the curtain went up I was getting thirty dollars a week. When it descended I was down to fifteen dollars'.[3]

Jeanne Russell and her Company were a lively bunch. Jeanne Russell Alford was born in Salt Lake City in 1875, the daughter of a salesman.

Ray Fowler Brandon, the company manager married her in around 1906. In 1907 they ran their own theatre in Denver and the stock company was set up in 1908.

They were sued by Broadway playwrights for stealing plays, sued for failing to pay an orchestra, and they in turn sued the *Edmonton Journal* for libel. They also seem to have displeased *The Grand Forks Gazette*, which complained:

> Travelling theatrical companies are noted for their exalted opinion of themselves and the Jeanne Russell company managed by Tay Brandon is no exception … The opera house rates didn't suit them, they had trouble with their hostelry, they had trouble with their bill poster, and they paid their printer's bill in court.

Jeanne Russell died in 1920 at the age of 44 of tabes dorsalis, a spinal infection caused by an untreated syphilis infection. Brandon remarried and had two children. He was killed in a car accident in Oregon in 1933.

While Karloff was a member of the troupe, they travelled through western Canada staying in hotels or rooming houses where, according to the American newspaper columnist Samuel Grafton, 'Karloff was a profound student on the business of living cheaply', for a stock-company actor 'had to learn to fry an egg on the bottom of an electric iron … Canned soup, always mulligatawny (because it had meat in it) was cooked in a dresser drawer over a canned-heat fire.'

In June 1912 the company arrived in Regina, capital of the province of Saskatchewan. Nobody had any money and the manager declared that the finances were so dire that they could no longer carry on. The following day – Sunday, 30 June – a tornado devastated the city, the deadliest and most powerful in Canada's history, killing twenty-eight people and leaving hundreds homeless. It also marked the end of the road for the Jeanne Russell Company.

Karloff moved on to join the Harry St Clair Players based in Prince Albert, Saskatchewan. St Clair needed a young leading man. After a year Karloff tried his luck in Chicago, arriving in October 1914, a few months after the outbreak of the First World War. But there was no work to be had and the British Army rejected him when he tried to join up because he had a heart murmur. He returned to St Clair's company where he stayed until 1916.

In 1919 after working for a succession of different companies across the Western states he arrived in Los Angeles and made his first appearance on film, as an extra in a crowd scene. He was paid five dollars. The title of the film has never been established but he was under the director of Frank Borzage (1894–1962). Borzage was the first director to win the Academy Award for Best Director for his film *Seventh Heaven*, at the first ever Academy Awards held in 1927.

Karloff's love of the theatre never left him and he regarded those years in stock companies as formative. His daughter Sara Jane says that perhaps his only real regret is that he never appeared in London's West End theatre.

* * *

By the mid-1930s, when Peter Cushing was a stage-struck surveyor's assistant with Coulsdon and Purley Urban District Council, the world of theatre was in slow decline. Property investment had shifted to cinema building, and with each passing year more and more theatres closed or converted to cinemas. Yet repertory theatre still offered actors regular work and a kind of security – even if members of the cast were expected to provide their own wardrobe for modern dress dramas (as often happened).

Cushing's dogged passion for a profession of which, in truth, he knew very little, was not unusual. Many actors then (as now) were prepared to work for nothing. Theatre companies would advertise, offering roles to starry-eyed would-be actors in return for a financial contribution to the production. In 1920 Ralph Richardson, then without any acting experience, invested a small inheritance in a local theatre company simply to get a role and appear on stage. Even prestigious theatres such as the Old Vic paid poorly. But it was worth it because of the exposure and the range of roles. For instance between 1932 and '33, Peggy Ashcroft earned £20 a week but she played Rosalind, Miranda,

Portia, Perdita, Juliet, Shaw's Cleopatra, Kate Hardcastle, Lady Teazle and the title role in Drinkwater's Mary Stuart.

The actors' union, the British Actors' Equity Association was set up in 1929 reflecting concerns about the treatment of performers by unscrupulous or incompetent managers who exploited the hunger for work and experience. But their closed shop policy meant that novice actors were still caught in that familiar bind – without experience they could not get an Equity card and without a card they couldn't get any work.

Peter Cushing attended London's West End theatres on Saturdays and sent countless letters answering advertisements in *The Stage*. He even changed his name to Peter Ling for a while but this caused confusion as it was often thought that he was Chinese, so he changed his name back again.

He was a good-looking young man with his hair Brilliantined in the style made popular by Rudolph Valentino (long dead but still influential). He attended Tango-Tea Dances which had become popular in the Edwardian era when the Argentine tango arrived in London. He went to the cinema a lot. He had a girlfriend. His life sounds full, but he says he was deeply depressed and felt a failure. He planned his suicide on a Bank Holiday afternoon when his parents had gone to visit his brother David's farm. He caught a train to Exmouth intending to throw himself off a cliff. Distracted by the sight of a wheatear among the plentiful birdlife, he changed his mind.

He applied to take acting classes at the Guildhall School of Music and Drama and was interviewed by one of the school's directors, the well-known actor Allan Aynesworth (1864–1959) who was not impressed with Cushing's 'lazy drawl' and sent him away to take elocution lessons. The lessons paid off and Cushing was eventually accepted to the Guildhall.

He continued to bombard repertory theatres with letters begging for work. Among them was the Connaught Theatre in Worthing. Unusually, the history of the Connaught reversed the usual trend of theatres converting into cinemas inasmuch as it was built in 1914 as a Picturedrome Cinema and then became the home of the theatre (established in 1931) in 1935. It is a handsome Art Deco building in the Streamline Moderne style, still in use today and – since 1987 – operating as a dual use cinema and theatre.

Finally it looked as though Cushing's policy had paid off when he received a letter from the theatre's director Bill Fraser inviting him to what he assumed was an interview. Fraser (1908–1987) was a Scot born in Perth who would become familiar to television audiences from the 1950s to the 1970s in the sitcoms *The Army Game* and *Bootsie and Snudge*, in which he took the role of the preposterous Sergeant-Major Claude Snudge. He had begun his working life as a bank clerk and came to London looking for acting work. His early experience was even more dispiriting than Cushing's, for Fraser ended up sleeping rough on the Embankment.

Cushing was dismayed to find that Fraser had only summoned him to the theatre to tell him in no uncertain terms to stop writing letters. Perhaps Fraser felt sorry for him, perhaps Cushing turned that fine, suffering face towards him. In any event, Fraser gave him a non-speaking role in J.B. Priestley's play *Cornelius*, which starred Ralph Richardson in the main role. After this 1935 production, the play was not revived until 2012 at London's Finborough Theatre. Reviewing it in *The Guardian*, Michael Billington described it as 'an intriguing piece that not only offers a vivid picture of office life, but also addresses the dire problems facing small businesses in the economic blizzard of the 1930s'.

In June 1936, Cushing was offered the job of assistant stage manager at the Connaught and paid 15 shillings a week. An assistant stage manager is the lowliest of the low in the theatre hierarchy, but for Cushing it represented a foot in the door and led to more acting roles in which his talent could shine. One of an ASM's jobs is to source props of productions and he showed great ingenuity in this. Sometimes, edible food was required (known as 'practical' food) and Cushing always looked forward to that because it meant there would be free leftovers for him to eat when the curtain went down.

The manager of the Grand Theatre in Southampton, Peter Coleman, invited him to join the company. The Grand had opened in 1898 and could seat 1,800. The stories of these magnificent old theatres are rarely happy ones. During the Second World War it was used as accommodation for troops. After the war it staged striptease shows. In 1960 it was demolished to make way for an office block. That in turn has now been knocked down and a student hall built on the site.

Cushing worked at the Grand for a few months before joining the William Brookfield Players who performed at the Theatre Royal, Rochdale and the Opera House, Scarborough.

One of Cushing's roles in this period was as Andy Hardy, the character played by Mickey Rooney in the series of MGM films that ran from 1937 to 1946. They were gentle, sentimental comedies celebrating American domestic life. To enhance his comically goofy appearance, Cushing borrowed a jacket that was several sizes too small for him, with sleeves that came half-way up his arms. It was an early sign of his acute and creative awareness of the value of props and visual details. It was also an indication of his comic skill, not something usually associated with a godfather of horror.

When he was filming Hammer's *The Abominable Snowman* (1957), his obsessive eye for detail concerning his props was described by his American co-star Forrest Tucker. In an interview in 1974 Tucker said that Cushing 'had to know where the string on his mittens was tied and when he could take his mittens off at that altitude, how long he could have his hands out of his mittens before they would be frostbitten.'[4]

Though he took care to be accurate with bits of business and to know how to use his props correctly and convincingly, he was happiest when he was in the highly artificial world of the film set – where the film crew were reading newspapers, eating sandwiches and taking cigarette breaks – rather than on location. On location the sense of reality oppressed him. The world of make-believe was where Peter Cushing liked to be. A childlike world of 'let's pretend' was to him, the very essence of acting.

Actors must not only look the part, they must also have a range of skills especially if they are appearing in the movies. When he first went to Hollywood he pretended that he was a skilled fencer when he had a small part in *The Man in the Iron Mask* (1939). In *The Skull* (1965) he had to play snooker convincingly before bludgeoning Christopher

Lee to death. He had to ride horses on many occasions and it was his wife Helen, an accomplished equestrienne, who gave him a few pointers. He had always fancied being in a Western but admits that the nearest he came to it was a shooting and brawling British adventure film called *Fury at Smuggler's Bay* (1961) co-starring Liz Fraser and George Coulouris. This also required him to be filmed on horseback. His friend Christopher Lee said sarcastically that the expression on Cushing's face when he died in the movie was exactly the same as when he found out what his fee for the film was going to be. It wasn't always horses either. In *She* (1965), Cushing rides a camel.

His roles as a mad or (occasionally) sane scientist – usually in Hammer films – often required him to show a familiarity with medical techniques, which made him jokingly compare himself with the heart transplant pioneer Dr Christiaan Barnard. In *Cone of Silence* (1960), which is about the aftermath of a civilian airline crash, Cushing had to make it look as though he knew how to fly a plane.

Though a great film actor, he was always drawn to live theatre, even though he suffered so badly from nerves and anxiety. But in 1975 – as he coped with his wife Helen's death in 1971 – he made a return to the stage after an absence of nearly ten years. In 1965 he had played Sir Hector Benbow in Ben Travers's farce *Thark*, directed by master-of-farce Ray Cooney. For his return he played Dr Austin Sloper in a production of *The Heiress* based on Henry James's *Washington Square*, staged by the Horseshoe Theatre Company at the Haymarket in Basingstoke, which was then run by Guy Slater and Helen Ryan.

* * *

After a slow start Christopher Lee had an action-packed war, but like many young men who emerged from the military, he did not know what to do with himself in peacetime. He certainly could not face going back to a clerical job. It was his cousin Nicolò Carandini, who had been a member of the Italian resistance and was now the Italian Ambassador, who said over lunch: 'Why don't you become an actor?' Count Carandini (1896–1972) – who would be the first president of

Italy's national airline Alitalia, from its foundation in 1948 until his retirement in 1968 – introduced him to former lawyer Filippo del Giudice, who was head of Two Cities Films, a film production company founded in 1937 which operated in London and Rome. Del Giudice, along with his partner Mario Zampi, had been briefly interned as 'enemy aliens' in 1940. He was released to relaunch Two Cities and to work on Noel Coward's 1943 film *In Which We Serve* with a secretary, Ann Elwell, who had been supplied by MI5.

In 1944, to raise the finance for Laurence Olivier's expensive production of *Henry V* (1944), Del Giudice surrendered a controlling interest to the Rank Organisation and that is how, in 1947, Christopher Lee signed a seven-year contract with what the press mockingly called the Rank Charm School, but which was officially known as the Company of Youth. The Methodist millionaire J. Arthur Rank, described by the late (and great) film critic Barry Norman as 'the first and indeed the last tycoon of the British film industry', recognised that with more and more films being made each year in the UK there was a real need to bring on young British talent. The idea of putting young players under contract (for about £10 a week) originated with the producer Sidney Box. We tend to think of the Charm School as being dedicated to fostering the talents of young women, but virile British male leads were also needed. Many of the young men were, like Lee, were just out of the armed forces.

The idea was that the home-grown talent would in some way resemble an A-list Hollywood counterpart. Lee was said to be the new James Mason.

In a documentary made about the Rank Charm School in 1982, which was presented by Barry Norman (and in which Lee takes part), Olive Dodds, director of artists between 1949–1959, says that they were looking for people with looks and personality who actively wanted to be film stars. Acting talent was not always necessary.

The school was based in a grim church hall in Highbury, north London with no loo. Diana Dors, one of the Rank 'starlets' at 15, had expected chandeliers and glamour and was a little disappointed. The students learned deportment, movement and mime, and rehearsal techniques. In many ways it was similar to a finishing school and Christopher Lee did not think much of it, telling Norman: 'I was not prepared to walk round the room with a book on my head which a lot of the girls had to do and a lot of the men, because they simply did not know how to move.'

One of the criticisms of the school is that while they sent their students (wearing borrowed mink coats and jewellery) out to make personal appearances at fetes, premieres and garden parties, there was no pressure on Rank's directors and producers to actually cast these inexperienced youngsters. There was a Rank connection with (coincidentally) the Connaught Theatre in Worthing where Peter Cushing had appeared and Lee recalls being sent there, which while it provided some understanding of live theatre did not seem very useful for these would-be film stars. Lee played the butler in a production of Margaret Kennedy's best-selling 1928 novel *The Constant Nymph*. It was not a very happy experience. Early in the run the producer made his way to Lee's dressing room, furious at the way the butler was upstaging everyone else, and tore into him, suggesting that as he seemed intent on playing every part the rest of the cast could go home.

Often the only real experience of film-making that the Rank students ever had was in 'stooging', which meant that they stood in for a star while others were screen-tested. Lee claims this was very valuable. He stooged for Stewart Granger in screen-tests for the Basil Deardon film *Sarabande for Dead Lovers* (1948), standing in for the actor as a succession of leading ladies went through their paces, including Flora Robson (who did get the part), Coral Browne and Moira Lister. The process of responding to each of their different performances interested him and made him think deeply about the craft of acting.

The Charm School was expensive to run and in 1949 many of the contract players were dropped, among them Christopher Lee, who says he breathed a sigh of relief. There was an attempt at resurrecting the Company of Youth in the mid-1950s but it did not last long. The Rank starlets in their borrowed minks (and in Diana Dors's case, the famous mink bikini worn at the Venice Film festival in 1955) had lent some innocent glamour to dreary post-war Britain. But though the alumni of the Company of Youth did produce some stars – Jean Simmons, Petula Clark, Honor Blackman, Patrick McGoohan and Donald Sinden among others – it was, from the outset, treated as a joke. What's more, the attempt to reproduce the Hollywood system from a bygone age was doomed. The contract system had had its day.

Lee was living in a basement flat in Chelsea and spent what money had had buying old 78rpm records of opera recordings at the shops on the Charing Cross Road. He believed he had inherited a decent singing voice from his great-grandfather, Girolamo Carandini, 10th Marquis of Sarzano. Carandini was a singer at the Modena Opera House and the woman he married was a celebrated soprano.

In an interview in *Gramophone Magazine* Lee recalled the night he met the Swedish tenor Jussi Björling at a student party in Stockholm in 1948 where everyone, including Lee, was drinking and singing. Björling told him to come the next morning to the Opera House and sing to him. Lee protested that he hadn't been trained, but Björling insisted. The following day, as instructed, Lee found himself on the stage. Björling was sitting in the stalls next to Joel Berglund (then head of the Royal Swedish Opera). Lee, unaccompanied, sang Don Giovanni's *Serenade* and everything he knew from the opera. Björling and Berglund conferred at length. The upshot was that Björling offered to train him if he stayed in Stockholm. Lee couldn't accept because he didn't have the funds to live in Stockholm. It remained one of the greatest regrets of his life. He always believed he was born to be an opera singer.

Meanwhile his film career was progressing slowly. His first film role (one line of dialogue) was in *Corridor of Mirrors* (1948). Both Lee and Peter Cushing had tiny roles in Olivier's *Hamlet* (1948), though they did not meet at the time. He is in *Song for Tomorrow* (1948) directed by Terence Fisher, who would go on to direct many Hammer horror films, and in a B-film about a Second World War fighter who suffers from amnesia. In *Scott of the Antarctic* (1948) directed by Charles Frend, he plays a member of the British Antarctic Expedition alongside John Mills, Kenneth More and James Robertson Justice. He was not required for location filming in Norway, braving instead the icy wastes of Ealing

Studios, where the blizzards were made of salt and acrylic resin, put through a sieve and blown across the set by an aeroplane engine. He was in a comedy musical *One Night With You* (1948) directed by Terence Young, and *Trottie True* (1949) starring Jean Kent as a Gaiety Girl in the 1890s. Lee plays the Hon Bongo Icklesham and the cast included another up-and-coming young actor, Roger Moore, cast as Stage Door Johnny.

Christopher Lee was in work but he did occasionally wonder if he was 'too tall to be an actor and too old to be a singer'.

Chapter Three

Hollywood

In 1934 the novelist and playwright J.B. Priestley (1894–1984) published English Journey, billed as 'a Rambling but Truthful Account of What One Man Saw and Heard and Felt and Thought During a Journey Through England During the Autumn of the Year 1933'. His journey took him from Southampton, to the Black Country, to the North East and Newcastle, to Norwich and finally back to home in Hampstead. He observes England as the Depression bites with high levels of unemployment. But he also has a keen sense for a new mood of modernity. Priestley was a theatre man through and through. His plays such as *An Inspector Calls* (ever a favourite GCSE set text), *Time and The Conways* and *When We Are Married* are still performed. But in *English Journey*, like a dog with a bone, he worries away at the threat posed to live theatre by cinema. Reading this book makes you appreciate just how the age of the movies transformed life for people in the middle decades of the twentieth century.

Stopping in Romsey in Hampshire he notes: 'This road with its new lock-up shops, its picture theatres, its red brick villas might have been anywhere: it is the standard new suburban road of our times'. He also understood that this new way of living was essentially American and that the blending of our two cultures was inevitable, adding that the streets 'only differ in a few minor details from a few thousand such roads in the United States where the same toothpastes and soaps and gramophone records are sold, the very same films are being shown'.

Even the pubs, ostensibly a very British institution, are at risk from Americanisation. In the Midlands he finds that some hostelries are 'admirably designed and built; others have been inspired by the idea of Merrie England, popular in the neighbourhood of Los Angeles'.

In Leicester he becomes grumpy when he goes in search of live theatre:

In the whole of Leicester that night there was only one performance being given by living players, in a touring musical comedy. In a town with nearly a quarter of a million people, not without intelligence or money, this is not good enough. Soon we shall be as badly off as America, where I would find myself in large cities that had not a single living actor performing in them, nothing but films, films, films. There, a whole generation has grown up that associates entertainment with moving pictures and with nothing else; and I am not sure that as much could not be said of this country. I rather like films, but not in my capacity as an enquiring traveller. They do not offer you any knowledge of the town you are visiting, only an escape from it; once inside a picture theatre, you might be anywhere, from Iowa City to Preston. A theatre or a music-hall not only has real performers but it also has real audiences, and so can tell you something about the local people, who come alive and are not merely deeper shadows in the murk. This is yet another reason for deploring the growing scarcity of proper theatres.

America, he accepts, is the model for England after the First World War. 'This,' he explains,

is the England of arterial and by-pass roads, of filling stations and factories that look like exhibition buildings, of giant cinemas and dance-halls and cafés, bungalows with tiny garages, cocktail bars, Woolworths, motor-coaches, wireless, hiking, factory girls looking like actresses, greyhound racing and dirt tracks, swimming pools, and everything given away for cigarette coupons.

Priestley was, in truth, a bit of a snob. How very withering is the phrase 'factory girls looking like actresses'. He means Hollywood actresses of course, whose beautiful powdered faces gazed out from the gossipy movie magazines that purported to tell fans what the stars were up to and offered them a vision of impossible glamour in a land of sunshine and oranges. One influential American magazine was *Photoplay*, founded in 1911. A promotion leaflet for potential advertisers reads: '*Photoplay* ... is outstandingly tributary to the great sales-making, building influence of the screen ... During that hour or two in the romantic world of make-believe, potent influences are at work. New desires are installed, new wants implanted, new impulses to spend are aroused.' It is impossible to overestimate the influence of Hollywood (in particular) and America (in general) on British culture in the 1920s and '30s. Even today, if a British star moves to Hollywood that is usually seen as indicative of a step-up in terms of success.

By 1934, when *English Journey* was published, Boris Karloff – a man who in the 1900s thought he was going to Canada to make his mark in live theatre – had become a Hollywood star thanks to *Frankenstein* (1931). He had been in Los Angeles since 1917 and *Frankenstein* was his eighty-first film, made when he was already in his mid-40s. This is one of the details which links Karloff, Cushing and Lee. In an industry which was – like the age in which it flourished – obsessed with youth, these three stars were middle-aged before they knew global fame. They were late developers.

At 40, Peter Cushing, was told by his father that he was a failure. Christopher Lee commented in his autobiography that at the age of 35, most of the men in his family had become cardinals or colonels, chairmen or ambassadors. Whereas, after ten years in the film business he was as unknown as when he started.

In the end their maturity became their unique selling point, the roles they played defied ageism and made a virtue of the longevity of their careers. They were the exception that proved the rule succinctly laid down in *Motion Picture Magazine* in 1926. 'Stardom is at best short-lived in motion pictures,' it declared, '...the stars of the cinema heaven are eclipsed and fade into obscurity quicker than do those of its nearest rivals in American favour – baseball.'

Karloff pounded the pavements looking for acting work in Hollywood. By the 1920s he had found a niche playing dark-skinned characters – among them, Arabs, Indians and South Sea Islanders – making the most of what he referred to as his 'tan'. He was never afraid of being 'typed' as it meant paid work. In 1923 he was in two Universal pictures, playing a cowboy in *The Gentleman from America*, and cast as Prince

Kapolski in *The Prisoner*. To make ends meet he had to take work as a warehouseman and truck driver. He appeared in a silent horror film *The Bells* (1926) adapted from an Edgar Allan Poe story with Lionel Barrymore in the lead.

In 1929 he appeared in his first sound film, *The Unholy Night* (1929) made by MGM based on a Ben Hecht story *The Green Ghost* and directed by Lionel Barrymore. Karloff had a small role as Abdul, the lawyer. The setting is foggy London where members of an army regiment are being killed off.

In 1930 Karloff came to the attention of the director Howard Hawks who gave him a part in the gritty prison movie *The Criminal Code* (1931), which he made for Columbia, in which Karloff had taken a part when the stage version was produced at LA's Belasco Theatre. In an article in *Film Weekly*, from 18 April 1936, Karloff says that this was 'the first talkie I made that really meant anything ... The high spot was a prison scene in which I had to come on to kill a stool-pigeon". It was a gripping scene.' Karloff persuaded Hawks to let him play the scene in exactly the same way as he had played it on stage – in silence and with no distracting close-ups.

By now he had worked for Universal and Columbia, Warner Bros, RKO and MGM. In the summer of 1931 he was back at Universal making a picture called *Graft*, while the bosses were trying to persuade Bela Lugosi to follow his success in Tod Browning's *Dracula* with a new horror spectacular – *Frankenstein*.

Bulk retailer Carl Laemmle had observed in the 1900s that 'the basic idea of motion pictures and Mr Woolworth's innovation were identical', and had opened his first nickelodeon (an early picture house), the White Front Theatre, on Chicago's Milwaukee Avenue in 1906. Successful though he was, he was thwarted by the poor technical quality of film prints, unscrupulous distributors and a shortage of material. So in 1909 Laemmle's Independent Motion Picture Company produced its first film, a one-reel adaptation of Longfellow's poem *Hiawatha*, and in 1912 Laemmle plus his associates launched The Universal Film Manufacturing Company. In 1915 Universal City Studios opened, on a 230-acre converted farm just over the Cahuenga Pass.

Laemmle was a shrewd businessman. Among other innovations was the novel practice of giving screen credits to the actors, which pleased actors and created the star system. Universal was a vertically integrated company with movie production, distribution and exhibition venues all linked. This was a key element of the studio system but this would eventually fall foul of America's anti-trust laws.

Karloff was taking a break in the canteen when an assistant to the director James Whale approached him. Would he be interested in testing for the monster in *Frankenstein*? As ever, Karloff was grateful for any work that came his way. Jack Pierce, make-up artist extraordinaire, spent weeks creating the iconic monster look. Laemmle Sr and his producer son Carl both approved and noted that, 'Karloff's eyes mirrored the suffering we needed'.

The painful and excruciatingly slow business of preparing Karloff to play the monster, and the equally slow business of taking the make-up off at the end of the day have become legend. In an article in *Picturegoer* from April 1932, Helen Weigel Brown describes the daily regime:

> Each time the monster was created, Karloff had to sit in the make-up chair for three and a half hours. First his eyes had to be given that heavy, half-dead, insane look – a matter of applying coats and coats of wax to his eyelids to weigh them down.
>
> Next invisible wire clamps were fixed over his lips to pull the corners of his mouth out and down. Then the overhanging brow and high, square shaped crown of the head, supposedly 'grafted' from the head of another man. These, as well as his face and neck, were shaped and built up by means of thin layers of flesh. Then the greyish make-up on top of all. Bolt-like plugs were placed on the side of the neck and held there by means of more layers of cotton and adhesive liquids ... Removing the make-up was not much simpler than putting it on, and certainly more painful. It required and hour and a half of prying, pulling and coaxing, plus special oils and 'a great deal of bad language,' adds Karloff.

Pierce's career had been far from straightforward. He had come to California from Chicago in 1908 to break into Coast League baseball. He was good but not good enough, so he took a job as a projectionist in a nickelodeon picture house and joined Universal in 1914 as an actor and assistant cameramen, before finding his way to the make-up department. Pierce said that he didn't depend on his imagination when devising the look of the Monster. He researched into anatomy, surgery, criminology, burial customs ancient and modern, as well as electrodynamics. He found out that there are six possible ways of removing a brain from a skull that would be used by trained brain surgeons. Frankenstein, being a scientist rather than a surgeon, would (Pierce figured) simply cut the top of the skull across like a lid and peel it open, like the hinge lid of a box. Whatever the method, Karloff's sessions in the make-up chair were always torture.

The hardships actors face are part of movie history and make for entertaining anecdotes. Almost any actor required to change appearance will give details of how they suffered for their art. In Karloff's case it was not only the hours in the make-up chair which wore him down physically. The filming of *Frankenstein* began on 24 August 1931, and California was sweltering. Karloff felt as though he was being partially cooked in his heavy padded suit and boots. He often worked a sixteen-hour day, though in theory the Academy of Motion Pictures Arts and Sciences (set up in 1927) stated that no actor work more than twelve hours a day. In one scene Karloff has to carry his creator, Dr Henry Frankenstein (played by Colin Clive), up a steep hill. There were a dozen takes and no stand-ins, as that would have stretched the budget. Sara Jane Karloff believes that this extreme exertion contributed to the mobility problems that plagued Karloff for the rest of his life.

What is more, you had to keep in with the right people – even if they kept you awake at night. Relatively early in his career Karloff was living next door to a Hollywood celebrity who threw a noisy party. Karloff had to be at the studio at dawn for a session in the make-up chair which took, on average, three hours. After tossing and turning for hours he decided to call the cops, but with the receiver in his hand he suddenly asked himself the question – which was more important, his Hollywood career or a good night's sleep? It was a no-brainer.

Karloff was one of the lucky ones. Thousands of would-be movie stars made their way to Hollywood in the 1910s and 1920s. Most had no experience of acting but had been sold the Tinseltown dream in which a complete unknown would be found to have a natural rapport with the camera and achieve overnight stardom. The film historian Kevin Brownlow estimates that the chances of finding work in the studios were around one in a hundred. Karloff always quoted the silent star Lon Chaney, whom he admired tremendously. Chaney had told him that 'the secret of success in Hollywood lies in being different from anyone else. Find something that no one else can or will do – and they'll begin to take notice of you.'

Encouraging words, and very apt in Karloff's case. But for the thousands of would-be actors a day's work as an extra was a dream come true. Extras employed on D.W. Griffiths film *Intolerance* (1916) received $1.25 per day plus some travel expenses and (crucially) a free lunch. For many this was the best part of the deal as a lot of Hollywood hopefuls knew real hunger.

The studios had the upper-hand at all times. In the 1920s and '30s, it was common for actors to receive informal job offers and then find they had been withdrawn without explanation or compensation. In a sad irony, only the most successful practitioners were allowed to join the Academy of Motion Picture Arts and Sciences, intended to improve relations within the film industry.

By 1933, the Depression had hit hard and box office takings were down. Film historian Kathryn Fuller-Seeley estimates that by 1932, about 8,000 of the nation's 23,000 movie theatres were closed. The studios announced temporary 50 per cent wage cuts, but when after the stated eight-week period neither Warner Brothers nor Goldwyn reinstated the wages, several members of the Academy resigned.

Actors Equity had been set up in 1913, a union for theatre performers. But it had no agreement with the film studios. In protest against the studios' exploitative actions, members of a Hollywood actors' social club called The Masquers along with disaffected Academy players joined forces to set up the Screen Actors Guild (SAG) early in 1933. Karloff was a founder member. Bela Lugosi joined soon after. In his native Hungary, Lugosi had been active in championing actors' rights. Far from being rivals, the two great horror stars – Karloff and Lugosi – were political allies.

Initially SAG was very circumspect, the founding members reluctant to draw attention to their activities and risk being blackballed by the studios. In June, upon hearing that his weekly salary from Universal of $1,000 would be cut, Karloff parted company with the studio – though only briefly. In 1934 he was back to star in an adaptation of Edgar Allan Poe's *The Black Cat*, co-starring with Bela Lugosi.

With his fame and his commitment to SAG, Karloff was now very much part of the Hollywood establishment, living with current wife Dorothy at 2320 Bowmont Drive in the Beverly Hills estate in a farmhouse that had previously been owned by Katharine Hepburn. In July 1935 he became a member of the Motion Picture Hall of Fame and sat on the committee of the California Pacific International Exposition in San Diego along with Joan Crawford, Bette Davis, James Cagney (a great personal friend), Clark Gable and Fredric March.

Boris and Dorothy left Hollywood briefly and enjoyed a stay in Europe where he filmed *The Man Who Changed his Mind* (1936), for Gainsborough Pictures, a sci-fi horror, co-starring the 'British Bombshell' Anna Lee and directed by her husband, Robert Stevenson. She plays a scientist who goes to work with the sinister Dr Laurience (Karloff) who claims he can switch the brains of chimpanzees.

Early in 1937, and back in Hollywood, filming began for *Night Key*, a Universal sci-fi film starring Karloff as the inventor of a burglar alarm who wants to take revenge on the hoodlum who stole his profits. The alarm is sabotaged by the gangster, who turns it into a device that will make burglaries easier.

During the shoot Boris took issue with Universal's attempt to make him work more than an eight-hour day. It was part of a mood of discontent which in April culminated in a film-industry strike. On 1 May, 3,000 technicians and other staff picketed the big studios, with the support of SAG. Some big stars crossed the picket line – among them, Clark Gable, William Powell, Jean Harlow and Greta Garbo. Jack Benny, Bing Crosby, Irene Dunne, Jean Arthur and Randolph Scott did not cross the picket line. SAG was instrumental in negotiating pay rises with RKO, Paramount, MGM, Twentieth Century Fox, Universal and Columbia and an end to the industrial action.

There was another strong inducement to leave Hollywood in 1941 when Karloff was lured to Broadway to play Jonathan Brewster in a production of Joseph Kesselring's *Arsenic and Old Lace*. The black comedy was long-running and the Karloff family briefly relocated to Darien, Connecticut. After the show Boris could catch the 11 pm train and be home by 1.30 am. In the winter they moved to a house in Manhattan on East 62nd Street.

The outbreak of war and the play's long run meant that Karloff did not return to Hollywood until 1944 and had only appeared in one film in almost four years. The 1940s saw him turn increasingly to radio and TV. Eventually, in 1950 – by now divorced and remarried to Evelyn – the couple moved east to New York. Hollywood was in the grip of the Communist witch hunt and the House Committee on Un-American Activities (HUAC), which began in 1951. Boris was, as his biographer Cynthia Lindsay claimed, 'on the liberal side', which put him under suspicion. But he was no longer permanently in Hollywood and had ended his work with the Screen Actors Guild.

In 1959 he moved back to England where he would spend the last decade of his life. Boris Karloff had risen to fame through the studio system of the Golden Age of Hollywood but also conquered TV, radio and theatre in New York, while remaining indelibly British.

* * *

Peter Cushing wanted to go to Hollywood because it was where his childhood hero – the movie cowboy Tom Mix – came from. Even in a 1972 TV interview he still said: 'I would love to do a western above all else; they're my favourite films'.

His father George, who had never shown any enthusiasm for his son's career choice, gave him a one-way ticket to America, which you could either read as a statement of faith in Cushing's ability to prosper, or as a way of washing his hands of him. Cushing set sail from Southampton on the SS *Champlain* on 18 January 1939. He was vaguely aware of Neville Chamberlain's 'peace for our time speech' during the Munich Crisis and (showing a touching faith in politicians) put all thoughts of war out of his head.

On arrival in New York he stayed for a week in the YMCA and met the actor Robert Morley (1908–1992) who was making his debut on Broadway at the Fulton Theatre. Morley suggested he simply went to Hollywood for a holiday as it was very crowded with movie hopefuls.

Nevertheless, Cushing bought a train ticket to Los Angeles, a journey which took five days, arriving on 10 February 1939. Wearing his thick tweed suit he walked the four miles from the station to Hollywood and checked in to stay at the YMCA on North Hudson Avenue.

He had a letter of introduction from Larry Goodkind of Columbia Pictures, who he met during his short stay in New York. Goodkind's letter got him an interview at the Edward Small Studios. Edward Small (1891–1977), born Edward Schmalheiser, had been raised in Brooklyn and moved to the West Coast in 1917 where initially he set up business as a talent agent. He began producing films in the 1920s, making *I Cover the Waterfront* (1933), *The Count of Monte Cristo* (1934) with Robert Donat, and *The Last of the Mohicans* (1936).

When Cushing arrived, Small was about to start shooting *The Man in the Iron Mask* (1939) starring Joan Bennett and Louis Hayward, directed by James Whale. The two leading male roles are twins and Hayward was playing both parts. In the scenes where one twin spoke to the other twin, there was need for a stand-in who would never be seen on camera.

Cushing was paid $75 a week with the promise of at least two months employment. Not a bad start for someone who had just got off the train. He also had a small name part in the film as The King's Messenger, which involved a sword fight with D'Artagnan (played by Warren William) and the three Musketeers (Alan Hale, Bert Roach and Miles Mander). He told James Whale that he had done a lot of fencing before meeting the film's fencing master Fred Cavens, when he admitted that he needed the job so badly that he had lied about his skills. He also lied about his abilities on horseback. The horse he was allocated bolted and threw him to the ground. As he lay dazed on the ground, he heard the director asking after the welfare of the horse rather than its rider.

Cushing was dazzled by being in Hollywood, thrilled to see so many luminaries who became a part of his new life, while also realising that they were merely human. He became close friends with Louis Hayward who was married to Ida Lupino. Hayward had been born in Johannesburg but educated at Latymer Upper School in West London.

Cushing was a regular at Schwab's Drugstore on Sunset Boulevard, a place where actors hung out and where F. Scott Fitzgerald suffered a heart attack in 1940 when he was standing in line to buy cigarettes. While enjoying a milk shake, Cushing learnt that Hall Roach needed English actors for a new Laurel and Hardy film *A Chump at Oxford* (1940). It was only a week's work but he enjoyed watching these two comic geniuses in action.

His friendship with Ida and Louis meant that he was invited to tennis parties, pool parties and beach parties. The test cricketer turned actor C. Aubrey Smith invited him to play in the Hollywood Cricket Club he had founded in 1932. The team included Basil Rathbone, David Niven and Boris Karloff. Cushing was bowled out first ball on his debut match and missed several easy catches. He was not invited to play again but claims he was put off his stroke by the presence of all those Hollywood stars.

Ida and Louis would take him to Ella Campbell's Restaurant on Sunset Boulevard which specialised in traditional English food and was very popular with the expat stars. He kissed Loretta Young's hand (it was ever his traditional greeting for beautiful women) and went to a bullfight in Tijuana with Adolphe Menjou (which he hated).

He had a small but significant part in an RKO production *Vigil in the Night* (1940), a hospital drama based on a story by A.J. Cronin, starring Carole Lombard and directed by George Stevens. After this he appeared in only four more Hollywood films before the outbreak of the Second World War changed the course of his career. His last one would be *They Dare Not Love* (1941), which was also *Frankenstein* director James Whale's final film.

When war was declared in Europe on 3 September 1939, all British subjects in the US had to attend a medical. By now Cushing – already homesick – was desperate to return to Britain, and began what would turn out to be a very long and difficult journey in January 1941. His Hollywood career was over before it had properly begun. It's a fascinating 'what if' question. Peter Cushing had obviously begun to make a name for himself and who knows what would have happened to him if he had stayed, and how would the British film industry have managed without him?

* * *

Christopher Lee had his first summons to Tinseltown just after his daughter Christina's traumatic birth late in 1963 – 'one of these freaks of bad timing which are incidental to an actor's life', he observed. He was offered a role in an episode of *The Alfred Hitchcock Hour*.

On arrival in California he was met by a car and a driver and taken to a half-completed motel right across the street from Universal Studios. It was not the sort of luxury Hollywood hotel that Lee had imagined where stars lazed on sunbeds. There was a swimming pool but it was so shallow that a man of Lee's height would have risked his life had he attempted to dive in. But even with the studios just 50 yards away Lee's insistence on arriving on foot caused consternation among the security officers. In LA, nobody walks.

The episode he was cast in was adapted from a story by Robert Bloch who had scripted *Psycho*. In his memoirs, Bloch insists that Lee's motel was 'infested by termites and supporting actors'. Robert Bloch (1917–1994) was horror's go-to writer who had received early encouragement from the horror fiction writer H.P. Lovecraft. He wrote many episodes of *The Alfred Hitchcock Hour* also known as *Alfred Hitchcock Presents* and films such as *The House That Dripped Blood* (1971) starring Lee and Cushing, *Asylum* (1972) with Cushing, and the 1998 remake of *Psycho* directed by Gus Van Sant. He and Christopher Lee would later become good friends and Bloch tells us that their wives went shopping together.

Hitchcock did not direct these episodes himself. He was far too grand for that. But he topped and tailed them with his arch introductions. 'The scene of tonight's drama is Hollywood, California, that bizarre town,' he announces – an appropriate introduction for Hollywood newbie, Lee.

It opens with three jaded Hollywood types watching a European film featuring Lee climbing from a sarcophagus and engaging in some satanic mumbo jumbo with sulky women in black robes and devil's horns. Chants are chanted. Goblets are drained.

The Hollywood people want Lee's character, Karl Jorla, to come to Hollywood to appear in a horror movie. Lee arrives, averse to publicity and flashbulbs, because the satanic cult who made the original film is now out to get him. 'Would you like to see your dressing room?' he's asked. 'It's a bungalow.' Ooh, the glamour.

Jorla becomes increasingly fearful and having fought off a satanist in the bungalow, he disappears. His corpse is finally tracked down in an insalubrious house in Topanga Canyon, a suburb in the Santa Monica mountains. By the 1960s Topanga Canyon was becoming popular with artists and rock stars such as Neil Young and Dennis Wilson of the Beach Boys. For a while it was also Charles Manson's address.

While Jorla had an unhappy visit to Hollywood, Lee's fortnight was a success. He'd been given Marlon Brando's dressing-room, he had caught sight of Hitchcock and he had played golf at Bel Air. His hope was that this visit would lead to greater things. Planning to leave behind his Hammer roles, by this stage he had moved to Switzerland to become a star in European movies, but though there had been parts in a number of Italian films he was not – during the 1960s – getting the exposure nor the range he had hoped for. Even his role in the Bond movie *The Man with the Golden Gun* (1974) did not move the dial as far as Lee was concerned.

Friends, including Billy Wilder and the actor Richard Widmark (with whom he had starred in the 1976 Hammer film *To The Devil*

... *a Daughter*), insisted that Lee should relocate to Los Angeles. In 1977 Christopher, Gitte and Christina made the move.

Lee bought an eighth-floor apartment on Wilshire Boulevard with a smog-bound view of the Hollywood Hills and was quickly offered a role in the disaster movie *Airport '77*. The cast was as Hollywood A-List as one could hope for – Jack Lemmon, James Stewart, Olivia de Havilland, Jospeh Cotten and George Kennedy. The costumes were by the great Hollywood designer Edith Head. Lee plays a solemn oceanographer on board the luxury 747 on its inaugural flight. Lee Grant plays his discontented wife with a glass always in her hand.

The unique selling point of *Airport '77* is that the plane spends most of its time under the ocean with the surviving passengers trapped in an air bubble.

The producer Bill Frye explained that Lee would have to go down into the 747's hold with the chief pilot (Lemmon) but the door blows, a tsunami of water pours in and Lee's character drowns.

For Lee, the prospect of doing a key scene with Jack Lemmon made it all worthwhile. He was coached by former Olympic swimmer Manfred Zendar (who also worked on *Jaws*) in the pool on the Universal lot. It was by no means a risk-free part for Lee who had to do several scenes underwater playing dead. On one occasion he ran out of breath and was handed the oxygen bottle. That was empty. Thankfully there was a spare. At the end of the picture the stunt men gave Lee a Stunt Men's Association belt buckle. He was deeply touched.

Part of the deal with being a Hollywood actor was that Lee agreed to fly to New York to appear on *Saturday Night Live*, which had premiered in 1975. This confection of skits, satire and variety went out (as it said on the tin) live, something which Lee hated, but he enjoyed doing a comic turn. He also knew it was something he had to do, mostly because it would be watched by up to 35 million viewers.

He was in Disney's *Return from Witch Mountain* (1978) with Bette Davis. In Steven Spielberg's movie *1941* (1979) he played Captain Wolfgang Von Kleinschmidt. Now considered a cult comedy the film received mixed reviews at the time. Vincent Canby of *The New York Times* wrote: 'I've seldom seen a comedy more ineptly timed.'

His next movie was *Bear Island* (1979), based on an Alistair Maclean Arctic climate change thriller (way ahead of its time), a British production co-starring Richard Widmark, Donald Sutherland and Vanessa Redgrave, directed by Don Sharp. Lee plays a Polish scientist with a spectacular moustache. Filming took place on location in Alaska and at Pinewood Studios.

Lee was aware that his typecasting as a horror star had a negative impact on his earning potential. And, perversely, being obliged to take a lower fee did not make him any more appealing to casting agents. In the film business the most expensive candidate is the one who is most likely to get the job.

He kept working, doggedly, making some forgettable TV films and totally forgotten TV pilots. He and Alan Arkin had fun in the superhero film *The Return of Captain Invincible* (1983) and he starred with Sally Kellerman and Tuesday Weld in *Serial* (1980), a comedy based on a bestseller about the hippie culture in San Francisco.

Lee describes Los Angeles rather well as a 'collection of suburbs in search of a town'. Film people, he observed, live close together for only the truly great stars can afford to live at a distance where they are not immediately available if their agent or the studio calls. The film community was tiny. Everyone read *Variety* and *Hollywood Reporter* and went to the same parties and talked about who was paid what.

Lee made some forty films when he was in Hollywood before deciding – in the mid-1980s – to up sticks again and return to Europe. But some of his biggest movies were still ahead of him.

* * *

Chapter Four

Television

Sara Jane Karloff has devoted much of her life to keeping alive her father's legacy. Every year there are conventions, websites, symposiums, podcasts, documentaries personal appearances by Sara Jane herself. But will this interest be maintained into the future? She is not convinced that it will because she knows that her sons have their own lives to lead and that her three grandchildren may not have the time nor the inclination. She may be right, but the fact is that even today – almost hundred years after *Frankenstein* was made – the image of Karloff's monster is known worldwide. It is instantly recognisable, endlessly reproduced and affectionately spoofed. It is a staple of Halloween costumes while the monster's unsteady gait and staring eyes are the understood code for 'horror'. Bolts in the neck? We know at once what character we are talking about. Dracula's incarnation in the shape of Christopher Lee in the films made by Hammer is equally iconic, even though there have been very many Draculas.

Yet *Frankenstein* was made in 1931 and the Hammer *Dracula* films were made in the late 1950s through to the early 1970s. These cultural totems owe their survival and enduring popularity to television, to late-night repeats of low-budget films, a practice which began in the US in the 1950s and in Britain in the mid-1960s with BBC2's Saturday night *Midnight Movie*, which usually started at about 11.15 pm. Restrictions on broadcasting hours on BBC1 and ITV could be sidestepped by BBC2 which broadcast for fewer hours than the permitted eight hours per day and therefore could use up more airtime with this late-night programming.

It was once feared that television – that diabolical box in the corner of the sitting-room – would mean the end of cinema. Any new medium leads to what has been called 'media panic', contrasted unfavourably with older media and condemned as a threat to society's morals and even its health. Young people are always assumed to be more at risk because they are the more enthusiastic adopters of the new medium, whether it be TV or TikTok. It was feared that television would drug the masses into passivity, destroy family life, and reduce all creative output to the 'lowest common denominator' in its ruthless drive for commercial domination.

Even in the 1930s – during the golden age of Hollywood – there was concern about television's potential. In 1935, the same year that Karloff starred in *The Bride of Frankenstein*, a movie was released called *Murder by Television*, involving the battle for control of a new device which allows live broadcasts to be beamed from every place in the world. The inventor – who believes that 'television is the greatest step forward we have ever made in the preservation of humanity' – refuses to sell his device, with tragic results. Though the sight of this new breed of TV executives wearing wing collars and evening dress is hilarious, it is a prescient little film. Bela Lugosi, who starred in Tod Browning's *Dracula* (1931) and whose supposed rivalry with Boris Karloff was endlessly talked up by Universal Studios, appears as the movie's villain.

Public service broadcasting began in Britain in 1936, though it closed down during the Second World War. In America, the late 1930s saw a burgeoning of interest in the medium. In 1938 NBC screened several prestigious telecasts from New York, including scenes from the Broadway hit *Susan and God* starring Gertrude Lawrence. In the same year NBC showed a live news event – a mobile unit which just happened to be passing captured a fire which broke out in the New York borough of Queens. The station also transmitted the official opening of the World's Fair in New York on 30 April 1939. Franklin D. Roosevelt gave the opening address which made him the first American President to appear on TV.

Scheduling was very informal but NBC inaugurated the first ratings system. The company kept a card index listing every set owner and sent out postcards each week describing the programmes that would be shown and asking the viewer's opinion of them.

New York was the capital of American TV just as Hollywood was the capital of American film. But the Second World War halted the ascendancy of the small screen as it did in Britain and it was not until 1946 that there was a regular network service. The growth of TV was phenomenal. The percentage of US homes with TV sets went from 1 per cent to 50 per cent between 1948–53, and exceeded 90 per cent by the early 1960s.

Boris Karloff realised quite early that both radio and TV had much to offer him. In January, 1949 he had opened in Edward Percy's play *The Shop at Sly Corner*, which closed after just five performances. The New York critics agreed that his performance had been the one redeeming feature of the production. Before he returned to Los Angeles Boris appeared in his first TV production in the anthology series *The Chevrolet Tele-Theatre*, a live broadcast from the NBC Studios on 7 February in a half-hour drama called *Expert Opinion*.

His move into TV coincided with the landmark Supreme Court anti-trust case United States v Paramount Pictures, Inc. (1948), which led to the Paramount Decree preventing film production companies from owning exhibition companies. The studios were forced to divest themselves of their movie theatre chains. This, combined with the growing popularity of TV, led to a severe downturn in the film industry and was the death knell for the old Hollywood studio system.

With this in mind Karloff and his wife Evie were keen to move to New York and he jumped at the offer of his own thirteen-week ABC series *Starring Boris Karloff* which began on 22 September 1949 – airing on both radio and TV, which was a common practice at the time. An anthology of stories of mystery and horror, it was hosted by and occasionally starred Karloff. The first one, titled *Five Golden Guineas*, sets the tone. A hangman, paid five guineas per execution, takes an unseemly pleasure in his work causing his pregnant wife to leave him. Twenty years later he executes a young man, who turns out to be his own son. His wife reveals to him what he has done. He strangles her and is duly sent to the gallows himself. The series wasn't a great critical success but it was the harbinger of Karloff's future career, a combination of theatre, TV and radio work.

The concept of the 'guest appearance' worked well for TV, adding a sprinkle of Hollywood stardust to the homely medium, whether in drama, chat shows or panel games. *Inside USA with Chevrolet* was a variety series launched in 1949 in which there was a 'star of the week'. Karloff was one. Others included Lucille Ball, Ethel Merman and David Niven. *Suspense*, made by CBS, ran between 1949 and 1964 and was a shoo-in for Karloff. *Lights Out* was another suspense anthology made by NBC between 1949 and 1952, variously featuring Karloff, Burgess Meredith, Leslie Nielsen, Basil Rathbone, Eddie Albert, Raymond Massey and Yvonne de Carlo. A short-running but star-studded *Masterpiece Playhouse* in the summer of 1950 offered live broadcasts of seven classics (Ibsen, Shakespeare etc) with Karloff in Chekhov's *Uncle Vanya*. *Tales of Tomorrow*, made by ABC between 1951 and 1953 was a sci-fi series in which he appeared along with Franchot Tone, Lon Chaney Jr, Veronica Lake, Eve Gabor, Leslie Nielsen and Lee J. Cobb. Karloff was a regular on *Down You Go*, a word game which ran between 1951 and 1956, in which the contestants had to guess a word or phrase submitted by a viewer. *The Elgin TV Hour* was another drama series, screened between 1954 and 1955 featuring Karloff, along with big stars such as Franchot Tone, Ralph Bellamy, Polly Bergen and John Cassavetes.

In 1956 he appeared on CBS's *The $64,000 Question*, answering every question about his special subject – children's fairy tales – correctly. He got to the stage where he could try for the $64,000 jackpot. But on the advice of his lawyer he refused, as the income tax would have reduced the winnings below the $32,000 that he had already won.

A year later he was in a ninety-minute NBC version of Lilian Hellman's *The Lark*, co-starring with Julie Harris, Eli Wallach and Basil Rathbone. It was a colour broadcast which was seen by 26 million viewers

Well into the 1960s, as a symbol of classic horror cinema, Boris Karloff was much in demand on TV. Whereas in the 1930s movie-goers had been challenged to brave a screening of the *Frankenstein* films, television audiences were now invited to regard Karloff with affection, as a slightly camp survivor of old Hollywood and an English gent. He gamely played up to this image.

Between 1960 and 1962 he hosted an American NBC series called *Thriller*, appearing in suit and tie to unveil the action, introduce us to the cast, and add a frisson to proceedings. For instance, in a 1961 episode called *The Grim Reaper*, starring a young William Shatner, he observes that, 'Someone is in mortal danger as surely as my name is Boris Karloff' (just in case there was any doubt).

His other TV work included the title role in *Colonel March of Scotland Yard*, which was a British production by Associated Television which was shown in both Britain and the US. It was based on John Dickson Carr's 1940 book *The Department of Queer Complaints*. Karloff played the Colonel wearing good tweeds and (never explained) an eyepatch. Among the directors was Terence Fisher, who would make many Hammer films. Christopher Lee, then 31, was a guest actor in one episode titled *All Cats Are Grey at Night*. TV critic Bernard Levin did not warm to the series, saying in the *Manchester Guardian* in 1955, that its intellectual content was 'the nearest thing to a hole that I have ever seen'.

The Veil (1958) was another anthology of supernatural stories presented by Karloff, sitting before a roaring fire in more fine tailoring. 'Good evening,' he says, 'tonight I'm going to tell you another strange and unusual story of the unexplainable that lies behind the veil.' The series was never broadcast but was later compiled into three feature-length films which showed up on late-night TV in the 1960s and were later released on VHS.

Out of This World (1962) was made for ITV by ABC Weekend, adapted from sci-fi stories and a steal from America's *The Twilight Zone*. Only one episode survives, *Little Lost Robot*, based on a story by Isaac Asimov. Karloff wears a black tie and tux to perform the hosting honours.

As a chat- or game-show guest it was essential that the host or the other guests affected a terror of the star in their midst. Karloff was always happy to play along. He appeared on *I've Got a Secret* made for CBS in 1952. His secret was that he was afraid of mice.

In 1957 he was a guest on *The Rosemary Clooney Show*. Rosemary jumps in faux alarm when he appears next to her. Karloff admits that he is terrified by the sight of himself in the shaving mirror these days, adding archly: 'How would you react to the sight of a razor held to your throat by ... Boris Karloff?' But now, so he tells Rosemary, he wants to break out of the horror mould and do a storytelling series for children. He performed much the same routine on CBS's *The Entertainers* in 1965 hosted by Carol Burnett. She screams when she sees him and he says: 'You're making the mistake of mixing me up with the parts that I play in films. In real life, my great interest is gardening. Why, only today, I planted a new flower bed.' 'Who's under it?' asks Carol.

In 1957, on his 70th birthday, he appeared on the American version of *This Is Your Life* in which an unsuspecting celebrity was gently ambushed and taken to a studio to meet friends and relatives from his or her past. Both Christopher Lee (in 1974) and Peter Cushing (in 1990) appeared on the British version of the long-running show hosted by the ever genial Eamonn Andrews. Whether or not Karloff really recognises that old schoolfriend from Uppingham is not entirely clear but, ever the gentleman, he acts as though he does.

In the Swinging Sixties he was a guest in a 1966 episode of *The Girl from U.N.C.L.E* starring Stefanie Powers, one of many ageing Hollywood stars who appeared in both this and *The Man From U.N.C.L.E.* By this time he was in considerable pain from his legs and back but always, according to Powers, 'a beguilingly lovely man'.

* * *

Peter Cushing's life in Hollywood was halted by the outbreak of the Second World War which caused him to return to England; he returned to working mostly in the theatre and so his career moved in a different direction. Increasingly he found the demands of live theatre unbearably stressful and during rehearsals for Laurence Olivier's 1950 production of Bridget Boland's *The Damascus Blade*, he suffered a nervous breakdown and was replaced. Olivier paid him in full, which Cushing always regarded as a great kindness.

Though he did manage to return to the stage he also began to appear on TV partly as a result of his wife Helen, who wrote to a string of TV producers announcing that her husband was available for work. As a result he appeared in his first TV play in 1951, J.B. Priestley's *Eden End*. All programmes were transmitted live from Alexandra Palace, Muswell Hill, and subsequently from the Lime Grove Studios in Shepherd's Bush.

Eden End went out on 2 December, following three weeks of rehearsal. The pressure of live TV, with actors dependent on cameras and mics can only be imagined, and far more daunting in some respects than was live theatre. There was no chance of the director shouting 'cut' and doing the scene again. There was no chance of fudging a mistake as actors can do on stage. The scrutiny of the cameras was all-seeing. If one of the actors forgot his or her lines, the best that could happen was that an assistant floor manager (AFM) would press a button which cut off the viewers' audio and allow the AFM to give a prompt. Cushing, never the most laid-back of performers, found the whole process excruciating.

The first performance in *Eden End* left him feeling depressed. As soon as the VISION ON sign came on he felt he had gone to pieces. He went home in despair. Helen had gone to see the TV play at a friend's house and when she came home she was in raptures about his performance. The next morning the phone rang with congratulatory messages and offers of more work. Subsequently, Cushing would always request that Helen would be in the studio during transmission to boost his confidence.

In 1951 there were about a million TV sets in Britain and just one BBC TV channel. The panel game *What's My Line* debuted along with *An Evening at Home with Bernard Braden and Barbara Kelly*. The first TV adaptation of Sherlock Holmes was made starring Alan Wheatley as Holmes and Raymond Francis as Watson.

In 1952 Peter Cushing played Mr Darcy in an adaptation of *Pride and Prejudice* and in March 1954 he took the title role in Anatole de Grunwald's play *Beau Brummell*. Barney Keelan in the *Radio Times* wrote: 'In this production style is in the safe-keeping of Peter Cushing.' An indication of just how often Cushing appeared on British TV in the early 1950s was evident in a radio comedy show in which television was described as 'Peter Cushing with knobs on'.

In 1954, he won the Daily Mail Outstanding Actor of 1953–54 and the Best Play award went to *Anastasia*, in which he had also starred. The romantic comedy *Tovarich*, written by Jacques Deval, was shown in January 1954. Cushing played Prince Mikhail Alexandrovitch Ouartieff with Ann Todd as his wife Grand Duchess Tatiana Petrovna – two down-on-their-luck Russian aristocrats trying to get by in exile after the revolution. This popular and prestigious production earned Cushing the accolade of his first *Radio Times* cover on 22 January 1954.

But it was an adaptation of George Orwell's *Nineteen Eighty-Four* that transformed Cushing into one of Britain's biggest stars. It was directed by Rudolph Cartier who had been impressed by Cushing's performance in *Anastasia* the previous year. The adaptation was by Nigel Kneale (who the year before had written the sci-fi horror *The Quatermass Experiment* for the BBC). It was shown on 12 December 1954 with Yvonne Mitchell playing Julia to Cushing's Winston Smith. Some 'inserts' were shot in advance but most of the two-hour production was broadcast live from the Lime Grove Studios.

The play caused controversy with some viewers appalled by the scene where Smith is tortured by rats. A report in the *Daily Express* claimed that a woman in Herne Bay had died of shock while watching. There were even questions in Parliament and a group of MPs chose to deplore 'the tendency, evident in recent British Broadcasting Corporation television programmes, notably on Sunday evenings, to pander to sexual and sadistic tastes'. It was perhaps TV's first 'water cooler moment'. The Queen and Prince Philip let it be known that they had enjoyed the play.

Adding fuel to the flames the BBC went ahead with its plan to re-stage the live broadcast on 16 December, with an introduction by Head of Drama, Michael Barry, to defend the production. Seven million viewers tuned in to this second sitting, the biggest TV audience since the Coronation the previous year.

In 1955 Cushing appeared in a BBC play called *The Moment of Truth*, directed by and starring Peter Ustinov. Ustinov plays a national hero and old soldier who believes he can lead his country out of a war. Cushing is the prime minister who believes that lives would be saved and the war ended if his country surrendered. Donald Pleasance plays the foreign minister.

After this, Cushing and Ustinov would carry on a long and playful correspondence by letter in which they pretended to be spies. Ustinov explained it thus: 'Although we didn't know each other very well, we had quite a correspondence going as spies, a typical example of the inherent shyness of actors who only lose their inhibitions by infiltrating into alien skins.'

Before *The Curse of Frankenstein* changed Cushing's life (but after he had filmed it), he appeared in a BBC adaptation of Patrick Hamilton's play *Gaslight* – about the mental torture of a Victorian wife – which had already been made for the big screen in the 1944 production starring Ingrid Bergman. Cushing of course plays the sadistic husband, Mr Manningham, with Mary Morris as his wife Bella.

Plays such as *Pride and Prejudice*, *Beau Brummell* and *Nineteen Eighty-Four* (Winston Smith's doomed relationship with Julia) showed that Cushing was good-looking and charismatic enough to play the romantic lead. They also demonstrated the BBC's commitment to strong single dramas on television, which are very rarely made now. Dramas are now stretched out (sometimes pointlessly) as 'seasons' on the main streaming services, to maximise audience loyalty and minimise costs.

Cushing's next major role on TV in *The Creature* was a move towards the horror genre. Again it was produced by Rudolph Cartier and written by Nigel Kneale telling the story of a Himalayan expedition to find the Yeti. Cushing and Stanley Baker play the expedition leaders Dr John Rollason and Tom Friend.

Cartier and Cushing worked together for the last time on a BBC production of Terence Rattigan's play *The Winslow Boy*, shown on 13 March 1958. Cushing plays the barrister Sir Robert Morton, fighting for justice when a young naval cadet is wrongly accused of stealing a postal order. It is based on the true-life Archer-Shee case of 1910 which became a national *cause-célèbre*.

Hammer would make their own version of *The Creature* titled *The Abominable Snowman* (1957) with Cushing in the same role. Producer Anthony Hinds said: 'Never were any other actors considered. Cushing was one of Britain's first real TV stars ... and whatever he was in would empty all the pubs and bring people home to their TV sets. We wanted him and we got him.'

Nevertheless, Cushing's TV career continued to run in tandem with his film commitments, something that was quite unusual at a time when actors tended to be pigeonholed as either TV or movie stars.

Keith Michell, who played Mark Antony, gave an interesting insight into Cushing's working practices in an interview with the Peter Cushing Association. 'Most actors' scripts tend to have notes scribbled over them hastily and usually illegible during rehearsals. But his, I remember, were covered in meticulously neat entries of moves, character notations, relevant historical research information or emotional subtext of lines, vocal inflections or anything else that would make his performance.'

In 1962 Cushing was in an ITV drama, *Peace with Terror*, playing a religious fanatic planning to end all wars by blowing up the War Office. A year later he appeared in the BBC's nine-part *The Spread of the Eagle*, an adaptation of three of Shakespeare's Roman plays – *Coriolanus*, *Julius Caesar* and *Anthony and Cleopatra*. Cushing played Cassius in the *Julius Caesar* sections. *The Spread of the Eagle* followed on from *The Age of Kings* (1960) which had performed a similar type of TV adaptation for Shakespeare's history plays. Foreign sales for both of these prestigious productions were important to the BBC and Peter Cushing, now known in both the UK and USA as a film star, was a formidable asset.

The launch of BBC2 in the spring of 1964 was a major event in television history with a remit to 'broadcast programmes of depth and substance', in contrast to the more mainstream BBC1. A new drama strand called *Story Parade* specialised in adaptations of modern novels. Cushing starred in *The Caves of Steel*, based on an Isaac Asimov science fiction story. It was scripted by Terry Nation (who had given the world Daleks in *Doctor Who*) and directed by Peter Sasdy. Music came from the BBC Radiophonic Workshop. Sadly, as was the normal practice in those days, the master tapes were wiped. So this little gem can no longer be seen.

Cushing plays suave and villainous in 'Return of the Cybernauts', an episode of *The Avengers* broadcast on 30 September 1967. He flirts with Mrs Peel (Diana Rigg) and makes Steed (Patrick Macnee) jealous.

In 1968, Cushing took on the role of Sherlock Holmes again for a BBC series produced in colour, with Nigel Stock as Watson. He had not been the first actor under consideration. John Neville and Eric Porter were also contenders. Cushing, worried about Helen's health, was not happy with his performance because he was not not able to receive her comments during filming.

In 1974 he played an ancient alien Raan in an episode of *Space 1999*, wearing gold face paint and long white hair. His friend Christopher Lee would wear a similar wig in other episodes. When *The Avengers* was brought back to TV under the new title *The New Avengers* starring Joanna Lumley and Gareth Hunt, Peter Cushing was invited to be the first guest star in an episode titled 'The Eagle's Nest'.

The late 1970s and early 1980s saw the emergence of the made-for-TV film. In 1980 Cushing played Dr Alexander Manette in *A Tale of Two Cities*, with Chris Sarandon in the dual roles of Charles Darnay and Sydney Carton. At the same time Hammer, unable to compete with big budget horror such as *The Exorcist*, made a return to TV with the thirteen-episode *Hammer House of Horror* series in 1980 on ITV. Cushing is in episode seven, titled 'The Silent Scream', playing a pet shop owner, Martin Blueck, who befriends young ex-con, Chuck (played by a very young Brian Cox), for his own evil purposes. Elaine Donnelly plays Chuck's wife.

Blueck claims to be a former prisoner in a concentration camp but it turns out he was one of the guards. In the shop he sells pets. In the basement he has a snarling menagerie of big cats and a fondness for electrifying every surface. Cushing looks a lot less cadaverous than he had a few years previously and his transformation from mild-mannered old gent to sinister nutcase is magnificent, and the twist at the end is very clever. The director was Alan Gibson who worked for Hammer on its last two Dracula titles 'The Satanic Rites of Dracula' and 'Dracula A.D. 1972'.

Like Karloff, Cushing did the rounds of chat shows on British TV. He was a willing stooge more than once on *The Morecambe and Wise Show* where the joke was that he was never paid for his appearances. Eric pretended he didn't know who he was. 'I don't seem to remember you at all Mr *Crushing*,' he protested. It was the ultimate accolade. The biggest stars lined up to be insulted by Eric and Ernie. Cushing appeared four times on Terry Wogan's chat show in the 1980s, often reminiscing about 'dear old Chris' (Christopher Lee) and pointing out that the Hammer films the youngsters enjoyed (on late night TV) had all been made twenty-five years ago.

Peter Cushing became a household name as a television star which is why Hammer wanted his star quality. Later in his career Cushing returned to TV as a veteran of those much-loved horror films. It was quite a journey.

* * *

In 1968, around Halloween, Alan Whicker, whose *Whicker's World* Series ran from 1958 to 1994, turned his urbane gaze on the horror film business and why we like to be scared. The investigation began in a mocked up Poe-esque torture dungeon, with Whicker lying on a slab wrapped in chains about to have a stake driven through his heart. He then proceeded to interview Christopher Lee, smoking furiously (as people still did on TV shows) and wearing his usual immaculate tweeds. Reacting to Whicker's suggestion that horror films catered for the 'lowest instincts' and were 'dangerous', Lee declared this to be 'absolute nonsense'. They offered 'escapism' and an 'emotional safety valve' he stated.

In another film a few years later, in which␣Whicker went to meet the wealthy British expats in California (a tough job but someone had to do it, and Whicker was a genius at that kind of stuff), he talks to Christopher Lee as the pair ride around in a golf buggy. Lee, who decamped to Hollywood to reboot his career and escape from *Dracula*, explains that the social scene is 'bizarre' and entirely based on 'money and power', and that he is 'not the least interested in belonging'. You rather wish that you could hear what these two clever and perspicacious men said to each other when the cameras and microphones were turned off.

He was co-opted to appear on *This is Your Life* in April 1974, just as Richard Lester's *The Three Musketeers* opened with a premiere where Lee – who plays the Comte de Rochefort – was introduced to the Queen Mother. His pals who contribute to the show included Oliver Reed, Charlton Heston, Peter Cushing (of course), Sammy Davis Jnr, Trevor Howard and (representing Dracula's late night snacks) Joanna Lumley, Veronica Carlson and Valerie Van Ost. Vincent Price arrives in person to tell a funny story about being mistaken for both Boris Karloff and Christopher Lee. Lee's old prep-school chum Patrick Macnee pays tribute to his career and says that his career will doubtless bloom and expand in the coming years. That same year Lee played the Bond villain Scaramanga in *The Man with the Golden Gun*, but he would never quite escape from Dracula's shadow (which is odd, because as vampirologists will tell you, a vampire casts no shadow).

Lee appeared in various TV roles. In 1975 he wore a long white wig and interesting eye make-up to appear as a guest star in the cult sci-fi series *Space 1999*. In 1997 he was in a mini series based on Sir Walter Scott's *Ivanhoe*, and an adaptation of Melvyn Peake's *Gormenghast* novels in 2000. In this he played Flay (another white wig), Lord Groan's peculiar manservant. Lee had known Mervyn Peake personally and used to meet him at the old Harrod's Library, remembering him as quiet but highly charismatic and otherworldly.

For all the varied work that Lee did both here, in Europe and in Hollywood, he was still the 'horror legend', and the Hammer films still turned up regularly on late-night TV scooping up a new, young audience.

It was a mixed blessing. James Whale (1889–1957), the British director of *Frankenstein*, was well aware of the fleeting nature of fame in Hollywood and when he died his name was more or less forgotten. Had he lived another ten years he would have seen his fame rekindled as the movies he made for Universal – *Frankenstein* (1931), *The Old Dark*

House (1932), *The Invisible Man* (1933) and *The Bride of Frankenstein* (1935) – appeared regularly on late night TV both here and in the US.

Television, once the upstart medium, has now been itself transformed in the digital age. Broadcast television is now as familiar and unthreatening as a pair of carpet slippers. Streaming services such as Netflix, Prime and Apple TV have changed the way we consume screen drama and movies. Viewers no longer have to rely on scheduled screenings or taping video recordings. Countless B-movies are available on YouTube, on the Horror Channel and Warner Bros. UK Horror, among others. In 2015, Talking Picture TV was launched in Britain, specialising in older classics, B-films and TV series. It is a family business, available on Freeview, run by producer Noel Cronin and his daughter Sarah Cronin-Stanley. Their mission has been to save the smaller, more obscure titles because mainstream TV now rarely shows anything other than big titles. Currently Caroline Munro, the former Hammer star presents a late night Friday horror film in a slot called *The Cellar Club*.

The box in the corner of the room may now be an iPad or a smartphone. But television in its various incarnations has kept the classic horror film alive and kicking for more than half a century.

* * *

Chapter Five

Hammer

In 2023, Hammer and that other British horror studio, Amicus, returned from the dead. Again. Hammer has been taken over by the appropriately named John Gore Organisation, a producer of West End and Broadway stage shows, responsible for award-winning productions such as *Moulin Rouge – The Musical* (2020), *Oklahoma!* (2019) and *Dear Evan Hansen* (2017).

In an interview in *The Guardian* in October 2023, Gore, a Briton born in 1962 and educated at Harrow and London University, said: 'My first ambition was film, but theatre took over. And I have loved Hammer since I was a kid, since I first saw Christopher Lee and Peter Cushing in *Dracula*.'

The latest Hammer revival was launched with a production of *Doctor Jekyll* (2023) starring Eddie Izzard. Meanwhile Amicus, described by the BBC in 1971 as Britain's 'tiniest film studio' has been disinterred by Lawrie Brewster, Scottish film-maker, who says: 'Our mission is to craft films that celebrate the golden era of British horror, paying respect to the rich traditions of yesteryear.'

This is not the first time an attempt has been made to revive Hammer. In 2000, the studio was bought by a consortium including advertising executive Charles Saatchi and publishers Neil Mendoza and William Sieghart. The company announced plans to begin making films again, but none was produced.

In 2007 Hammer was again relaunched under CEO Simon Oakes. The new organisation acquired Hammer's film library of 295 pictures. Interviewed by *The Independent* in February 2012, Oakes said: 'Hammer was very much of its time'. 'We asked ourselves the question: if Hammer had carried on from the late 1970s, where would it be today? How would it have progressed?'[6]

In 2010 the new Hammer made a vampire movie, *Let Me In*, followed in 2011 by a creepy thriller called *The Resident*, starring Hilary Swank and featuring a final performance by Christopher Lee before this death in 2015. In 2012 the *Harry Potter* star Daniel Radcliffe (a great admirer of Peter Cushing) appeared in a production of Susan Hill's *The Woman In Black*.

The nostalgic affection for British horror films remains undimmed. Hammer is one of the few film studios that people can name apart from the American giants such as Paramount or Twentieth Century Fox, yet they only produced horror films for a period of about fifteen years from the mid-1950s through to the early 1970s. Nobody under the age of 70 can have ever seen a Hammer film on first release in the cinema, but the films won a new audience from the 1970s onwards on late-night TV, at film festivals and – latterly – on YouTube and Freeview's Talking Pictures TV.

The legend that is Hammer first came to life in 1934 when William Hinds, a successful London jeweller who had moved into music hall and variety, registered his own film company, Hammer Productions Ltd, and began work on his first film, *The Public Life of Henry Ninth*. Hinds had used Hammer as a stage name because he lived in Hammersmith at the time. He met Enrique Carreras and they formed Exclusive Films, a film distribution company. Hammer was forced into liquidation (the first of its many ups and downs) in 1937 but Exclusive continued to trade. In 1947, James Carreras (1909–90), son of Enrique, relaunched Hammer and went into business with William Hinds's son Anthony (1922–2013). James was the chairman of Hammer Film Productions from 1949 to 1980. He was made MBE in 1944 and knighted in 1970.

The company's early output had nothing to do with horror. James Carreras knew that in the age of the cinema double-bill there was a market for 'quota quickies', as low-budget support features. Hammer acquired the rights to the *Dick Barton* stories, shooting the films at the Marylebone Studios in 1947. The company soon realised that it was cheaper to move to premises out of London and in 1951 found a permanent home at Down Place on the banks of the Thames in Berkshire. This became known as Bray Studios, with the grounds used for location shooting and contributing to the inescapable Home Counties look of Hammer horror films.

Hammer's first horror film was an adaptation of Nigel Kneale's *The Quatermass Experiment*, which had been made for BBC television a couple of years previously. The title was changed to *The Quatermass Xperiment* (1955) to make the most of the appeal of the new X-rated certificate. The success of that film led to *Quatermass 2* (1957).

But why horror? The British fondness for Gothic literature found expression in novels such as Horace Walpole's *The Castle of Otranto* in the late eighteenth century, Mary Shelley's *Frankenstein* in the early nineteenth century, Bram Stoker's *Dracula* in the late nineteenth century and the ghost stories of M.R. James in the early twentieth century. Yet by the late 1930s, Hollywood believed that Britain – its most important export market – had lost interest in the horror films of Bela Lugosi and Boris Karloff, even though Boris Karloff (when he briefly parted company with Universal) had come to Britain to make *The Ghoul* in 1933 for Gaumont British, which also starred Cedrick Hardwick, Ernest Theisger and Ralph Richardson. Karloff plays a renowned Egyptologist who comes back from the dead. The cinematographer was Gunther Krampf who worked on Murnau's *Nosferatu* and Pabst's *Pandora's Box*. In true German Expressionist style it is full of shadows and half light, and while it is rather ponderous it is undoubtedly creepy.

Yet for a while horror was seen as box office poison. *The Raven* (1935) starring Karloff was often cited as a film that had caused sufficient outrage to end the horror boom. And in May 1936, in its distinctive clipped industry-speak, *Variety* reported: 'Universal is ringing curfew on horror picture production for at least a year following release of *Dracula's Daughter*, just completed … Reason attributed by U [Universal] for abandonment of horror cycle is that European countries, especially England, are prejudiced against this type of product.'

Dracula's Daughter, starring the stately Gloria Holden in the title role is not a bad film and is said to have been admired by Anne Rice, the American author of *Interview with a Vampire*. But we have to remember that Hollywood was churning out dozens of horror films in the 1930s, hoping to cash in on the popularity of Bela Lugosi and

Boris Karloff's movies. Many of them were substandard and audiences grew tired of them.

The British Board of Film Censors (BBFC) was also flexing its muscle on the lookout for unsuitable American products. Karloff's *Frankenstein* fell foul of the British censor in the scene by the lake where he accidentally drowns a little girl. Partly as a result of this the BBFC introduced the H certificate in 1932, which stood for 'Horrific' not 'Horror'. In 1935 Edward Shortt, President of the BBFC, delivered a speech titled 'The Problems of Censorship' to the Cinematograph Exhibitors Association, and expressed concern about the number of H films coming from Hollywood, saying:

> I cannot believe such films are wholesome, pandering as they do to the love of the morbid and horrible ... Although there is little chance of children seeing these films, I believe they will have a deleterious effect on the adolescent. I hope that producers and renters will accept this word of warning and discourage this type of subject as much as possible.

It is easy to think of the BBFC as a committee of old fusspots because their pronouncements often sound like that. But before the Hays Code was more strictly enforced in America (around 1934) a great deal of American material would seem shocking even today. Films depicting animal cruelty and pornography were fairly commonplace. One of the best known practitioners was Dwain Esper (1894–1982) whose 'documentaries' such as *Reefer Madness* (1936) and *Sex Madness* (1938) purported to deplore the perils of marijuana and syphilis, but did so in the most salacious manner. Another of Esper's classics was *How to Undress In Front of Your Husband* (1937), which was a how-to manual for the 'super snooper'. His mad-scientist film *Maniac* (1937) which includes a rape scene is regularly referred to as the worst film ever made. Again, it's nasty sleaze masquerading as an educational film about mental illness.

Nevertheless, the BBFC did not ban any American horror films between 1936 and 1941 and there is very little evidence that European countries, or Britain, were 'prejudiced' as the *Variety* article claims. So though the British censor may have complained, it did not actually censor anything and many films (such as *Dracula's Daughter*) were given a mild 'A' certificate.

It is often said that the onset of the Second World War led to an unofficial moratorium on horror films, but this is not really true either. Jim Ivers, in an article on the 'Horror Film Hiatus' claims that Joseph Breen, a staunch Catholic and conservative appointed to the Production Code Administration (PCO) of the Movie Picture Producers and Distributors of America (MPPDA), began to exaggerate the antipathy towards horror films in the UK. His reason for doing this was simply that he loathed horror movies and wanted to discourage American studios from making them.

In 1938, much to the surprise of the film industry, a Los Angeles cinema facing bankruptcy put on a triple bill of *Frankenstein*, *Dracula* and *Son of Kong* (films that were by now more than five years old). The audiences queued round the block. Universal then reissued *Frankenstein* and *Dracula* as a double feature nationwide with similar results. A return to horror film production proceeded with *Son of Frankenstein* (1939), Karloff's final outing as the monster. It was a a huge box office hit both in the US and in Europe.

It was not until 1945, however, that the British horror film industry restarted with the Ealing Studios anthology horror *Dead of Night*, which takes the well-established scenario of a group of middle-class people who meet in a country cottage and tell their stories. Michael Redgrave's turn as a ventriloquist with a psychopathic dummy is particularly memorable.

The polite guests, the country cottage setting and the general air of stifled unease make this a very recognisable kind of English horror story. But it was Hammer, through its canny financial arrangements with American production companies such as United Artists and Twentieth Century Fox, which developed the idea of the genre film, of horror as a trademark and selling point. And through both luck and judgment the success of *The Quatermass Xperiment* set the studio on its path to win a place in cinematic history.

The big question is why did Hammer's distinctive brand appeal? Certainly, after the end of the Second World War, there were calls for breaks with the past, and an embrace of all that was modern and new. But while there was a mood of optimism this was also the moment when the chill of the Cold War descended, ushering in an age of anxiety and dread. Hammer reflected this in the *Quatermass* films, but in its subsequent movies added that comforting touch of 'Home Counties Gothic' and Swinging Sixties' permissiveness. What was not to like about that?

Yet even making the right films at the right time might not have been enough if they hadn't secured their two big stars – Peter Cushing and Christopher Lee.

In his great book *A New Heritage of Horror – The English Gothic Cinema*, Dave Pirie writes:

> But the two men who did as much to build Hammer as anyone else (indeed it is difficult to imagine the company without them) remain Peter Cushing and Christopher Lee. It is remarkable that they were both discovered and used for the first time in the key breakthrough picture *The Curse of Frankenstein*. For, as the years went by and despite repeated attempts, Hammer was never able to find another actor to match either of them, let alone two at once. Both Lee and Cushing have the presence which is the rare but indispensable gift of great film acting.

Hammer did operate as a kind of repertory company, a reserve of talent which included directors Terence Fisher, Freddie Francis, Roy Ward Baker, Peter Sasdy, Don Sharp and Peter Sykes; screenwriters Tudor Gates, John Gilling, Anthony Hinds (pen name John Elder) and Jimmy Sangster; composers James Bernard, Malcolm Williamson, John Hollingsworth and Harry Robertson; set designer Bernard Robinson. Apart from Cushing and Lee, the family of players included Ralph Bates, Veronica Carlson, Michael Gough, Francis Matthews, André Morell, Ingrid Pitt, Oliver Reed, Barbara Shelley, Madeline Smith, Thorley Waters and Hazel Court. It does seem that there was a kind of family atmosphere. In an interview on the Classic Film and TV Café website in 2014, Veronica Carlson (who died in 2022 aged 77) said of the atmosphere at Bray: 'Happy, very happy. It was a very convivial, light-hearted atmosphere, though very serious when we were working. The crew was so obliging. It was just a happy family. There was no dissent. There were no problems. There was no grumbling.'

James Carreras and Anthony Hinds wanted Peter Cushing because by the mid-1950s he was a very well-known TV star. Cushing was of course familiar with James Whale's film of *Frankenstein*, and when he heard that Hammer was contemplating a remake he was keen to play the part of the Baron. Since 1953 he had been represented by the agent John Redway and it was Redway who facilitated this move to Hammer. Cushing would play Baron Frankenstein in five more Hammer films, and five as Professor Van Helsing in the *Dracula* films opposite Christopher Lee.

Cushing and Lee had both appeared in Olivier's film of *Hamlet* and in *Moulin Rouge* (1952) directed by John Huston, which had been filmed at Shepperton Studios. But they only met when they worked on *The Curse of Frankenstein* in 1956.

Hammer immediately ran into difficulties when Universal Studios heard about the project. They threatened a lawsuit if anything was copied from the original Boris Karloff film, including the word 'monster' and the iconic make-up devised by Jack Pierce. But Jimmy Sangster, who had been commissioned to write the script, immediately steered the film in a different direction because he made it plain that he was more interested in the character of Baron Frankenstein than in the monster. He also had no intention of having scenes of villagers storming the castle because 'we couldn't afford it'.

While Cushing was the first choice for the part of Baron Frankenstein, Lee was not the only actor in the frame for the role of the monster. Bernard Bresslaw (at six foot seven inches, even taller than Lee) was also considered.

Lee had no lines, which dismayed him at first. But from the moment he met Cushing on the set of *The Curse of Frankenstein* at Bray, they became friends. Their first encounter began with Lee storming into

Cushing's dressing-room and announcing his absence of lines. Cushing looked up, and said with his trademark dry wit, 'You're lucky. I've read the script.'

The monster's make-up was created by Phil Leakey. The idea for the Creature's look was to give the impression of someone who had been in a road accident and had been kept in a holding tank. Putty, cotton wool, and wax were used to build layers, and Lee wore a contact in his right eye to create a cataract effect. Altogether, it took three hours to be made-up.

As befits the bigger star, Peter Cushing had a slightly larger dressing-room than his co-star. If Lee wanted a quiet lie down he had to put cushions in the bath and stretch out. But he says that the atmosphere on set was the happiest he had ever known. There was a sense that they were creating something very good so the filming schedule was extended from five weeks to six. Lee also said that playing the monster made him realise how skilful was Karloff's interpretation of the part.

The critics dismissed *The Curse of Frankenstein* as they generally dismissed all horror films. C.A. Lejeune of *The Observer* wrote that it was 'Among the half-dozen most repulsive films I have encountered in the course of some 10,000 miles of film reviewing.' The British Film Institute's *Monthly Film Bulletin* said: 'The immense possibilities of the Frankenstein story have here been sacrificed by an ill-made script, poor direction and performance and, above all, a preoccupation with disgusting – not horrific – charnelry.'

Yet the public loved it. Hazel Court recalled the premiere at the Empire in Leicester Square, when the stars (nervous of the film's reception) arrived wearing scarves and sunglasses so they would not be immediately recognised. In one scene, Cushing, having just cut up some cadavers, is having breakfast and says to Hazel: 'Pass me the marmalade, darling.'[7] At that, the entire audience clapped and screamed with laughter. This was the strange alchemy of the Hammer films. They made you laugh even as you happily succumbed to the full Gothic.

Just as Universal had followed up Bela Lugosi's *Dracula* with Boris Karloff's *Frankenstein*, so Hammer follow the same path, but in reverse. The box-office success of *The Curse of Frankenstein* convinced James

Carreras that Hammer must make its own *Dracula*, (known as *Horror of Dracula* outside the UK), which would also be scripted by Jimmy Sangster and directed by Terence Fisher. There was no thought of casting anyone but Christopher Lee in the title role with Peter Cushing as Doctor Van Helsing.

The popularity of Hammer was also good news for Boris Karloff, who by the mid-1950s was more often seen on TV than on the big screen. Other British companies wanted to capitalise on the new horror boom and Anglo-Amalgamated had a role perfectly suited to what was billed as Karloff's comeback.

Anglo-Amalgamated was set up in 1945 by Nat Cohen and Stuart Levy. It produced the first twelve *Carry On* films along with British classics such as *Peeping Tom* (1960), *A Kind of Loving* (1962), *Billy Liar* (1963) and *Poor Cow* (1967). It had a distribution arrangement with Roger Corman's American International Pictures (AIP) and they jointly produced *The Masque of The Red Death* and *The Tomb of Ligeia* (both 1964). *The Grip of the Strangler* (1958) starred Karloff as a nineteenth-century novelist and social reformer reopening the case of a serial killer – the notorious Haymarket Strangler – only to find (spoiler alert) that he was the man responsible. Karloff would go on to make another nineteenth-century thriller horror, *Corridors of Blood*, with Day, whose work he admired. The film also features Christopher Lee as the arch villain and the two men became friends, talking about cricket but tactfully avoiding the subject of their shared experience as Frankenstein's monster.

Just as it is difficult to watch silent films with the same pleasure as the people who watched them before the talkies, it is impossible to watch a Hammer film with a mind unencumbered by the knowledge of what Hammer would come to mean as a totem of British and cinematic culture. That is why the generally negative reviews of Hammer films when they were first released strike us as so wrong-headed. But what we have to remember is that these films were not immediately seen as 'horror classics'. Mostly, they were seen as silly and exploitative, which makes Cushing and Lee's performances that much more extraordinary. It is a given that British horror films are to be made light of, yet both actors injected a seriousness into Hammer films which defies glib criticism.

As Hammer lost its way in the 1970s, one of its least appealing films was *The Horror of Frankenstein* (1970), directed by Jimmy Sangster, in which Ralph Bates took the part of the Baron. It was a spoof on *Curse of Frankenstein*, with Kate O'Mara and Veronica Carlson. In the interview that Carlson did in 2014 with the *The Classic Film and TV Cafe* blog, she describes her dismay at the film's tone:

> I was so upset ... because I took Hammer seriously. I felt that very keenly. Jimmy [Sangster] knew that. It was a sort of 'laughing at Hammer' reaction. I didn't want it to be that way. You always get people that sneer at horror films anyway. But this was sort of sitting up and begging for it. Jimmy was a light-hearted, serious man – an adorable man – but he had to have this nudge-nudge, wink-wink humour in the film. I thought it was so degrading to Hammer.

Christopher Lee looks upon *Dracula* as the film that changed this life, securing him 'a name, a fan club, and a second-hand car'. He was paid £750. He chose not to watch Bela Lugosi's interpretation of Dracula, in advance, to avoid being influenced. But he immersed himself in Bram Stoker's 1897 novel and created a Dracula who is not only urbane, but seething with sexual energy.

According to Wayne Kinsey's book *Hammer Films: The Bray Studio Years*, Bernard Robinson's sets for *Dracula* almost led to him being fired. There had been an expectation of cobwebs and crumbling stone as in Murnau's *Nosferatu* or Tod Browning's *Dracula*. But Robinson's castle was rather cosy and well-appointed, a Home Counties mansion with handsome balustrades and polished candelabras. When the hapless Jonathan Harker (payed by John Van Essen) is shown to his room, it looks positively inviting.

Always a stickler for bits of stage business and the use of props, Cushing found himself rather encumbered by the number of vampire-repelling crucifixes that he was required to have about his person. In his final showdown with Dracula, Cushing had the idea of jumping on a table, pulling down the curtains to let in the vampire-killing sunlight, seizing a couple of metal candlesticks and clashing them together in the form of a cross. In another scene he conducts a person-to-person blood transplant between Arthur and his wife Mina (who has been almost drained of blood by Dracula). We can be sure that (as was always his practice with any medical procedure he was required to perform in a film), he consulted a doctor to make sure he did it correctly.

His action-man portrayal of Van Helsing was intentional. In an interview for the 1987 documentary *Hammer: the Studio That Dripped Blood*, Cushing says of Van Helsing:

> In the book by Bram Stoker, he's described as a very old, little, withered man who speaks almost double-Dutch. And this was going back 25 years when I was younger and prettier. When I was offered the part, I said, 'Well, instead of making me up, I think we'd better play it as myself' and they agreed to that.

Melissa Stribling (1926–1992), who was married to Basil Deardon, plays Mina. First seen as Arthur's frumpy wife she is transformed by her first encounter with Dracula. The director Terence Fisher told her: 'Imagine you've had one hell of a sexual night ... Give me that in your face.'[8] Lee's erotic appeal was so great that a cinema manager in the north of England wrote to him complain that an usherette claimed to have become pregnant by Dracula as a result of seeing the film five times a day. In the summer of 1958, a *Picturegoer* feature about Lee was headed 'Scream Boy? No – Dream Boy.'

The filming of *Corridors of Blood* (also known as *The Doctor from Seven Dials*) in which Christopher Lee stars with Boris Karloff, was briefly halted so that Lee and Cushing could fly to the US for the New York premiere of *Dracula*. It was Lee's first transatlantic trip and he was suffering from a knee injury as a result of stabbing Karloff's character to death before crashing into a metal stove.

It was late May, with Peter's birthday falling on the 26th and Christopher's on the 27th. They celebrated together at the top of the

Empire State Building. There was a picture of him as Dracula, 50ft high, holding a limp girl in his arms, in Times Square.

Hammer made eight Dracula movies, only two of which starred both Lee and Cushing – *Dracula A.D. 1972* (1972) and *The Satanic Rites of Dracula* (1973). Cushing appeared in *The Brides of Dracula* (1960). Lee starred in *Dracula: Prince of Darkness* (1966), *Dracula Has Risen From the Grave* (1968), *Taste the Blood of Dracula* (1970), and *Scars of Dracula* (1970).

Hammer made five more Frankenstein movies with Cushing after *The Curse of Frankenstein*. *The Revenge of Frankenstein* (1958) began production three days after filming wrapped on *Dracula*, starring Peter Cushing and Francis Matthews. *The Evil of Frankenstein* (1964) stars Cushing with the monster played by Kiwi Kingston in a make-up that seemed to resemble Boris Karloff's trademark flat-headed look.

Terence Fisher directed *Frankenstein Created Woman* (1967), a movie picked by Martin Scorsese in 1987 as part of a National Film Theatre season of his favourite films, saying: 'If I single this one out it's because here they actually isolate the soul ... The implied metaphysics are close to something sublime.' In the film a woman with a scarred face and her lover – Christina and Hans – are killed. Frankenstein (Cushing) merges the two of them into a single perfect body and the new-look Christina (Susan Denberg) sets about seducing and murdering the men responsible for her father and Hans's death.

In *Frankenstein Must Be Destroyed* (1969), which was one of director Terence Fisher's favourites, Peter Cushing is on laboratory manoeuvres with Freddie Jones. *Frankenstein and the Monster From Hell* (1974) was an ailing Terence Fisher's final film and the last of Hammer's Frankenstein movies.

Everyone has their favourite Sherlock Holmes, be it Basil Rathbone, Jeremy Brett, Ian Richardson, Benedict Cumberbatch or any of the other distinguished actors who have taken the role. Both Peter Cushing and Christopher Lee played the great detective several times.

Hammer's *The Hound of the Baskervilles* (1959), directed by Terence Fisher, teamed Peter Cushing with Christopher Lee as Sir Henry Baskerville. The plot calls for him to find a large and deadly spider crawling over his person and a bird-eating spider from South America was duly cast. Lee drew the line at having it crawl over his neck and settled for it inching up the arm of his tweed jacket. Lee's look of terror was not acting.

The hound is well described by Arthur Conan-Doyle but always poses a problem for film-makers. In an effort to make the dog seem of gigantic proportions the designers dressed three small boys in clothes resembling those worn by Dr Watson (André Morell), Sir Henry and Holmes, and placed them on a miniature replica of Dartmoor. When the rushes were viewed it was obvious that it was indeed three small boys with a cheerful dog in the middle of the toy scenery. The sequence was scrapped.

The Mummy (1959) was an arduous shoot for Lee who had been thoroughly bruised and battered. He tore a muscle carrying leading lady Yvonne Furneaux through a swamp because fainting heroines in horror films cannot put an arm round a monster's shoulder. They have to hang limply, which turns them into a dead weight.

Cushing, ever with an eye for detail, was bothered by the poster which showed a beam of light passing through a hole in the Mummy's body. He was unhappy because this event didn't occur in the script. As Egyptologist John Banning, he is attacked by Karis, the Mummy. Cushing asked director Terence Fisher if he could grab a harpoon which was hanging on the wall of Banning's study and drive it through the monster, thus giving some verisimilitude to the poster.

In 1964 Hammer made *The Gorgon*, with Lee as Professor Karl Meister and Cushing as Dr Naramoff investigating a series of murders where the victims are turned to stone. Barbara Shelley, another familiar Hammer beauty plays Namaroff's assistant Carla Hoffman. As a reimagining of the Greek Medusa myth, this was the first time that Hammer had introduced a female monster.

In *She* (1965), the entire focus of this expensive-looking Hammer adaptation of Rider H. Haggard's novel was the divine Ursula Andress. She is Ayesha, the goddess-y ruler of a remote realm visited by archaeologists led by Peter Cushing's Professor Holly. Christopher

Lee, all dressed up in a striking gold helmet, plays Ayesha's high priest, Billali.

During filming he admits in his autobiography that he was carrying his problems with him, his daughter Christina's physical difficulties and Gitte's traumatic experience of the birth. There was one scene in Ayesha's throne room where her victims were being flung through a hole in the floor to the flames beneath. Lee was suddenly overcome with claustrophobia and ran off the set. He felt no better in his dressing room even when he opened the window. It was only when he went outside into the cold rainy day that he was able to walk around and calm down.

Not all the films that Lee and Cushing made together were Hammer films. There were two other small companies – Amicus and Tigon – which made horror thrillers. Between 1962 and 1977, Amicus produced twenty-eight movies, and the best ones were the portmanteau films where several stories and characters are yoked together. Where Hammer films tend to be set in the nineteenth century, Amicus movies were set firmly in the present in all its 1970s' tackiness, which has proved irresistible to fans. Steve Coogan made an Amicus-spoofing show in the 1990s called *Dr Terrible's House of Horrible*. A few years later, Richard Ayoade and Matthew Holness offered up the tongue-in-cheek horror anthology *Garth Marenghi's Darkplace*. The Simpsons' *Treehouse of Horror* episodes owe everything to Amicus.

The company, based at Shepperton Studios, was founded by two New Yorkers – screenwriter Milton Subotsky (1921–1991) and lawyer turned producer Max Rosenberg (1914–2004). It had originally been Subotsky's idea to remake *Frankenstein* in 1955, an idea which eventually materialised as Hammer's *The Curse of Frankenstein*, so it can be safely assumed that relations between the two horror houses were a little strained, though in the years to come Amicus would employ many members of the Hammer team.

Lee and Cushing both starred in Amicus's *Dr Terror's House of Horrors* (1964) directed by Freddie Francis, in *The Skull* (1965) and in *Scream and Scream Again* (1970), where they are joined by Vincent Price (the first time all three had been in the same film).

The House That Dripped Blood (1971) is an anthology film also starring Nyree Dawn Porter, Ingrid Pitt, Denholm Elliott and Jon Pertwee.

Tales from the Crypt (1972) won Peter Cushing the Licorne d'Or Award for best actor when it was shown at a film festival in France some years later. In this portmanteau film – offered to him shortly after the death of his wife Helen – he plays Mr Grimsdyke, a lonely old recluse, with great pathos. Ralph Richardson plays the Crypt Keeper with Joan Collins putting in a memorable performance as a brittle sophisticate who has murdered her husband and hopes to blame a homicidal maniac who is currently on the loose dressed as Father Christmas.

And Now The Screaming Starts (1973) is much better than its title would suggest (director Roy Ward Baker thought it 'silly'). It's 1795; Catherine (Stephanie Beacham) arrives at the estate of her wealthy fiancé Charles Fengriffen (Iain Ogilvy). The screaming starts almost at once within minutes of Catherine being shown the family portraits. The screaming continues when Catherine is attacked on her wedding night. But is it all in her mind? Peter Cushing plays Dr Pope, a specialist in psychiatric disorders. There's a severed hand creeping around too.

Amicus returned to the anthology format with *From Beyond the Grave* (1974) with Peter Cushing as the proprietor of Temptations Ltd, an antiques shop. Four customers steal and … as we know they will … pay a heavy penalty. A glorious cast includes Diana Dors, David Warner, Ian Bannen, Donald and Angela Pleasence, Ian Carmichael, Margaret Leighton and Lesley-Anne Down.

Madhouse, released the same year (sometimes known as *The Revenge of Dr Death*) teamed Vincent Price with Peter Cushing again. It's a kind of tribute to Price, who plays Paul Toombes, a horror actor. Peter Cushing is cast as the ominously named screenwriter Herbert Flay. The 'special participation' of both Basil Rathbone and Boris Karloff (who had died in 1967 and 1969 respectively) are mentioned in the title credits. And the film includes scenes from AIP's films *Tales of Terror* (1962) and *The Raven* (1963), in which they had appeared with Price.

A millionaire big game hunter assembles six people at his mansion in *The Beast Must Die* (1974), announcing that he suspects one of them to be a werewolf. Peter Cushing is in a familiar professorial role as lycanthropy expert Christopher Lundgren. Charles Gray and Michael Gambon join in the fun. *At The Earth's Core* (1976) is a fantasy science fiction film based on the 1914 novel by Edgar Rice Burroughs. It was an attempt to reprise the success of *The Land That Time Forget* (1974) which also starred wholesome Doug McLure. Cushing – in his final role for Amicus – plays scientist Dr Abner Perry and scream queen Caroline Munro is Princess Dia. She said of Cushing:

> He exuded a peaceful calm and an almost saintly air; he was wonderful when my grandfather died during the making of *At The Earth's Core*. Very supportive and kind, he even took me aside and we said prayers together. He really understood the way I was feeling at that sad time.

Tigon was another small British production company which at various times employed the talents of Boris Karloff, Peter Cushing and Christopher Lee. It inhabited the niche world of the British exploitation films of the 1970s, trashy money-spinners for a number of small Soho-based companies. By the 1980s they had vanished, superseded by videos and changing tastes.

Described by the critic Matthew Sweet as one of the 'wild men' of Wardour Street, Tony Tenser (1920–2007), who ran Tigon, was a Londoner born of Lithuanian immigrant parents. One of seven siblings, he grew up in a two-room tenement flat in Shoreditch and won a scholarship to grammar school. During the war he was a technician with the RAF. When the war ended he joined the ABC cinema chain as a trainee manager at the Central Cinema, Cambridge, and pulled off some hilarious publicity stunts. To promote *Challenge to Lassie* (1949) he staged a sheepdog trial. He pretended that his bosses were trying to prevent him showing a second run of the Margaret Rutherford comedy *The Happiest Days of your Life* (1950) and asked the patrons to sign a petition in protest. Naturally the film played to full houses.

Working for Miracle Films in Soho, a distribution company which acquired Brigitte Bardot's film *La lumire d'en face* (*The Light Across the Street*, 1955) he brought Bardot to London and coined the term 'sex kitten'. Her next film was called *En Effeuillant la Marguerite* (1956) which Tenser translated as *Mam'selle Striptease*. He borrowed some strippers from the Gargoyle club and paid them to stage a 'protest' outside the cinema. The press and the punters loved it.

Tenser went into business with Michael Klinger who ran the Gargoyle and in 1960, they leased the basement of a Soho office block, installed 170 seats and a projector, and called it the Compton Cinema Club. Cheekily they persuaded John Trevelyan, head of the BBFC to become a founder member. They also went into film production with a film about a nudist colony, *Naked as Nature Intended* (1961), made by George Harrison Marks (1926–1997), a big name in soft porn British films in the Sixties and Seventies. In 1964 Tenser produced his first horror film called *The Black Torment*.

Tenser and Klinger went their separate ways and Tenser's Tigon made *The Sorcerers* (1968) with Boris Karloff and Ian Ogilvy, directed by Michael Reeves. Reeves made the (now) cult horror film *Witchfinder General* the same year with Vincent Price.

In Tigon's *The Blood Beast Terror* (1968) Peter Cushing plays Inspector Quennell, investigating a string of gruesome murders of handsome young men in Victorian England, apparently perpetrated by a giant moth woman who is played by Wanda Ventham, now more famous as Benedict Cumberbatch's mum. *The Creeping Flesh* (1973) teams Peter Cushing and Christopher Lee in a lush and enjoyable Victorian melodrama, directed by Freddie Francis. By this period Hammer was scraping the barrel and *The Creeping Flesh* looks like the sort of film that the Bray bunch should have been making, but weren't.

Tigon had no particular interest in the horror genre and in the 1970s they focused on the seedy soft porn, low-budget and profitable. Films such as *Come Play With Me* (1977) and *Mary Millington's World Striptease Extravaganza* (1981) conjure up a lost world of Soho sleaze, nylon lingerie-clad housewives and priapic window cleaners.

Tyburn Films, founded in the 1970s by Freddie Francis's son Kevin, was hailed as the 'next' Hammer. *The Ghoul* (1975) with Peter Cushing, John Hurt, Veronica Carlson and Alexandra Bastedo, was directed by his dad Freddie. In *The Plague of the Werewolves* (1975) Cushing faces up to ... well not so much a plague of werewolves in nineteenth-century France. There is just the one.

Tyburn then disappeared until 1984 when *The Masks of Death* showed up on Channel 4. Peter Cushing (by now 71) plays Sherlock Holmes, coaxed out of retirement, to investigate three deaths in London's East End. Roy Ward Baker directed a solid cast that includes John Mills as Dr Watson, Anne Baxter as Irene Adler, Ray Milland, Anton Diffring, Gordon Jackson and Susan Penhaligon. This was the third time that Cushing had played Holmes, and also his last. He said that Holmes was his all-time favourite role, but by now he felt he was too old for the part. There were plans for a sequel called *The Abbot's Cry*, but Cushing's failing health meant that it was never made.

For around two decades, Hammer, and the small companies that arrived in its wake – Amicus, Tigon and Tyburn – flew the flag for a type of British film-making which nobody took very seriously. Horror seemed part of a downmarket exploitation package which included soft porn and extended to *Carry On* films and low-budget kung fu movies. Yet there is quality amid the laughable dross, and Cushing in particular can elevate the poorest material.

But a new sort of horror movie was hovering in the wings. In 1968 George Romero's *Night of the Living Dead* was released, both cool and subversive. Meanwhile, Hollywood studios was returning to horror with big budget horror with films such as *Rosemary's Baby* (1968) and *The Exorcist* (1973).

In some ways this was a dire period for British cinema. Throughout the 1960s the number of cinemas fell from 3,034 to 1,530. Just as, in the 1930s, J.B. Priestley had mourned for the theatre that had been turned into cinemas, now the cinemas were being turned into bowling alleys and bingo halls. Such British film-makers as there were always had to turn (as did Hammer) to foreign sources of capital, particularly the United States.

Frankenstein and the Monster From Hell (1974) was Hammer's last Frankenstein movie and director Terence Fisher's last film. By then James Carreras had sold the company to his son Michael, who managed to secure funding from Paramount. Peter Cushing is back as the Baron, pursuing his inquiries in another lunatic asylum.

At the end of the film the monster is of course destroyed, and the Baron prepares himself for new ventures. There is such a poignant last line in the final scene – 'We must get this place tidied so we can start afresh,' he says, 'Next time we will need fresh material.'

Chapter Six

Love

On screen, love tended to elude Boris Karloff, Peter Cushing and Christopher Lee. They were all tall and good-looking but, alas, the role of romantic lead was not really an option once you had made your name in horror films. What's more, Lee always thought that at six foot four inches, his height counted against him. As he observed in his autobiography, not many leading ladies wanted to address their remarks to an actor's belt buckle. Tall, dark and handsome is one thing. *Too* tall is quite another in the eyes of casting directors.

In *The Bride of Frankenstein* (1935), Elsa Lanchester plays the female mate constructed for Boris Karloff's monster. Their first meeting does not go well. 'Friend,' says Karloff hopefully. The Bride screams her head off. Then Karloff's monster makes a lunge for her and she recoils in horror, screaming again. 'She hates me,' the monster says. And he's not wrong. It is a scene of extreme pathos.

There is a little more chemistry in *The Mummy* (1932) in which Karloff plays the Ancient Egyptian priest Imhotep, buried alive almost 4,000 years ago for the crime of attempting to bring back his lover Princess Anck-es-en-Amon from the dead. The Romanian-born Broadway actress Zita Johann plays the Princess, reincarnated as society beauty Helen Grosvenor. Karloff again evokes sympathy and pity as Zita Johann's character is alternately repulsed by, and attracted to, him.

In real life Karloff was perhaps luckier in love but much married. On 23 February 1910, a few months after he arrived in Canada, he married Jessie Grace Harding who had been born in Croydon in 1885, just a few miles from Karloff's Camberwell birthplace. On the marriage certificate Karloff (still going by the name of William Pratt) lists his profession as that of real estate broker. Grace's parents, Harry Laurie (a chartered accountant) and Mary Jessie Maria Harding, had married in Kingston in 1885 and later emigrated with their daughter to New Zealand. In 1904 they moved on to Canada and finally settled in British Columbia. The marriage took place in Vancouver's Holy Rosary Cathedral, with Grace's mother Mary as one of the witnesses. But it was not to last.

Karloff's peripatetic life as an actor undoubtedly put a strain on the relationship and while touring with the Jeanne Russell Company he had an affair with Jeanne's half sister Helene Ripley.

On 8 January 1913, Grace petitioned for divorce citing Helene with Karloff as co-respondent and the marriage was dissolved. Neither party appeared in court. Karloff, who was generally broke at the time, was ordered to 'pay the petitioner her costs of this action as between Solicitor and client after the taxation thereof'. Grace remarried ten days later to a realtor called Cecil Angus Hadfield and the couple moved to Calgary.

The existence of this, Karloff's first marriage, had not been known until Stephen Jacobs produced his biography of Karloff in 2011, drawing from newly digitised British Columbia archives.

Helene also went by the name of Margot Beaton and when the Jeanne Russell Company had performed in Nelson in February 1912 this is the name she used to check in to the Queen Hotel, with Karloff signing his name as 'B. Korloff'.

Cynthia Lindsay, a previous biographer of Karloff, says that: 'From the time Boris disembarked [in Canada] he laid a trail as difficult to follow as if he had deliberately obliterated it.' But in those days it was easier to disappear, to start a new life, to ditch a wife that you couldn't afford, and generally evade official scrutiny at a time when so many immigrants were making their way across the globe in search of new opportunities.

On 12 October 1913 he crossed the border from Canada to Portal, North Dakota, in the USA, entering as 'an immigrant for permanent residence,' still apparently accompanied by Margot Beaton who claimed (probably falsely) to be his wife. His next marriage was to Olive de Wilton (1898–1968). Born in Ropeley, Hampshire, she was the daughter of a retired Captain in the Royal Scots Greys and had grown up in

Western Canada, making two early marriages when she was very young. After her relationship with Karloff ended she returned to England, but eventually settled in Montreal where she acted on stage and in films.

In 1920 – after he had settled in Los Angeles – Karloff married 'Montana' Lauren Williams, a 24-year-old musician. They split up in 1922 and in 1924 he married again to Helene Vivian Soule. She was an actress and dancer known as Polly, who had been brought up in Massachusetts before coming to Hollywood to find fame. It was another brief relationship. In November 1928, a Los Angeles judge ordered Karloff to pay alimony to her, which apparently he failed to do. The dispute dragged on until July 1929 when some sort of settlement was reached.

Karloff's next marriage – after another very brief courtship – was to Dorothy Stine in 1930. The ceremony took place at the Hollywood Presbyterian Church on 12 April. Dorothy was a librarian for the Los Angeles City Library Central Supply System. He did not tell his new wife about his previous ones and throughout his life would be remarkably secretive about his personal life. Rather astonishingly, all his wives were also complicit in this circumspection, neither complaining nor explaining.

After the marriage (a honeymoon was unaffordable as Karloff had still not become a star) the couple moved in to what Dorothy referred to as a 'shack' above Laurel Canyon in the Hollywood Hills, where they lived for the next two years. In those days Laurel Canyon – an address which became infested with rock stars in the 1960s – was a bohemian neighbourhood favoured by Hollywood's bit-part players. 'There was very little money,' said Dorothy, 'and it was Prohibition but we always loved to entertain, so we made beer in the bath.' This was not just romantic poverty. Many of the thousands of actors in Hollywood went hungry, often.

The couple had one child, daughter Sara Jane, born on 23 November 1938, which was also Boris's 51st birthday. On 21 April 1946 Karloff and Dorothy – once seemingly a strong and happy couple – divorced. In the latter part of their marriage Karloff was travelling continuously with the hit stage production of *Arsenic and Old Lace* which ran to

1,444 performances over three years. This undoubtedly put a strain on this relationship too.

The end of the marriage was sealed when Karloff sold his house to the director Robert Siodmak and Dorothy and Sara Jane moved into 714 Foothill in Beverly Hills. Dorothy formed an attachment to an attorney, Edgar Rowe, who she would subsequently marry. Karloff, meanwhile, had become involved with family friend Evelyn Helmore, who had recently divorced her husband, English actor Tom Helmore. She had worked as an assistant to producers David O'Selznick and the English Shakespearean actor Maurice Evans. The day after his divorce from Dorothy was finalised, Karloff married Evelyn.

Evelyn Hope had been born in Putney in 1904, the oldest of three sisters. After school she worked at a dry cleaners set up in London by Maurice Evans and Tom Helmore whose acting careers had stalled. Evelyn had a good business brain and ran the company for a year or so before she and Tom married. She sounds a formidable woman. 'My wife is a woman of great taste,' Boris once said. 'She has seen very, very few of my pictures.'

Even after his own divorce from Evie, Tom had nothing but good words about Boris, describing him in a letter to Evie's mother Lina as 'the nicest person I have ever met'.

Sara Jane Karloff remembers little about the divorce and remarriage but she recalls her mother Dorothy saying to her: 'Your father and I are divorced. Your father married Evie this afternoon.' Then she stood up and left the room.

Cynthia Lindsay, a friend of Karloff's and one of his biographers, recalls receiving a phone call from him on the day of the wedding. They had not been in touch for about a year. He was in Las Vegas and and told her he would be bringing his 'bride' Evie to the Miramar in Santa Monica and would she mind putting some flowers in the room. 'Darling, I guess I didn't tell you. Dorothy and I were divorced … Evie and I are married.' Cynthia was stunned but did as he asked, adding some champagne, caviar and a Gideon Bible.

The new Mr and Mrs Karloff went to live in a house previously owned by Gregory Peck on Mulholland Drive. He and Dorothy were

The cinema in the High Street, Thornton Heath which Peter Cushing visited as a child. Currently playing is *Orphans in the Storm* (1921) directed by D.W. Griffiths, a drama set during the French Revolution starring sisters Lillian and Dorothy Gish. (*Wikicommons*)

The Church of St Mary's in Bramshott dating from 1220, in the Hampshire village where Boris Karloff lived during the last ten years of his life. His widow donated a new set of church bells. (*Jennifer Selway*)

Boris Karloff's house in Bramshott, known as Roundabout Cottage. (*Jennifer Selway*)

The art deco house on St James's Road, Purley, south London, that was Peter Cushing's childhood home (*Wikicommons*)

Christopher Lee and Peter Cushing wonder if Telly Savalas has bought a valid ticket in *Horror Express* (1972). (*Moviestillsdb*)

Christopher Lee in *The Brides of Fu Manchu* (1966) – the second in the series – based on the stories of Sax Rohmer. (*Moviestillsdb*)

Gloria Stuart and Boris Karloff in James Whale's *The Old Dark House* (1932) based on J.B. Priestley's 1927 novel Benighted. (*Moviestillsdb*)

Karloff plays depraved Baron Gregor in *The Black Room* (1935), as well as his clean-living twin Anton. (*Moviestillsdb*)

The notorious scene in the original *Frankenstein* (1931) when the Monster (Boris Karloff) encounters little Maria (Marilyn Harris) and (spoiler alert!) inadvertently drowns her. (*Moviestillsdb*)

Elsa Lanchester and Boris Karloff will fail to make a go of it in *The Bride of Frankenstein* (1935). Lanchester also takes the role of Frankenstein creator Mary Shelley. (*Moviestillsdb*)

Peter Cushing gets out the chemistry set in Hammer's *The Curse of Frankenstein* (1957). (*Wikicommons*)

Publicity poster from the original *Frankenstein* (1931) with Colin Clive and Boris Karloff. (*Moviestillsd*

Christopher Lee's school, Wellington College. (*Wikicommons*)

Christopher Lee in the title role for Hammer's first outing into undead territory, *Dracula* (1958). (*Moviestillsdb*)

A make-up free Boris Karloff, from the 1942 comedy *The Boogie Man Will Get You*. (*Moviestillsdb*)

Is that a pepper pot I see before me? Peter Cushing and Jennie Linden in *Dr Who and the Daleks* (1965). (*Moviestillsdb*)

Veronica Carlsen and Christopher Lee in Hammer's *Dracula Has Risen From The Grave* (1968). (*Moviestillsdb*)

Look behind you! Christopher Lee as arch villain Francisco Scaramanga and Roger Moore as 007 in *The Man with the Golden Gun* (1974). (*Movisetsillsdb*)

Christopher Lee and Lee Grant in the disaster movie *Airport '77* (1977). Lee may be looking glum but he was delighted to appear with this star-studded cast led by Jack Lemmon. (*Moviestillsdb*)

Peter Cushing and director Freddie Francis on the set of the Hammer film *The Creeping Flesh* (1973) distributed by Tigon British Film Productions. (*Moviestillsdb*)

Peter Cushing as General Spielsdorf goes to work in Hammer's *The Vampire Lovers* (1970) directed by Roy Ward Baker. Based on the 1872 Sheridan Le Fanu novella Carmilla. (*Moviestills Db*)

Peter Cushing as stern Puritan leader Gustav Weil in *Twins of Evil* (1971). The twins were played by real-life identical twins and former *Playboy Playmates*, Mary and Madeleine Collins. Mary is the one in this picture. (*Movistillsdb*)

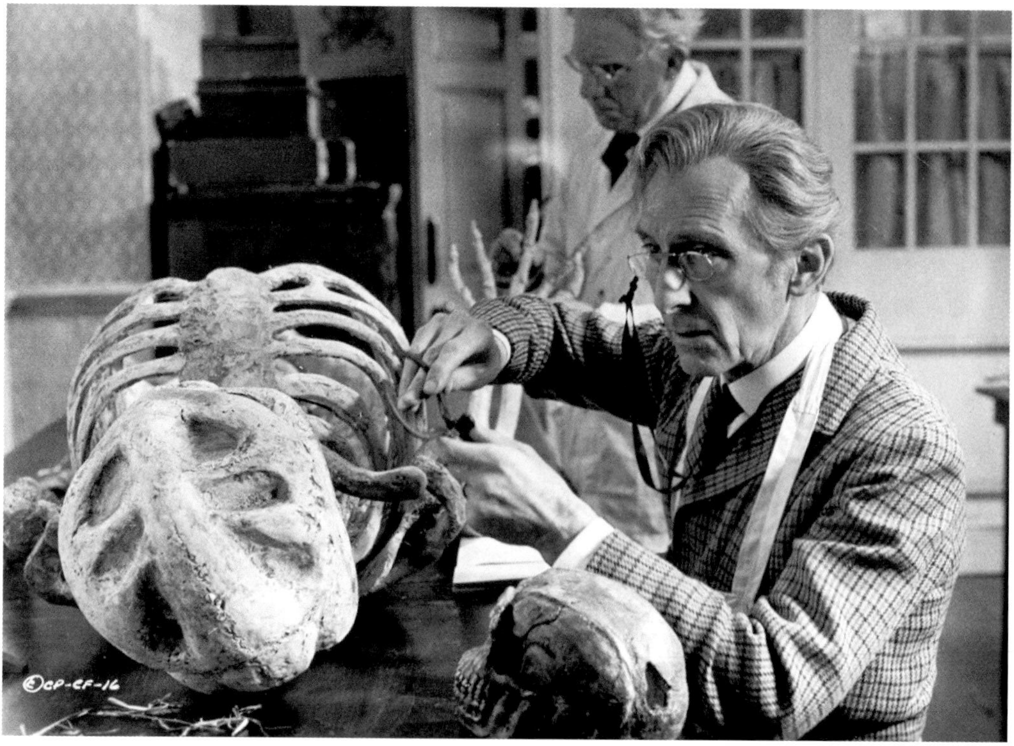

Peter Cushing examines his latest paleontological find in *The Creeping Flesh* (1973) which also stars Christopher Lee. (*Moveistillsdb*)

Basil Rathbone, Boris Karloff, Peter Lorre and Vincent Price take a break from filming *The Comedy of Terrors* (1964) to catch up on the latest showbiz news. (*Moveistillsdb*)

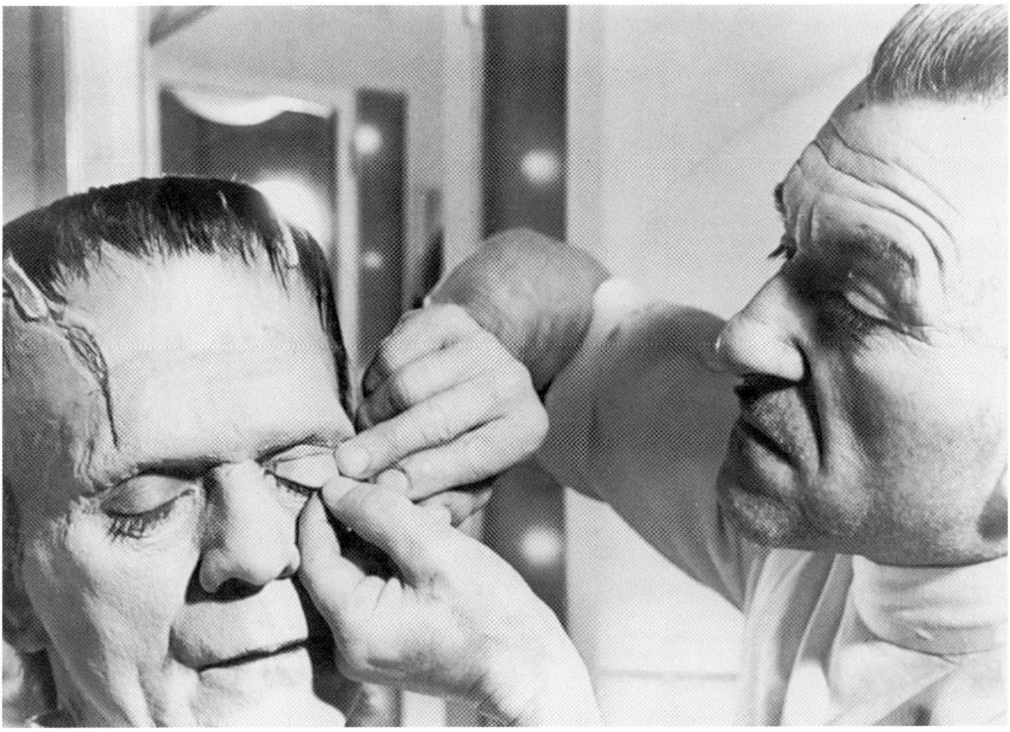

Make-up genius Jack Pierce applies eyelids to Boris Karloff during the making of *Son of Frankenstein* (1939). (*Moveistillsdb*)

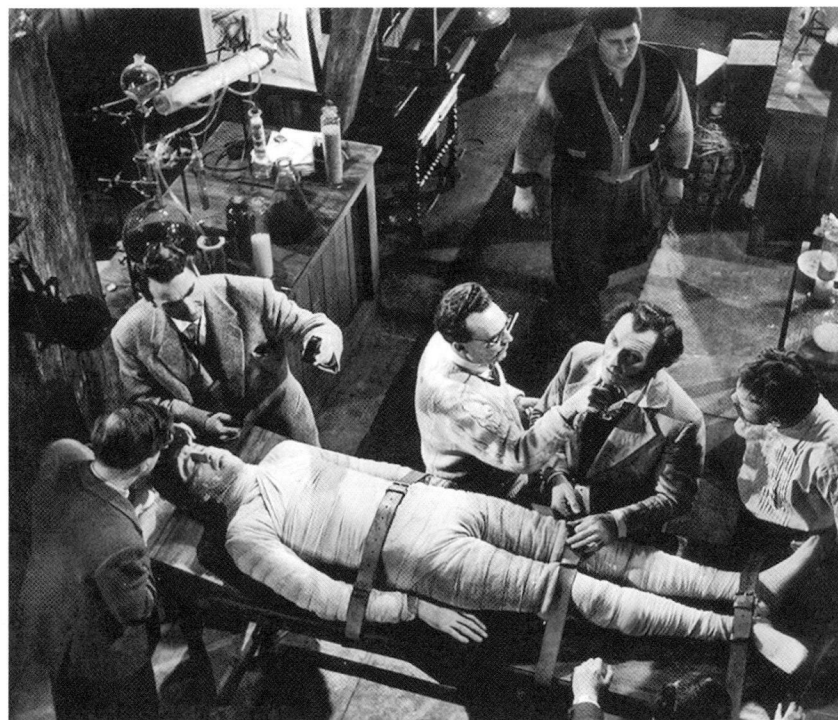

On the set of *The Curse of Frankenstein* (1957) with Christopher Lee as the Monster and Peter Cushing as Baron Frankenstein. (*Moveistillsdb*)

Peter Cushing gets a head of himself while making *The House That Dripped Blood* (1971), made by Amicus Productions and also starring Christopher Lee. (*Moviestillsdb*)

Donald Pleasence and Peter Cushing as Syme and Winston Smith in the controversial BBC TV production of George Orwell's *Nineteen Eighty-Four* (1954). (*Moviestillsdb*)

This isn't going to hurt! Christopher Lee and Caroline Munro in *Dracula AD 1972*, made by Hammer Films. (*Moviestillsdb*)

Christopher Lee in *The Wicker Man* (1973) the folk horror cult movie also starring Edward Woodward and Britt Ekland. (*Moviestillsdb*)

Christopher Lee as Count Dooku wields his trusty light sabre in *Star Wars: Episode II – Attack of the Clones* (2002). (*Moviestillsdb*)

The pub in Whitstable named after Peter Cushing on Oxford Street (formerly a cinema). (*Wikicommons*)

not especially friendly by now and there was conflict over his hectic working schedule which prevented him from seeing very much of his daughter.

Boris's increasing health and mobility problems meant that Evie began to take on the role of her husband's carer, often accompanying him to film sets to fuss over him. Many of Boris's old friends found her a little cold and controlling. Sara Jane has always been diplomatic about Evie, but she acknowledges that she organised his life so that Sara Jane played a very small part as though, 'I was just someone left over from another era.'

When Sara Jane became engaged to 26-year-old American Air Force pilot Richard Cotton, she asked Karloff to give her away at the wedding, due to take place in January 1958. Boris refused, saying that his presence would cause too much attention. Said Sara Jane: 'I rather snippily wrote back that usually most eyes are on the bride, not on the bride's father.' She was, she admits, both disappointed and relieved; and she was happy to call on her stepfather Edgar Rowe to give her away.

Much later, Evie also failed to inform Sara Jane about Boris's death and funeral arrangements.

From the late 1940s Boris's work became ever more centred on TV, radio and theatre. The couple moved to New York, living at the top floor of the Dakota Building on West 72nd Street on Manhattan's Upper West Side, then as now one of the most sought-after residences in the city. It was first celebrated because it was one of the only New York buildings to have elevators, and latterly because of the famous people who have made it their home. It is quite a roll call of New York and showbiz aristocracy – Judy Garland, Lauren Bacall, Rudolf Nureyev, Paul Simon, John and Yoko Lennon, Lilian Gish, the author Harlan Coben, Leonard Bernstein and Rosemary Clooney.

Boris and Evie spent the last ten years of his life in England, moving first to a top floor flat at 43 Cadogan Square in Knightsbridge (Christopher Lee lived next door), and then to a cottage in Bramshott in Hampshire. It is not the only village to be dubbed 'the most haunted village in Britain', but it is one of them. An appropriate home for the old horror master.

In 1968 when he made *Targets*, the young director Peter Bogdanovich wrote about Boris's relationship with Evie:

> They were very warm, like a real old English couple ... proper and cozy. She was mad about him. Took really good care of him, and he was very deferential and warm to her. They were very much in love. She loved him a lot ... I think they were very happy.[9]

Karloff's relationship with his wider family was made difficult by distance and circumstance. His desire to be an actor was troubling to his successful and conventional siblings, as he was painfully aware. After he left England for Canada and Hollywood he made his first return in 1933 when the film *The Ghoul* was released. A reception was given, attended by three of his brothers – Sir John Pratt, former Vice-Consul in China, Consul in the Far East and in charge of all Chinese affairs at the Foreign Office; Charles Pratt, who had worked as an administrator of the Argentinian Railway, and Frederick Pratt, retired, formerly of the Executive Branch of the Indian Civil Service. Edward, a high court judge in Bombay, David and Richard did not attend. George had died, as had half-sister Emma. Sister Julia was happily married to a vicar. Though Karloff was a world-famous star, he was nervous of asking his distinguished siblings if they would mind being photographed with him by the cameraman who had been sent along to mark the occasion. He thought they would consider it beneath their dignity. Of course they were delighted but even so, Sir John took his little brother aside at one point in the evening and assured him that the success of someone doing 'that sort of thing' (i.e. acting) could not possibly last.

Karloff was not the only member of the Pratt family who flouted convention and went into showbiz. His great nephew Anthony Pratt, born in 1937, is also the nephew of the actress Gillian Lind, born in India in 1904, who had a long career on stage, TV and film. Anthony is an art director who has worked on many of John Boorman's films including *Hell in the Pacific* (1968), *Excalibur* (1981) and *Hope and Glory* (1987). He was nominated for an Oscar for *Hope and Glory* and for *The Phantom of the Opera* (2004). Born in England, he had been evacuated to Australia when the Second World War started but returned to London when he was a schoolboy. He met Karloff once, in 1965, and remembers he was 'extremely nice', interested in what his great nephew was doing and knowledgeable about the whole business of production design.

He remembers his Aunt Gillian taking him to see *Unconquered* (1947), an epic adventure about the struggles between American colonists and native Americans in the eighteenth century. Gillian had a crush on Gary Cooper, who stars along with Paulette Goddard. But the film also features Great Uncle Boris in the role of Guyasuta, chief of the Seneca people. Glamorous Aunt Gillian made Anthony long to be an actor too. But after National Service he found his way into film design via a course in theatre design at the Regent Street Polytechnic, where he was mentored by the great art director Carmen Dillon who won an Oscar for her design for Olivier's *Hamlet* (1948).

With his many wives and abrupt divorces, Karloff's emotional centre is elusive. He never became an American national but for all his love of Englishness – cricket, roast beef and Noel Coward – he always seems pleased to return to California after visiting Britain. He seems to have had a disconnected though not particularly fractious relationship with his vast family. In the days before mobile phones and emails it was hard to stay in touch if you had emigrated to Canada when barely out of your teens and lived half a world away. Everyone pays tribute to Karloff's niceness. He was often referred to as Dear Boris. Who, what, did he love? It's difficult to know.

* * *

In April 1942, Peter Cushing took the role of Elyot Chase in a touring production of Noel Coward's *Private Lives* for the Entertainments National Services Association (ENSA). Established in 1939 when war broke out it was nicknamed 'Every Night Something Awful'. Cushing was paid £10 a week. It might not have been active combat but wartime touring was exhausting. 'We rarely knew where we were going or where we were when we got there,' said the stage manager

Joan Craft. When he joined the company his leading lady – playing Amanda Prynne – was Sonia Dresdel. In May, Dresdel took a break from the role and was replaced by Helen Beck.

Violet Helena Beck (she preferred to be called Helen) was some years older than Cushing. She had been born in 1905 in Imperial Russia and her early childhood – along with that of her three sisters and two brothers – was one of extreme privilege. Her father, Ernest Beck, was a Lancashire industrialist who ran the James Beck Spinning Company in St Petersburg, the largest firm of cotton spinners in Russia.

In the last half of the nineteenth century leading up to the Revolution of 1917, a number of foreign multinationals set up manufacturing companies in Russia at a time when the country was experiencing significant industrialisation. By 1915, the UK accounted for a quarter of foreign capital invested in Russian enterprises, with most British companies engaged in cotton spinning or textiles. By the end of the nineteenth century the Russian textile industry produced a third of the country's industrial output and employed a third of Russia's non-agricultural workforce.

The events of 1917 did not bring a halt to the industry but the Bolsheviks had continually attempted to force the workers to strike in the period leading up to the Revolution, which was also one of extreme political instability as a result of the Russo-Japanese War, the Balkan War and the First World War. After the Revolution the new government took control of production, pursuing a policy of protectionism. Ernest Beck, who could sense the way that events were unfolding, took his family back to England in 1915.

On her mother's side Helen was Swedish and Polish, educated – as were many wealthy English girls – in Switzerland, and she was fluent in French, Russian, English and German.

In 1929 Helen had married Kenton Redgrave Keitmayer, a disastrous marriage which she never spoke about. She had lost a child late in pregnancy which seems to have affected her health permanently.

Helen – a trained dancer – had toured America in the mid-1920s as part of Cochran's troupe of girls. Sir Charles Blake Cochran (1872–1951) (known as C.B.) produced revues and musicals in the 1920s and 1930s, often collaborating with Noel Coward and promoting the careers of stars such as Gertrude Lawrence, Jessie Matthews and Beatrice Lillie. He produced the Ballet Russes and ran the Royal Albert Hall for more than a decade.

Making her way to Hollywood Helen took a small role in the silent film *What Price Glory?* (1926) directed by Raoul Walsh. On her return to England she became English tutor to Yvette Labrousse, a beauty queen who became Miss France in 1930 and married the Aga Khan in 1944. Helen also worked as a secretary to the comedian and playwright Sonnie Hale, who was married to Jessie Matthews at the time.

In an interview in 1955, Helen described her first meeting with Peter when they met up on the ENSA tour. She saw him at the coach station wearing an old mackintosh, an old hat and carrying a battered suitcase. She said, 'He swept his hat off and greeted me as if I were royalty and seemed unconscious of his appearance. I thought, "This is the strangest individual I've ever met – but the most attractive."'

Their relationship blossomed as they learnt their lines together, playing Coward's brittle and sophisticated divorced couple. Helen was the first to fall ill, her persistent cough led to a haemorrhage. Cushing then fell ill with congestion of the lungs in Taunton and had to stop work while the rest of the company went back to the ENSA HQ in London. Helen happily stayed behind to nurse him back to health. Both were accordingly invalided out of ENSA. They were deeply in love and Peter Cushing insists that theirs was a spiritual union and that the physical side of their relationship was of little importance.

They married at Marylebone Register Office on 10 April 1943. Helen's parents attended the wedding but Peter did not even inform his own family. They set up home at Airlie Gardens, Camden Hill Road, renting a garden flat for £3 a week. From this point in her life Helen would shelve her own acting ambitions and devote her life to helping her husband. They had little money and she pawned her Fabergé Russian Easter eggs and some other pieces of jewellery. Among their friends at the time was the playwright Ronald Millar (1919–1998). His flat was uninhabitable so he moved in with the Cushings and slept in the bath.

Helen was more than ten years older than him. That isn't a great age difference but the armchair psychiatrist is bound to wonder whether Cushing, who was described by the perspicacious ENSA stage manager Joan Craft as 'not tremendously mature', was looking for a mother figure. Helen was determined but often in poor health. He was – by his own admission – neurotic. In one interview Cushing explained: 'As dear Helen said, except for certain photogenic looks and an obvious ability, you have everything against you. You're shy and you don't like people watching you when you work. You've got nerves like a racehorse and you don't like going abroad.' The marriage could have been a recipe for disaster. But Helen and Peter were the most devoted couple imaginable.

He appeared in several plays at the Q Theatre, near Kew Bridge, opened in 1924 by Jack and Beatie De Leon. Committed to new work, the theatre would stage the first plays by Terence Rattigan and William Douglas-Home. Cushing was appearing in a play called *The Dark Potential* by Joan Morgan when Helen was taken ill with severe abdominal pain and admitted to the Samaritan Hospital for Women in Marylebone Road. She underwent a hysterectomy and a dead foetus was discovered during the operation.

Helen did not only give Peter emotional support. Her linguistic skills enabled her to coach him in accents which helped him secure the part of Private Charles, a Frenchman in Anthony Asquith's *Happy Few*, which opened at the Cambridge Theatre in October 1944. This led to a role in Terence Rattigan's long-running comedy *While the Sun Shines* at the Globe Theatre (now the Gielgud Theatre), which also went on tour.

His success as a dashing Frenchman in the Rattigan play brought Cushing to the attention of Laurence Olivier and earned him the part of Osric in the film version of *Hamlet* (1948). Helen's older brother Reginald Beck (1902–1992) was an associate producer on the film. Having begun his career with Gainsborough Studios in 1927, he would work as a film editor for directors such as Carol Reed, David Lean and Jospeh Losey.

Olivier then invited Cushing to join the 1948 Old Vic tour of Australia and New Zealand. He only accepted when Helen was also included as a member of the company. Peter and Helen would appear together in Thornton Wilder's *The Skin of our Teeth*. In February 1949, back in London, based at the New Theatre, the company put on a production of Jean Anouilh's *Antigone* with Vivian Leigh in the title role, Helen as Eurydice and Leigh's then husband, Olivier, as the chorus.

Olivier then offered Cushing another French-accented role in *The Damascus Blade* but his fragile nerves got the better of him. A tart and inconsequential remark from Olivier reduced Cushing to tears, marking the start of another nervous breakdown. Helen once more nursed him back to health over a period of six months.

When Peter told Helen that he feared he would have to give up acting altogether because of the effect it had on his mental health, it was Helen who began studying the listings in the *Radio Times*, making a note of producers and writing them letters to the effect that Peter Cushing was available for work. As mentioned earlier, it paid off. Cushing first appeared on TV in 1951 in *Eden End*.

His fortunes were about to change but in the meantime Cushing had to go to his father, George Cushing, to ask for financial help. Cushing senior had never believe in his son's acting career and made the awful comment that his son was 'forty and a failure'. Apparently Helen took George to task for this and managed to pour oil on troubled waters. But it was a remark from which Cushing never quite recovered.

Yet now his career really was taking off. As noted earlier, he played Mr Darcy on TV in an adaptation of *Pride and Prejudice* (1952), Winston Smith in *Ninety Eighty-Four* (1954) and Andrew Crocker-Harris in *The Winslow Boy* (1955), rapidly establishing himself as one of Britain's biggest stars. This, in turn, was what made Hammer woo him. Whereas in America the presence of movie stars added lustre to TV, it also worked the other way. In Britain, a big TV star like Cushing would bring audiences back to the cinema. Cushing always said that he owed his success to Helen and it was no exaggeration. She would often accompany him on to a film set or a TV studio and take down the director's notes to the cast and to her husband in shorthand.

She was also aware of the limitations which resulted from her husband's success with Hammer in the *Frankenstein* films. The *New*

York Daily News said: 'Cushing is the new Karloff.' It is a good headline but it meant that Cushing could now say goodbye to playing romantic leading parts such as Mr Darcy.

In the 1950s Peter and Helen bought 3 Seaway Cottages in Whitstable, Kent, a town they had visited since the mid-1940s. The fresh sea air mean that Helen could gain some respite from her emphysema (she was a heavy smoker) which would lead to her death in 1971.

Helen was a semi-invalid for some years, sometimes requiring oxygen. She once took a correspondence course with William Knowles called *New Life Through Breathing*. Knowles was an internationally known 'breath therapist', and during the Second World War had been employed to teach his techniques to the Royal Air Force. Eventually a doctor told Helen – correctly – that Knowles's programme of exercises was a waste of time. Cushing is convinced that this brutal assessment speeded his wife's death. Her weight went down to six stone and Cushing says he himself lost three stone.

Early in 1971 she was taken into hospital in Canterbury for a check-up and was due to stay for three days. Not overly concerned, Cushing promised he would come the next day and bring a little picnic lunch of smoked salmon and avocado salad by way of a change from hospital food. But Helen then had a relapse. She was allowed home and died peacefully soon after.

Cushing was devastated by her death, often saying that he was born in 1913 and died in 1971. It took him eleven years to return to a normal social life. His loyal secretary Joyce Broughton said that he often became 'quite irrational' in his period of self-imposed purdah and ultimately it was only his diagnosis of prostate cancer in 1982 which gave him a new zest for life. As was the way then, Joyce and his closest circle decided it was best if Peter was not informed of the diagnosis for some time.

He considered suicide after her death, but also threw himself into his work. The first film he worked on was Hammer's *Twins of Evil* (1971), one of their best, with Cushing appearing gaunt and worn but giving a truly great performance. During his first Christmas without Helen he worked with Christopher Lee on *The Horror People*, filming in Spain, and he remembers how kind and understanding Lee was. In

1974, while working on *The Ghoul* with John Hurt and Gwen Watford, he had another breakdown. As a prop he had used a picture of his wife Helen at the age of 33 and it all proved too much.

The actor Barbara Leigh who dated both Steve McQueen and Elvis Presley had been chosen by Hammer to star in *Vampirella* in 1976, but unfortunately the film was never made due to Hammer's growing financial problems. Leigh remembers meeting Cushing at the Famous Monsters Convention in New York. 'One dinner was especially memorable,' she wrote in her autobiography *The King, The McQueen and the Love Machine*.

> We were to eat in his hotel suite and the table was set for three so I asked who else was coming. 'It's for my wife. I always set a place for her,' he replied. How odd, I thought, knowing that Peter's wife Helen had died in 1971. Then again, what a loving, devoted husband he must have been.

When *Star Wars* came out he gave an interview to *Weekend Magazine* headlined 'I can't live without my wife' saying: 'When Helen passed on six years ago I lost the only joy in life that I ever wanted. She was my whole life and without her there is no meaning. I am simply killing time, so to speak, until that wonderful day when we are together again'.

By the mid-1980s Cushing was too frail to make frequent visits to Helen's grave and having once helped with a request on the BBC show *Jim'll Fix It*, he wrote to Jimmy Savile explaining his problem and was invited to the show as a special guest. Savile had Christopher Wheatcroft of Wheatcroft Gardens invite Cushing to his Nottingham nursery to pick out a new rose which would be named after Helen. What a pity that this touching story is tainted by its association with the monster Savile.

Cushing had plenty to say about Helen, but love is a two-way business. Describing that initial attraction Helen wrote of the young, tall, shambolic actor who she called her 'beloved vagabond':

> His hands told me he was either a musician or an artist ... and when he bent over one of mine to kiss it, a faint and quite delightful

waft of tobacco and lavender-water hung upon the air. I knew I would love him for the rest of my days – and beyond.

Before Helen, there had been other women in Cushing's life. In 1936 he had accepted a job with Southampton Rep where he spent three years immediately prior to his departure for New York. While he was working in Southampton he met 18-year-old Doreen Lawrence, also an actor with the company. She took pity on him when she found he was living in damp and mouldy theatre digs in a house with no bath and an outside loo at the bottom of the garden. She was living with her parents and invited Peter to stay in the family home.

Doreen was attracted by his 'splendid profile and dark wavy hair' and they became engaged. It was Doreen who broke it off because she claimed that Cushing would often bring his parents along on dates and was prone to crying fits. It is said that during an argument he threw a plate of spaghetti in her face.[10] In 1947 Doreen married the actor Jack Hawkins who had previously been married to Jessica Tandy. Doreen and Jack, who died in 1973, had three children. Doreen died in 2013.

Another odd story came from actor and film director Bryan Forbes. Forbes and Cushing appeared in a TV play called *The Road* on 21 June, 1953. In his book on Cushing, Christopher Gullo quotes a letter from Forbes in which he says that after Helen's death, Cushing 'became very odd indeed. Possibly through guilt (he confessed to me that to his shame he had been unfaithful to her and now wanted to join her in heaven and make amends).' Cushing admits there were many times when he had 'erred', but that although Helen always forgave him, he could never forgive himself. Helen had said before they married that she did not want Peter to feel 'possessed', and that as far as she was concerned 'the things' had never happened.

* * *

We must take at face value Christopher Lee's claim that he was still a virgin at 25 and accept that the bromides in the tea during his military career did the trick. But all this was to change during the filming of *Scott of the Antarctic* (1948) starring John Mills as Robert Falcon Scott, with Lee as Bernard Day, an Australian member of the expedition. Not required for location filming in Norway Lee found himself passing the time in the Milroy nightclub in Stratton Street, Mayfair, where he hit the dance floor with a French professional skier called Jacqueline who was working on the film as a snow expert. She was tall (always a plus for Lee), 'looked very lithe and brown in her white halter-neck', and was staying at the Savoy Hotel.

She duly invited Lee to her room at three in the afternoon and he made his way there full of trepidation. He hadn't slept well, he was hungry and he wondered whether they would be talking in French which (mysteriously) would elevate the entire experience in his imagination. Jacqueline flung open the hotel room door wearing a peignoir, and nothing else.

The afternoon was a success and Lee recalls that more than once he fell off the bed. Later in the evening they walked to a restaurant in the King's Road for supper.

He met the Swedish aristocrat Henriette von Rosen in a nightclub called Riche in Stockholm on a blind date. She was 19, had flame red hair and green eyes. Lee was ten years older and immediately smitten. He had been filming the Hammer film *The Mummy* (1959) with Peter Cushing. Due to the strictness of Sweden's censorship laws on horror films, Henriette had never seen any of his previous movies. In spite of this (or perhaps because of it) she quickly agreed to marry him. Her father, Count Fritz von Rosen, was not delighted by the prospective union and immediately set a pack of private detectives on to Lee, attempting to check his credentials. The Count also contacted Lee's friends asking for references, among them Douglas Fairbanks and John Boulting (of the film producing duo the Boulting Brothers). Boulting's letter suggested to the irascible Count that actors were no longer the rogues and vagabonds of popular myth.

At Christmas time Lee embarked on an exhausting 'etiquette marathon', paraded among the family's castle and great houses, enduring lengthy toasts and speeches, interminable formal dinners, hostile servants. He didn't know quite what to wear, when to stand or sit and whether he should fold up his napkin at the end of a banquet. Lee enjoyed one small victory – when a perusal of the family trees revealed that Lee's Carandini family was hundreds of years older than the parvenu van Rosens.

After passing all the tests that Fritz could throw at the prospective bridegroom, it seemed that the wedding was about to go ahead. Henriette travelled to London to prepare herself for her new life. Lee is very vague about exactly what happened, but it was he who called it off, as they sat in his second-hand Mercedes in Eaton Square. She was upset and he never saw her again. Lee later found out that she went back to Sweden and married a wealthy man with whom she had three children and lived happily ever after. You can't help but feel that there is a lot here which went unsaid.

Lee and Birgit Kroencke (known as Gitte) met through a mutual friend, Harry Rabinowitz. Gitte's Danish family owned the Tuborg brewery in Copenhagen. Gitte, born in 1935, was a painter and a model who had worked for Balmain, Balenciaga and Dior. A mesmerising beauty, she was also a redhead with green eyes. They married on 17 March 1961 at St Michael's, Chester Square in Belgravia, and Gitte was 'beautiful in beige and a fur hat'. There was no time for a proper honeymoon as Lee was about to start filming *The Devil's Daffodil*, a British-West German crime movie based on an Edgar Wallace story in which Lee plays a Chinese detective, and had to speak lines in German with a Chinese accent. Fluent in German, the new bride was called upon to help with Lee's mastery of this difficult feat. These days it would not be the accent that was problematic, it would be the casting of a non-Chinese actor.

The couple were living in Switzerland when Gitte gave birth to their daughter Christina in 1963 in a clinic in Lausanne. It was a traumatic event. Lee had flu and a broken rib and as they checked into the clinic the news of Kennedy's assassination was coming through. Gitte's waters had broken but, ominously, they were green, indicating that the baby had emptied its bowels and might be suffocating, also putting Gitte's life in danger. Both mother and baby Christina survived, but Christina was born with her feet turned at right angles, almost facing backwards. For the first year of her life she was in splints, and would endure many procedures before she was able to walk and overcome her disability.

Gitte usually travelled with Lee though the couple agreed that they would never fly together in case there was a crash and Christina would be orphaned. They enjoyed, according to the press and Lee himself, 'a miraculous marriage'. He had asked her to marry him just days after they met. They barely spent a day apart.

* * *

Chapter Seven

Franchise

The film industry is always looking for something new. But since the early days of Hollywood it has also known the value of doing something ... again. The sequel, the prequel, the remake, the reboot and the franchise have always had an appeal to producers (a safe bet) and audiences (getting what you know you enjoy) alike. Somehow franchise is the word with the most businesslike air about it. It conjures up a world of corporate lawyers, contracts, intellectual property laws and shrewd commercial decisions. A reboot implies a cultural reassessment of an earlier film. A remake is a way of appealing to a younger audience. Sequels and prequels top and tail a familiar story.

We have all grown up with film franchises which become important cultural markers for us individually and for society – the Middle-Earth series encompassing the *Lord of the Rings* and *The Hobbit* films; *Pirates of the Caribbean*; the *Batman* films; *Star Wars*; *Rocky*, *Indiana Jones*; the *Alien* films; *Harry Potter*; the James Bond films; *Mission Impossible*; *Toy Story*; no end of Marvel MCU films; *Jaws*; *Shrek*; endless 'Nightmares' on Elm Street and on and on.

George Lucas, creator of the *Star Wars* franchise, calls the *Star Wars* films 'episodes', conceiving them as being in the tradition of the Saturday matinee serials shown across American picture houses from the early days of cinema up until the 1950s. One of the first of these was *The Perils of Pauline* (1914), devised by William Randolph Hearst with Pearl White (1889–1938) in the title role. Each episode of Pauline's all-action adventures usually ended with a moment of great jeopardy which helped popularise the word 'cliffhanger'. The marketing of *The Perils of Pauline* included merchandise – a key feature of all movie franchises – with sheet music available to fans. Pearl died of liver failure in her 40s. Rather like Boris Karloff, she too suffered from spinal problems as a result of the arduous physical nature of filming *Perils*, and self-medicated with alcohol for the rest of her life.

Universal Pictures, under Carl Laemmle Jr, created the horror franchise with the *Frankenstein, Dracula, Mummy, Wolfman* and *Invisible Man* series. More recently, Universal also made the *Fast and Furious* and *Jurassic Park* series. Even when horror films were in the doldrums in the late 1930s there was scope for a Frankenstein reboot. Filmed towards the end of 1938, *Son of Frankenstein* – starring Bela Lugosi as Ygor, the broken-necked blacksmith, Basil Rathbone as the son of Baron Frankenstein, and Karloff as the Monster (with second billing) – was not to Karloff's liking. But during filming the daughter of Frankenstein appeared – Sara Jane Karloff was born at Hollywood Presbyterian Hospital on 23 November. It was also her father's 51st birthday with a party on the film set, accompanied by a lavish birthday cake on Frankenstein's laboratory table.

Karloff was concerned that the stories were going 'downhill', that there was not much more to be squeezed from the Monster's character and that he would simply become 'an oafish prop'. It is perhaps the fate of all successful franchises which, like political careers, are doomed to end in failure. Nevertheless, when *Son of Frankenstein* was released early in 1939 it was a box office hit, proving that there was still life in the old monster.

No wonder Universal's tight control of its valuable property extended to preventing Hammer from reproducing Jack Pierce's iconic Frankenstein's monster make-up when the British company made *The Curse of Frankenstein* in the 1950s.

If proof were needed of how successful a franchise film can be, one can turn to *Abbott and Costello Meet Frankenstein* (1948), a comedy monster mash-up for Bud Abbott and Lou Costello which involved horror stars Bela Lugosi and Lon Chaney Jr. with Vincent Price as the voice of the Invisible Man. Frankenstein's monster was played by Glenn Strange because Karloff had declined to appear. He did, however, agree to promote the film when it opened at Loew's Criterion Theatre in New York. He said he would not be seeing the film because: 'I'm too fond of the Monster. I'm grateful to him for all he did for me, and I wouldn't want to watch anybody make sport of him.'

Nevertheless, this comedy became the most successful film in the *Frankenstein* series since the release of the original in 1931, even though there was a sense (as there tends to be with endless franchise follow-ups) that a dead horse was being flogged. Shortly after the film opened, Karloff returned to Universal to make *Abbott and Costello Meet the Killer, Boris Karloff* (1949). In this film Karloff plays a Swami, a part he seems to have had had no problem accepting. 'Bud and Lou are wonderful chaps to work with,' he confirmed, 'but we've all got to work, don't we? So the less said about this film, the better.'

Having played Chinese arch villain Fu Manchu in *The Mask of Fu Manchu* (1932) Karloff played the sympathetic lead in five of the *Mr Wong* films in the late 1930s. James Lee Wong was a fictional Chinese-American detective created by Hugh Wiley whose stories appeared in *Collier's Magazine*, a general interest periodical which was published in America between 1888–1957. It published fiction by some of America's greatest writers including F.Scott Fitzgerald, Ray Bradbury, Willa Cather, Sinclair Lewis and J.D. Salinger. As well as the *Wong* stories, *Collier's* also published Sax Rohmer's *Fu Manchu* serials.

William Nigh directed the *Wong* films which were produced by the low-budget Monogram studio. They were *Mr Wong, Detective* (1938), *The Mystery of Mr Wong* (1939), *Mr Wong in Chinatown* (1939), *The Fatal Hour* (1940) and *Doomed to Die* (1940).

* * *

Peter Cushing can be seen as a franchise man through and through, being a defining character actor in Hammer's *Frankenstein* and *Dracula* films. He and Lee also took turns in the *Sherlock Holmes* movies made by Hammer and other studios. They both starred in Hammer's first Holmes movie (and the first to be shot in colour) *The Hound of The Baskervilles* (1959) with Cushing as Holmes. Lee starred as Holmes in *Sherlock Holmes and the Deadly Necklace* (1962), directed by Terrence Fisher in a West German-French-Italian co-production. Lee – who had met Arthur Conan Doyle – thought it was both disastrous and dull. Lee played Mycroft Holmes in the 1970 production of Billy Wilder's *The Private Life of Sherlock Holmes* opposite Robert Stephens, then returned as Sherlock Holmes in the early 1990s in a pair of telefilms, *Sherlock Holmes and the Leading Lady* and *Incident at Victoria Falls*.

Dalekmania gripped the nation in the mid-1960s. *Dr Who* had debuted on the BBC in 1963 with William Hartnell in the lead taking on the might of the giant pepper pots with their sink-plunger attachments. The Dalek catchphrase 'Exterminate, exterminate, exterminate' (rising to an hysterical pitch of murderous intent) was heard across school playgrounds, the length and breadth of Britain.

In 1965 Cushing found himself starring in *Dr Who and the Daleks* and its follow-up *Daleks' Invasion Earth 2150AD* (1966). Dalekmania was a natural candidate for this full-length movie treatment and was released during the school summer holidays.

It was an Amicus production (though the name was changed to AARU), written by Milton Subotsky and filmed at Shepperton Studios. It was decided to drop William Hartnell in favour of a more recognisable name and face and Peter Cushing was cast, with Roy Castle as his comedic sidekick. Roberta Tovey and Jennie Linden play his grand-daughters. Though the look of the film is almost as low budget as the TV series, this would have been the first time that many children (still watching black-and-white TV) would have seen Daleks in glorious colour.

The sequel *Daleks' Invasion Earth 2150AD*, released the following year is an improvement with Peter Cushing's Doctor wearing a long blue scarf which would be copied by Tom Baker (in a multicoloured version) when he became the fourth Dr Who.

The BBC is now obsessed with the *Dr Who* legacy, forever patting itself on the back for the longevity of its time-travelling hero. But in the endless anniversary celebrations which come round with increasing frequency, Cushing seems to have been written out of history. Yet in some ways he performed a necessary service to the *Dr Who* canon by showing that another actor could play the role. Without him would there have been the subsequent manifestations of Dr Who and the confected excitement about who will play the 'next' Dr Who. Some franchises – like the James Bond films – depend on the lead character being 'refreshed' to keep the series alive.

Cushing says that George Lucas first asked him to play the Jedi Master Obi-Wan Kenobi in his new film *Star Wars* (1977). In the event he played the Grand Moff Tarkin, intended to provide a human face to villainy, because Darth Vader's face (his rival in malevolence) was covered. Darth Vader is played by Dave Prowse who had appeared with Cushing in *Frankenstein and the Monster from Hell*. Cushing says he accepted the role because he felt his fans enjoyed seeing him in science fiction films, ever a first cousin to horror.

But *Star Wars* was no ordinary science fiction film. The Bunsen burners and lurching revenants that Cushing dealt with in his usual man-of-science roles were nowhere to be seen. The wobbly sets of TV's *Dr Who* (only slightly improved on in the Amicus film) are replaced by the astonishing special effects. This was the beginning of the era of the blockbuster franchise, and Cushing – who had made his name in the world of low budget films, elevating them by his particular brand of screen magic – became a part of that. Nothing like it had ever been seen before. There have now been so many 'episodes' in the franchise and we are accustomed to its magnificence. But I remember going to a press screening of that first Star Wars film and I'm pretty sure my mouth hung open in amazement from start to finish.

As usual, Cushing charmed everyone on the set. Carrie Fisher said it was difficult to act as though she hated his character because he was so adorable. Mark Hamill, Harrison Ford and Fisher made their names in the film, but Cushing and Alec Guinness (as Obi-Wan Kenobi) were the bigger stars at the time. In 1980, when Peter Cushing made his final appearance on the *Morecambe and Wise Christmas Special*, his fellow guest was Alec Guinness.

Guinness was apparently irritated that, great classical actor that he was, *Star Wars* became the film with which he was most associated. During filming he wrote to a friend (Anne):

> I have returned to London this evening for my stint at the studio for the rest of the week. Can't say I'm enjoying the film – new rubbish dialogue reaches me every other day day on wadges of pink paper – and *none* of it makes my character clear or even bearable.

Another gripe was the way the young cast treated him as though he was an old codger in his 90s. His one consolation was the large amount of money he was paid.

Cushing – genuinely – never seems to have been bothered by the prestige (or lack of it) attached to the roles that came this way. He was handsomely paid too (though there is some dispute over these figures). Some sources say he earned £2,000 a day whereas Mark Hamill was on $1,000, Harrison Ford on $750 and Carrie Fisher on $850.

Cushing is terrific as the Grand Moff Tarkin ('I've often wondered what a Grand Moff is,' he observes mildly in one filmed interview). Watch him threatening to destroy Princess Leia's home planet if she does not tell him where the rebel base is. When she does tell him he destroys the planet anyway. His majestic malevolence is somewhat diminished by the oft-told anecdote about his footwear. He described Tarkin's costume as being similar to that of an 'Edwardian chauffeur' with riding boots. Unfortunately the bespoke boots were not big enough for Cushing's large feet. He duly requested that George Lucas filmed him from the knees up so that he could wear carpet slippers on the set.

Unfortunately, both Alec Guinness's and Peter Cushing's characters are killed, which prevented the two stars from appearing again. Cushing must have reflected that a minor inconvenience such as death never prevented characters in low-budget horror films from returning to life. And, as it turned out, the evil Moff would indeed rise again, but not before Cushing's own demise.

One role in a film franchise would escape Cushing. The director John Carpenter invited him to play the part of Dr Samuel Loomis in the film *Halloween*. Cushing's agent, confident that his client would have no need of low-budget shockers after his success in *Star Wars*, declined. The role went to Donald Pleasence.

Christopher Lee never seemed entirely at ease with his career trajectory. In this respect he was very unlike Peter Cushing who, apart from an occasional tart remark, never complained about the parts he was offered. 'I don't mind being known as a horror star,' Cushing said in an an interview. 'My heavens that would be like socking a gift horse in the face or whatever the saying is. It doesn't bother me at all.'

But it did bother Lee who – with his patrician air, his mastery of ten languages, and his friends in high places – was clearly irritated every time a journalist mentioned the D word. Dracula. When Matthew Sweet interviewed him in 2001 Lee told him that he had only continued to accept roles in Hammer's *Dracula* films because otherwise the company bosses pestered him with 'hysterical phone calls'. They would tell him that they had used his name to secure American funding, that if he wouldn't agree to appear then many British actors and film technicians would find themselves out of work. The idea that Hammer appealed to Lee's sense of patriotic duty may sound laughable, but there is some truth to it. It is difficult to imagine Hammer without Christopher Lee and it is equally hard to imagine the British film industry in the 1950s and 1960s without Hammer.

Lee also fell back on the accusation of 'sloppy journalism', ever popular with disgruntled actors who feel their oeuvre has been misrepresented. 'So why does the press refer to me as a horror actor?' he grumbled to Sweet.

> If you ask the press, or any casting directors, what Christopher Lee did when he was in America for ten years, they haven't a clue. I hosted *Saturday Night Live*. It was their third biggest audience of all time. Fact. You can't fiddle those figures. And I did a hell of a lot of comedy in America. Fact. It's right there on the screen. Now, are you prepared to accept the evidence of your own eyes, or are you going to deny it? And they deny it.

Yet try as one might, it is hard to see *Police Academy: Mission to Moscow* (1994) – in which he plays Commandant Aleksandr Nikolaevich Rakov – as a defining moment in his eminent career, especially as this film was the least successful in Warner Bros' *Police Academy* franchise. It was, though, produced by his old pal Paul Maslansky.

Long before he went to Hollywood in 1977, Lee had (in one of several attempts to escape his associations with Dracula) tried to position himself as a European actor in the 1960s. There was a certain cachet attached to the concept of European cinema in the 1960s, deliberately setting itself apart from the familiar Hollywood themes of love, adventure and heroism, with a focus on politics, sexuality, existentialism and individual experience. France had the New Wave, Italy had Neorealism with directors such as Antonioni, Fellini and Visconti. In Spain, Bunuel's *Viridiana* (1961) was an anticlerical satire starring Fernando Rey which was banned by Franco but won the Palme d'Or at Cannes. Though a popular setting for spaghetti Westerns, Spain did not participate in the new European cinema until Franco's death in 1975. New German Cinema came to the fore in the early 1970s, but until then had less of an identity. But there was still work to be had and British-German co-productions meant that Lee could use his fluency in German.

In search of this new 'European actor' identity, Lee and Gitte moved to Switzerland, finding a bungalow near Vevey on the northern shore of Lake Geneva. Charlie Chaplin, Noel Coward and Marlene Dietrich were close neighbours, while Deborah Kerr was at Mürren, David Nigel at Chateau d'Oex, the Burtons at Gstaad, James Mason at Corseaux, George Sanders near Lausanne, William Holden and Yul Brunner in Lausanne, and Brian Aherne was in Vevey.

Even with so much opportunity to name drop there were problems. Lee's Swiss residency meant that he had to limit the films he made in the UK and most of these were for Hammer, among them *The Gorgon* (1964). He made many films in Italy and a lot of them were very weird indeed. They included Mario Brava's *La Frusta e il Corpo* (1963) which translates as *The Whip and the Body*. The Italian censors did not respond well to its sadomasochist themes and it was banned from most cinemas in Italy. *La Vergine de Norimberga* (1964), in which Lee plays a scarred SS man turned chauffeur, includes a grisly iron maiden scene and a female corpse whose head has been covered by a cage imprisoning a rat that has gnawed her face away. On the plus side, the film abounds in pious anti-war sentiments.

One of Lee's better films in this period is *Castello dei Morti Vivi* (1964) produced by Paul Maslansky and directed by Warren Kiefer. Michael Reeves, who would make *Witchfinder General* and *The Sorcerers* before his tragically premature death, is credited as assistant director. Also starring was a young Donald Sutherland, who was good friends with Kiefer – so much so that Sutherland named his son after him.

Lee plays the sinister and charismatic Count Drago, a man who has developed a new embalming procedure which he is anxious to try out, so one fears for the cheery troupe of *commedia dell'arte* performers who have shown up at his castle. This was his first meeting with Maslansky, who he admired for his speed and efficiency – despite the fact that when Lee went to Rome for the post-synch and discovered that due to a cock-up of majestic proportions there was no sound at all on the film's print. Lee went ballistic but was rendered helpless with laughter by Maslansky who yelled: 'I'll have you know that I am not just any odd asshole that's rolled in off the street. I'm a Producer!'

These films, among others that he made during his European period, are indisputably horror films.

In fact, Lee's reputation for horror follows him across the Channel. After the *Castello* shoot ended, Lee and a pregnant Gitte were driving between Milan and Stresa on their way home when a tyre blew.

Lee put out the warning triangle and, while speaking to Gitte through the passenger window, he suddenly slid down into an unexpected cutting where a new road was being built. Although uninjured, he was covered in mud and sand. Leaving Gitte and Bongo (their dog) in the car, Lee went for help.

Wandering in the dark across a construction site and a turnip field, he finally reached a place of human habitation. A man opened the door, took one look at Lee, shrieked and fainted. His wife was also pretty distraught. It seemed that the previous night the couple had watched Lee in *Dracula*.

The five-film *Fu Manchu* franchise, based on the stories of Sax Rohmer, kept Lee busy in the 1960s. They were produced by another colourful chancer from the British film industry, Harry Alan Towers (1920–2009). South London-born Towers attended the Italia Conti Academy of Theatre Arts and became a child actor. During the war he served with the RAF and became head of the RAF radio unit on the British Broadcasting Service. He produced TV dramas for ITV from the mid-1950s, and in 1956 moved to New York where he clinched a deal with American DJ Alan Freed to do a Saturday night rock'n'roll show on Radio Luxembourg, which was transmitted throughout Western Europe.

In 1961 Towers and his girlfriend were charged with operating a vice ring at a New York hotel for a clientele of UN diplomats. His girlfriend, Mariella Novotny (real name Stella Capes), was part of the Christine Keeler set (in the 1989 film *Scandal* she is played by Britt Ekland) and is said to have had affairs with both John F. and Robert Kennedy.

Towers jumped bail and left for Moscow where he began producing films, financed in some devilishly cunning way through Lichtenstein. On a trip to Spain he met the director Jesus Franco and together they made a number of sexploitation horror movies as well as the *Fu Manchu* films with Christopher Lee as the oriental villain. Lee also appears in Franco's *Eugenie ... The Story of her Journey into Perversion* (1969) based on a Marquis de Sade story. 'Her body is bruised and embraced beyond her wildest dreams' reads the poster. Lee took the lead in Franco's *Night of the Blood Monster* (1970 – ostensibly a biopic of the notorious seventeenth-century Lord Jeffreys, the 'Hanging Judge'. 'Chained women, captives of pleasure', drools the trailer. Though in the event the film got a mild PG rating.

Towers scripted the *Fu Manchu* films under his pen-name Peter Welbeck. Don Sharp (who Lee admired) was director for *The Face of Fu Manchu* (1965) and *The Brides of Fu Manchu* (1966). British director Jeremy Summers made *The Vengeance of Fu Manchu* (1967). Franco directed *The Blood of Fu Manchu* (1968) and *The Castle of Fu Manchu* (1969).

Lee is equivocal about the oriental villain, saying he was not embarrassed to be associated with either the first *Dracula* or *The Face of Fu Manchu*. He felt far less happy about the subsequent follow-up movies but put his reservations aside in the interests of making a living. Again he says he went on appearing in the *Fu Manchu* films because of the many actors who would lose work if he declined to sign up for the next film in the franchise.

Sax Rohmer was the pseudonym of Arthur Henry Sarsfield Ward (1883–1959). Apparently he died in the Asian flu pandemic, which is a telling irony. The first Fu Manchu story, *Dr Fu Manchu*, appeared in 1913. His widow, Rose Elizabeth, was also a writer and visited the set of the first *Fu Manchu* film, made in Dublin – which convincingly resembled London's Limehouse in the 1930s. She told Lee that Rohmer conceived the idea for the stories when, one night in Limehouse, he had seen a Chinaman as tall as Lee getting out of a Rolls Royce with a beautiful young mixed-race woman.

Today, the casting of a European to play the immortal Chinese supervillain would in itself be enough to sink the film, let alone any concerns about the storyline's inherent racism or its artistic merit.

The Chinese actress Tsai Chin played Fu Manchu's evil daughter. Born in 1933 she has had an extraordinary career and is the sister of the restaurateur Michael Chow. The first Chinese student at RADA, she starred on the London stage in *The World of Suzie Wong* in 1959 and appeared in two Bond films, *You Only Live Twice* (1967) and *Casino Royale* (2006). She was Auntie Lindo in the 1993 film *The Joy Luck Club*. She helped Lee with what he describes as 'the Chinese bits' and 'reassured' him when Chinese communities across the world declared the *Fu Manchu* film to be offensive.

Lee was persuaded to take part in an elaborate publicity stunt to promote the second film, *The Brides of Fu Manchu*, which he describes as 'tosh'. Towers persuaded him to tour European countries choosing the winners of national beauty competitions, whose prize would be a part in the film. Filmed at Bray Studios, the plot finds Fu Manchu kidnapping the uniformly beautiful daughters of prominent scientists so that he can blackmail them into building a device which will transmit blast waves across the globe, enabling him to achieve world domination.

Before the 1970s, film franchises tended to mean low-budget, exploitation material – basically, doing something again and again because there's a known audience. But in the 1970s the franchise became an essential part of the film industry's business model. In a global but fragmented market the franchise provided a level of assurance. A nervous investor would have more confidence if there was a familiar star and a known brand.

It was in the 1970s that the James Bond franchise achieved the kind of global supremacy that the films' villains invariably crave. The casting of Roger Moore to replace Sean Connery took the franchise in a new direction – more comedic certainly (that raised eyebrow) but also with a reach beyond the post-war, Cold War preoccupations of Connery's 007.

Lee had hoped to be cast as Dr No in the 1962 film. After all, he was Ian Fleming's cousin (sort of) and it would have been, he admitted, a welcome change from German and Italian horror films. But unfortunately Joseph Wiseman won the role of Dr Julius No. Lee was dismayed, writing that 'the fantasy Ian created has been the most reliable vehicle in the story of the cinema that any actor would want to carry him round the world. And I had missed my chance.'

But then, in 1973, the director Guy Hamilton took him to lunch at the White Elephant Club in London's Curzon Street and offered Lee the role of Scaramanga in the upcoming 007 film *The Man With The Golden Gun*, (the Bond villain famous for having a third nipple), which would be filmed in Thailand. You sense that Lee – after a lifetime of low budget movies – was beside himself with happiness. He knew that a Bond film bestowed worldwide recognition and that the big budgets meant that the production values would be second to none. He was now in a world where producer Cubby Broccoli would drop by in a helicopter, bringing a champagne lunch to the idyllic location (Phuket).

But for all the kudos of being a Bond villain, it was horror business as usual for Christopher Lee in the years that followed and it was not until the next century that he had roles in films that were also part of huge film franchises. In 1977 he had turned down the role of the Grand Moff Tarkin in the first *Star Wars* film, which went to his friend Peter Cushing. But in 2002 he appeared as Count Dooku in *Star Wars: Episode II – Attack of the Clones*, followed in 2005 by *Star Wars: Episode*

III – Revenge of the Sith. In 2008 he supplied his voice for the computer animation *Star Wars: The Clone Wars*.

The Lord of the Rings trilogy, based on Tolkien's novels, was directed by Peter Jackson, under three titles – *The Fellowship of the Ring* (2001), *The Two Towers* (2002) and *The Return of the King* (2003). Between 2012 and 2014 it was followed by the prequel of *Hobbit* films – *The Hobbit: An Unexpected Journey*, *The Hobbit: The Desolation of Smaug* and *The Hobbit: The Battle of the Five Armies*. Lee, with a poker-straight white wig and impressive robes, was cast as the wizard Saruman, though he really fancied the role of Gandalf, which went to Ian McKellen. It has been said that McKellen and Lee were a little chilly with each other. McKellen was a great classical actor while Lee was a low-budget horror star. On the other hand Lee had actually met J.R.R. Tolkien (who died in 1973), something that nobody else involved with the movies could claim. It was in a pub in Oxford, The Eagle and Child. He really did love the books too, saying that he thought *The Lord of the Rings* was 'the greatest literary achievement in my lifetime'.

His cordial relationship with Peter Jackson was marred when Jackson cut him out of *The Return of the King*, the last in the trilogy. Lee was so upset that he boycotted the premiere.

The original plan in *The Return of the King* was supposed to show Saruman's death in a long sequence, the final confrontation between the Fellowship and their greatest enemy. But it wasn't in the final film, something the fans could not understand. Nobody who saw the film knew what had happened to Saruman. It was like ending Hamlet with a question mark. Did he die or didn't he?

Jackson justified this peculiarity, at least to his own satisfaction, and the scene is available as extra material on the DVD. In the footage, Saruman is stabbed by Grima Wormtongue and, falling from the tower, is impaled on a wooden stake projecting from a mill wheel, a visual nod to Lee's Dracula.

He returned to the role of Saruman in the last *Hobbit* film, *The Battle of the Five Armies*. It was the last of his films to be released before his death in 2015. *Angels in Notting Hill* and *The Hunting of the Snark* were released in 2016 and 2017 respectively.

Lee was by now too frail and elderly to travel to New Zealand where the *Hobbit* films were shot. The rest of the cast did the relevant scene in New Zealand and Lee did his scenes at Pinewood Studios in the UK. There is a video of Peter Jackson and members of the crew paying homage to the great man as he sits in his Saruman robes at Pinewood regaling them with stories about his long and illustrious career. Clearly the falling out with Jackson has been forgiven and forgotten.

Lee really did love to talk, and when he moved to Hollywood in the 1970s one acquaintance of his joked that 'the population of Los Angeles were dusting out their bomb shelters in anticipation of a barrage of anecdotes'. There is another story of an actress (unidentified, sadly) who got off a plane looking exhausted. Did she need medical attention? No, she said, but she had been sitting next to Lee and he had not stopped talking about himself for the entire ten-hour flight.

In the Jackson video you see the barely-concealed impatience on the face of one of the production assistants as he launches into another yarn. Time is money in the film biz, even when you are in the presence of a grand old man of cinema.

In a warm tribute to Christopher Lee, published in *Entertainment Weekly* after he died in 2015, the director Tim Burton says in admiration that Lee 'just kept going', making films almost back to back right through the first decade of the twenty-first century. One of the most positive relationships he had during this time was with Burton. Burton's body of work does not represent a franchise but it is so distinctive that Lee's small roles in five of his films make up a touching footnote to his career. He appears in *Sleepy Hollow* (1999), *Charlie and the Chocolate Factory* (2005), the animation *Corpse Bride* (2005), *Alice in Wonderland* (2010) and the vampire movie *Dark Shadows* (2012). For those who have tried to keep a tally of Christopher Lee's films (and even he had lost count) this is supposed to be his 200th.

Lee believed that Burton was one of the great directors of the modern age. While he had theoretically turned his back on horror films back in the 1970s, perhaps Burton's films showed him how the horror genre could be taken in a different direction, with movies that were indeed Gothic phantasmagorias but were also taken seriously by critics, were financed by major studios with big budgets and had elements of intentional comedy. Lee might have wondered to himself why this never happened in the Hammer era. Did the sight of the purposefully lurid fake blood that occasionally spatters through Burton's films remind him of the exciting scarlet of Hammer's fake sanguination, affectionately known as Kensington Gore?

Tim Burton (born in 1958) began his career at Disney after attending the California Institute of Arts, a training college set up by Walt Disney in the 1960s. His films have been produced by Warner Bros, Twentieth Century Fox and Columbia. The critic Jonathan Romney described him as 'Hollywood's pet maladjusted adolescent'. Yet while he has always presented himself as an outsider, he is also popular with cinema-goers who don't normally bandy around names of directors. His films are both weird and popular, arty but mainstream. They can be enjoyed by both adults and children, and that does not apply to many films these days.

Like many directors of the baby boomer generation such as Steven Spielberg or John Carpenter, Burton loved classic horror films and their melancholy monsters – such as Karloff's Frankenstein monster, Godzilla and King Kong – influenced the sad, freaky outsiders who populate his films. His film *Frankenweenie* (1984) is full of references to *Frankenstein* and *The Bride of Frankenstein*. In the animated version of *Frankenweenie* (2012) he sticks in a shot from Lee's 1958 *Dracula* because he was such an inspiration,

One of Burton's favourite Dracula films is *Dracula A.D. 1972*, which was always one of Lee's least favourites excursions into undead territory.

Dark Shadows is both an homage to horror in general and to an American daytime soap that ran from 1966 to 1971. Though it had contained the usual run of soap stories, the characters were ghosts, werewolves and vampires. Said scriptwriter Seth Grahame-Smith, better known as the author of the novel *Pride and Prejudice and Zombies*, said of *Dark Shadows*: 'It's a supernatural Gothic soap-opera action-comedy. It's that old bag of hammers.'

Johnny Depp, who has starred in many of Burton's films, became friends with Christopher Lee when they made *Sleepy Hollow* together.

Depp plays Ichabod Crane, a policeman investigating a spate of beheadings, and Lee is the Burgomaster of the troubled town.

It was Depp who presented Lee with his BFI Fellowship Award in 2013. It is very moving to see Lee on the video of the event, bowed, frail but with that beautiful voice undiminished, make his short acceptance speech. 'It's very kind, and unexpected, a great joy to me … and I think that's it.' Lee admired Depp and thought him a true star.

Christopher Lee's involvement with Burton began during pre-production for *Sleepy Hollow* in 1998 and a discussion about casting the small role of the Burgomaster. 'What about Christopher Lee?', he suggested. Someone said they thought he was dead. Burton wasn't sure but once he had established that Lee was not only alive but available for work, they met at London's Dorchester Hotel. Burton was awed by his presence. He felt like one of Dracula's victims, hypnotised and helpless by this screen legend who had been such a huge part of his cinematic life. Lee, always happy to have an audience, regaled Burton with stories about the Second World War, about 007 author Ian Fleming, and one about playing golf with Hervé Villechaize, his co-star from *The Man With The Golden Gun*.' Burton, (perhaps zoning out from some of the anecdotal detail) was seduced by the timbre and beauty of Lee's voice which made him aware of his – often underused – technical skills. Half-joking, he asked his guest if he would record his phone message.

While Lee could sometimes go on a bit, Burton found that talking to him reminded him why he, Burton, loved making films. He recognised his versatility and understood why he became tired and frustrated by being pigeonholed.

* * *

Chapter Eight

War

The First World War was the first to be caught on motion picture cameras. It also transformed the shiny new world of film-making, creating an industry in Hollywood while bringing it to a near-standstill in Europe. In France, Pathé and Gaumont had been power houses. After the war they ceased production and French cinema became a ragtag of independents jostling to sell their product. There were still some memorable triumphs, such as Abel Gance's *J'Accuse* (1919) about a poet who goes to the front and comes back shellshocked. The great German war film, G.W. Pabst's *Westfront 1918*, is comparable to Lewis Milestone's *All Quiet On the Western Front*, but both films were only released in 1930. By this time the mood music had changed. Before the 1920s the tone of most films about the war had been patriotic and propagandising. With the passing of time, the horror and folly of war came to be of more pressing concern to artists of all stripes.

The real victor of the First World War was Hollywood. Even by the early 1900s California was attracting industry, the aviation business, industrialists, railroad magnates and entrepreneurs. For film-makers it was paradise, with endless space and a miraculous landscape which could stand in for any location in the world.

In 1914, Mary Pickford (1892–1979), the Canadian actress known as 'America's Sweetheart', made the silent film *Hearts Adrift*, the first time an actor's name would be featured above the title. This and *Tess of the Storm Country* released a few weeks later propelled her into global stardom of a kind never experienced before.

When war in Europe broke out that same year, America was not taking sides. This was a country of immigrants and its citizens came from all the nations in Europe that were now in conflict. In his successful

1916 re-election campaign President Woodrow Wilson (1856–1924) promised to maintain American neutrality and focus on the economy. In Hollywood, the big-budget film *Civilisation* (1916) was a pacifist drama produced by Thomas H. Ince, but there was a perceptible change of tone in Cecil B. DeMille's film *Joan the Woman* (1916), in which a British officer summons the ghost of Joan of Arc to tell the story of how she led French troops to victory.

With the sinking of the *Lusitania* – torpedoed by German U-boats in 1915 with the loss 1,195 lives, including 128 US citizens – Americans began to pay more attention to the war. In 1917 British intelligence intercepted a telegram from the German State Secretary for Foreign Affairs, Arthur Zimmermann, to the German ambassador to Mexico, which proposed a military alliance between Germany and Mexico if the US entered the war. Mexico was too close for comfort and the telegram helped change American attitudes towards the distant war in Europe. On 4 April 1917, the US Senate voted in support of the measure to declare war on Germany.

American journalist George Creel (1876–1953) was made head of the quickly assembled propaganda organisation, the Committee on Public Information. Hollywood would be essential to the business of selling the war to America, yet initially film producers held out against his demands for them to produce pro-war propaganda. They tended to fall into line when he threatened them with export bans, with recruiting film employees into the army and with closing cinemas in the evenings.

Mary Pickford proved essential to the war effort. In *The Little American* (1917), directed by DeMille, she travels to occupied France and sees atrocities committed by German soldiers. She was also a key figure in the campaign for war bond subscriptions.

This was the first time that film stars used their popularity to influence the public. In a sense, the First World War not only wiped out the European competition in the filmmaking world also but also created Hollywood as a cauldron of superstardom.

In 1914 when war broke out, Karloff was still working in live theatre. In October, he arrived in Chicago and attempted to enlist in the British Army but was turned down because he had a heart murmur. His travels with Harry St Clair's stock company brought him into contact with Billie Bennett's company, which was going on tour with a production of *The Virginian*. Karloff went along and toured Minnesota, Iowa, Kansas, Colorado and Nevada, before finally ending up in Los Angeles, a few months after America had joined the war.

Karloff was not a star at this stage but if he had been it might have been harder for him, as a British citizen, to carry on as normal. Charlie Chaplin, for instance, was criticised by Lord Northcliffe's *Daily Mail* for staying in Hollywood. He received hundreds of white feathers when America entered the war in 1917, though he, like Mary Pickford, raised vast amounts for the war effort through war bonds.

Other stars of this era, who were Karloff's contemporaries, did see active service. Among them was the director Merian C. Cooper, who would direct *King Kong* (1933) and who flew DH-4 bombers for the US Army Air Service before being shot down and taken prisoner in 1918. After the war ended he volunteered for relief work in Poland, was captured by Cossacks and spent nine months as a prisoner before he escaped and walked 700 miles to freedom. He was rewarded with Poland's highest military honour, the Virtuti Militari.

Bela Lugosi, the man who would become Karloff's seeming rival, was a well-known stage actor in Budapest when war was declared. He volunteered for the 43rd Royal Hungarian Infantry and was wounded. Randolph Scott served with the 2nd Trench Mortar Battalion of the 19th Field Artillery in the spring of 1918.

James Whale, director of *Frankenstein*, and a fellow Brit, was posted to the Western Front as a second lieutenant in the Worcestershire Regiment in July 1916. He was captured and sent to the Holzminden PoW camp near Hanover, where there were 12,000 inmates and where he would remain until December 1918. To pass the time he played poker and bridge. He also staged Saturday night shows in the camp which were surprisingly ambitious. On one occasion costumes were sent for from Cologne.

America had been supplying supplies and military aid to the Allies since 1940, but there was considerable reluctance about greater involvement at the start of the Second World War. The Republican

Senator Gerald Nye led the isolationist movement and believed that a Jewish conspiracy was pushing the US into war. He was a key member of the Senate Investigation Into Motion Picture War Propaganda, claiming in September 1941 that Hollywood had made 'at least twenty pictures in the last year designed to drug the reason of the American people, set aflame their emotions, turn their hatred into a blaze, fill them with fear that Hitler will come over and capture them'.

The truth was rather different. There were a few pre-war anti-Nazi films such as *Confessions of a Nazi Spy* (1939) made by Warner Brothers with Edward G. Robinson and George Sanders. The Motion Picture Association (the trade association representing the major studios) recommended shelving the film because it would risk losing the German export market and was unduly critical of a world leader (Hitler). There was in Hollywood a great fear of offending foreign audiences and there were no films in favour of America joining the war until the Japanese attack on Pearl Harbor in December 1941 caused a swift U-turn and led to a unanimous declaration of war. Entertainment lawyers raced to copyright movie titles like 'Sunday in Hawaii', 'Yellow Peril' and 'V for Victory'. The use of searchlights at Hollywood premieres, criss-crossing the night sky, was banned, and premieres themselves were banned from August 1942.

Hysteria was not far behind. On the night of 25 February 1942, hundreds of anti-aircraft guns fired for hours into the Los Angeles night sky. Many civilians were injured by falling shrapnel; reporters, army officers and policemen were convinced they had seen swarms of Japanese aircraft flying overhead. There were none.

Two weeks after the attack on Pearl Harbor, President Roosevelt said that Hollywood could make 'a very useful contribution' to the war effort but that 'the motion picture industry must remain free … I want no censorship'. In 1942 the American government set up two bodies within the Office of War Information (OWI) to oversee the film industry: the Bureau of Motion Pictures which produced educational films, and the Bureau of Censorship, which scrutinised film exports. The Bureau of Motion Pictures produced *The Government Information*

Manual for the Motion Picture which encouraged film-makers to ask themselves: 'Will this picture help win the war?'

When America entered the war, Karloff had completed his first year in the long-running Broadway production of *Arsenic and Old Lace*. In a letter to his mother-in-law, Louise Stine, he wrote, 'The play is still wonderful and our business is steadily growing back to normal each week after the first shock of the war. We are lucky in that our show is one where people can really laugh and relax for a few hours, and that is always good medicine.'

Meanwhile, Karloff's wife Dorothy threw herself into the war effort by doing an Army course on aircraft spotting (scanning the skies was a wartime volunteer activity popular with people of all ages), selling defence bonds, and taking part in Red Cross drives.

Founded by Civil War nurse Clara Barton in 1881, the American Red Cross, was America's most influential volunteer force. Immediately after Pearl Harbor, the American Red Cross had announced a War Fund campaign similar to the one it launched when the United States entered World War I. The goal of this 1941–1942 campaign was to raise $50 million but the public responded by donating more than $66 million. By the end of the war more than 3,500,000 American women had volunteered with the Red Cross.

In February 1942 Mr and Mrs Karloff signed up for Civilian Defence work. Dorothy became secretary at Air Warden Sector headquarters. In the evening she would drop in at the Seamen's Institute to socialise with the sailors and Boris would occasionally join her after his evening performance.

On 10 March 1942, he took part in a Navy Relief Show at Madison Square Garden. Along with Vincent Price, Danny Kaye, Clifton Webb, Ed Wynn and Eddie Cantor, he formed a drag act called the Floradora Sextette. Sophie Tucker, Lenore Aubert, Luise Rainer, Tallulah Bankhead and Eve Arden dressed as men. Karloff wore a yellow dress made of sequins and a big yellow hat. Vincent Price retained the beard he had grown for *Angel Street*, the renamed Broadway production of Patrick Hamilton's play *Gaslight*. (It was as a result of this play that the term 'to gaslight someone' gradually entered the popular consciousness.)

A few days later the couple attended a cocktail party held onboard a ship at the Brooklyn Navy Yard. Moved by patriotic fervour, Dorothy thought it a wonderful sight to see all the destroyers, cruisers and airplane carriers under construction.

On 20 March, Karloff began his volunteer work as an air raid warden located in the basement of Manhattan Beekman Hotel. He was on duty every third Thursday from midnight until 8 am and would arrive for his shift with a pillow and a blanket.

One of his air-raid warden colleagues was New Yorker Nancy Farrell. She became very fond of him. In a letter to the *New York Times* published on 9 March 1969 she described how Karloff always appeared for his shift wearing his British tweed coat and his rimless glasses. He would often arrive early on duty and kindly urged the other wardens to take the opportunity to leave early for home.

In June 1942, Boris and Dorothy returned to California. Building on his success in *Arsenic and Old Lace* (the theme of eccentric characters and bodies in the basement) he was to appear in a comedy horror *The Boogie Man Will Get You* (1942) in which he plays the inevitable mad scientist, assisted by Peter Lorre in a project to create a race of supermen for the war effort.

Karloff was a big star by now but even he was adversely affected by the new direction of the Hollywood studios.

As a wartime austerity measure the Roosevelt administration had cut the amount of available film stock by 25 per cent and limited the amount of money that could be spent on sets to $5,000 per film. Most studios responded by focusing on the more prestigious films and reducing the number of B features. Karloff was signed up by Universal to appear in *The Climax* (1944), his first Technicolor movie. It is a sort of rehash of the *Phantom of the Opera* story. This was followed up with *The Devil's Brood*, sometimes called *The House of Frankenstein* (1944), starring Karloff, John Carradine and Lon Chaney Jnr. With Karloff as the mad doctor, the part of Frankenstein's monster went to Glenn Strange.

At this time Karloff negotiated a deal with Val Lewton at RKO with whom he made three pictures. Lewton had joined RKO in 1942 because they were in a financial mess following the expensive box office disaster that was Orson Welles's *Citizen Kane*. The company that had made Fred and Ginger musicals and *King Kong* was in need of a saviour. The war-time gag was, 'In the case of an air raid, go directly to RKO. They haven't had a hit for years.'

While other studios were putting their money into fewer but pricier pictures, Lewton did the opposite. His contract with RKO stipulated that his films would cost no more than $150,000 and none would be longer than seventy-five minutes. Lewton, who had a melancholy and somewhat Gothic disposition, obsessively watched old horror films to get a sense of what could be achieved. He knew that monsters and spectacular effects were out of the question on such a low budget, but he believed that a combination of light, sound and silence could work miracles. He would make eleven films for RKO, with the first being *Cat People* (1942), directed by Jacques Tourneur. At first he thought that putting Karloff under contract would highlight Karloff's association with Universal, whose products had become, in Lewton's view, increasingly trashy. But a meeting with Karloff – the greatest horror star – changed his mind. For his part, Karloff was delighted to work on films where the characters had a greater psychological depth.

In a book called *Icons of Grief: Val Lewton's Home Front Pictures*, the Yale art historian Alexander Nemerov argues that Lewton's wartime films – which he calls 'apparitions of sorrow' – articulate the daily trauma, anxiety and grief experienced by ordinary Americans sublimated by the morale-boosting war effort along with Hollywood's patriotic and relentlessly optimistic output. None of Lewton's films is directly about the war, says Nemerov, but 'it appears in them all the same even if we never catch a clear glimpse of it. Like a ghost moving through the house, it slams doors and tips over pottery ... in movies celebrated for their portrayal of the unseen, the war is the singular invisible beast.'

The underlying melancholy in all of Karloff's screen performances, throughout his career, is perfectly suited to his roles in Lewton's films. *The Body Snatcher* (1945), directed by Robert Wise (who would go on to direct *The Sound of Music*), is a reworking of Robert Louis Stevenson's Burke and Hare body snatcher story. It is Edinburgh, 1831. Karloff plays a cab driver with a sideline as a grave robber. In the first scene he is taking a small paraplegic girl to see an eminent doctor. He is kindness personified. In the next we see his stooped shadow making its way across a graveyard to smash in to a freshly dug grave.

Isle of the Dead (1945) takes its cue from Arnold Böcklin's eerie 1880 painting (he made six versions of it) of a funerary island of caves and rocky inlets, with – at its centre – a grove of almost black cypress trees (always associated with cemeteries and mourning). Hitler had bought one of the originals, and Vladimir Nabokov's 1936 novel *Despair* states that prints were 'found in every Berlin home'. Set during the First Balkan War of 1912 Karloff plays the austere General Pherides. He, accompanied by an American reporter (Marc Cramer), pays a visit to the Isle of the Dead where the General's wife is buried. Here they come across a disparate group of characters and the fear that a *vorvolaka*, (a malevolent being in Greek folklore) is among them. The next morning one of the party is found to have died of the plague. There are more deaths. One of the characters, Mrs St Aubyn (Katherine Emery), suffers from catalepsy and has a morbid fear of being buried alive. It is a thoroughly strange, morbid and yet profoundly serious film. The director Martin Scorsese rates it as one of the scariest movies of all time. Yet there is no real supernatural element.

Karloff's final film with RKO, *Bedlam* (1946), is inspired by Hogarth's series of paintings, *The Rake's Progress*. He plays the sadistic George Sims, overseer of the Bedlam asylum in London. Anna Lee is the plucky Nell Bowen, an actress who had become the mistress of the insane Lord Mortimer. Her growing social awakening and concern for the squalid treatment of the patients leads her into conflict with Sims, who has her committed.

Karloff regarded Lewton as the man who restored his soul as an actor. His last film, *Targets* (1968), endorses that sense in its depiction of a deranged Vietnam war veteran who kills his family and then embarks on a random murder spree. Karloff essentially plays himself – an old movie star who thinks retirement is the only option now that the news is so much more frightening than anything that can be found in a horror film.

Whereas the First and Second World Wars were broadly seen as wars that had to be fought, the Vietnam War was seen as pointless. There was no great evil to combat. Indeed, it was American imperialism itself which was seen as the monster. But the monster could no longer be slain by the forces of virtue and the victims were now simply unlucky, selected at random – as they are in slasher movie such as *The Texas Chainsaw Massacre* (1974).

'My kind of horror is not horror anymore,' says Karloff's character in *Targets*. He was right.

* * *

In 1913, with the Great War looming, H.G. Wells wrote *Little Wars*, a book laying out the rules of miniature war games with model soldiers. Its full title is the almost unbearably twee: *Little Wars; a game for boys from twelve years of age to one hundred and fifty and for that more intelligent sort of girl who likes boys' games and books*. His aim, though, was entirely noble. He wanted to present an alternative to armed conflict and he wrote: 'Here is a homeopathic remedy for the imaginative strategist. Here is the premeditation, the thrill, the strain of accumulating victory or disaster – and no smashed nor sanguinary bodies, no shattered fine buildings nor devastated countrysides …'

The rules are incredibly detailed. Here's an example. 'The length of time given for each move is determined by the size of the forces engaged. About a minute should be allowed for moving 30 men and a minute for each gun. Thus a force of 110 men and 3 guns, move day one plate, seven minutes is an ample allowance.'

Playing and painting model soldiers was Peter Cushing's passion from boyhood until the end of his life. It is easy to see why this pastime appealed to his pernickety nature, his obsession with detail and his utopian gentleness. As a man born near the start of a century scarred by two world wars and countless smaller conflicts, he was a profoundly peaceful man living in a belligerent time.

That is not to say he did not try to do his bit when war broke out in 1939, when he was 26. He was beginning to make his name in Hollywood, and had finished filming *Vigil in the Night* (1939) co-starring with Carole Lombard when war was declared. He had been in awe of this glamorous film star who, tragically, would die in an air crash in 1942. By then America had entered the war and she was returning from a war bond drive in Indiana. President Roosevelt posthumously awarded her the Medal of Freedom as the first woman killed in the line of duty in the Second World War.

After the declaration of war on 3 September 1939, all British subjects in America were told to report for a medical. Cushing, due to a perforated eardrum and torn ligaments in his left knee (rugby injuries), was given a low category 4c and told to 'stand by'. One of the medics said to him: 'They are not in need of cannon fodder yet.'

He would not have been much use to the military anyway at that time. A blister on his heel turned septic, the infection compounded by contact with contaminated water in the shower. There was talk of amputation but fortunately it did not prove necessary.

He continued to work but by 1941 was homesick and desperate to return to England. Travel was difficult because all ships had been requisitioned, and he did not have enough money in any case. He planned to go to New York to get at least a little nearer to home, intending to make his way up to Canada, which was a British dominion. He wrote to both the Office of the High Commissioner for the United Kingdom in Ottawa and to the Department of National Defence in Regina, Saskatchewan, explaining his predicament. Both replies informed him that '... no provisions exist to cover the cost of transportation from an individual's home to the point of enlistment'.

His friend, the actor Louis Hayward, lent him the money for the fare to New York. On arrival he saw a banner which read 'GIVE BLOOD FOR BRITAIN'. This scheme came about through the work of the African-American physician Charles Drew, known as the 'Father of the Blood Bank'. His research had focused on one of the most challenging medical problems of war time: how to 'bank' blood so it would be available for transfusions as needed.

In May 1940, the National Research Council (NRC) appointed a Committee on Transfusion to evaluate the status of blood supplies. As Germany began bombing England that summer, the British were in desperate need of medical supplies, including blood and plasma for transfusion. In response a relief programme (Blood for Britain) was organised to collect blood donations and ship blood plasma to England. Besides providing vital aid to England, Blood for Britain was intended to gather the data needed to launch a nationwide blood banking programme if the US entered the war.

Curiously, considering how crucial an African-American was to this valuable project, blood donations were segregated on the assumption that the British would prefer this. Naturally Drew objected, stating that there was no scientific evidence of any difference between blood of different races, and that the policy was insulting to African-Americans, who were eager to contribute to the war effort.

Cushing of course knew nothing of the background to the blood donor programme, volunteered and then passed out on the sidewalk. He was taken to hospital where he would spend two weeks suffering from nervous exhaustion.

He took a room at the Hotel St James just off Times Square and set about looking for casual work. A job parking cars at a summer resort on Long Island lasted for one day (he was sacked). He then worked as an illusionist's assistant in a nightclub off Broadway. He also found work reading radio commercials for laxatives.

Favourable reviews for *Vigil in the Night* opened the door to a job in summer stock theatre at a holiday camp called Green Mansions in Warrensburg in the Adirondack mountains. In 1933 the Group Theater had been invited to Green Mansions. Founded two years before by Harold Clurman, Lee Strasberg and Cheryl Crawford, the Group, had introduced 'method acting'. In exchange for four nights of entertainment each week, the Group received bed, board and an idyllic rehearsal environment. Cushing also received $100 at the end of the four month season. The plays presented included Robert E. Sherwood's *The Petrified Forest*, Arnold Ridley's *The Ghost Train*, Noel Coward's *Fumed Oak*, and a modern-dress version of *Macbeth*.

An offer to appear in a Broadway production followed, playing a London policeman wounded in the Blitz in *The Seventh Trumpet*. It opened on 21 November 1941 and closed on 29 November.

He hoped to appear in Rose Franken's play *Claudia*. The well-known English character actor John Williams (1903–1983), who played the role of Jerry, was leaving soon to join the Royal Air Force. After the war, Williams would return to the US where he had a long, successful career on stage and screen appearing in films such as *To Catch a Thief* (1955) and *Midnight Lace* (1960). Franken (1895–1988), a force in Broadway theatre at the time, interviewed Cushing and said that *Claudia* would enjoy a long run and she was concerned that Cushing would also leave to return to England. Cushing – keeping his options open – said he would not. A few days later he received a letter from her saying that she was disappointed that he did not want to 'do his bit' and would therefore not be offering him the part.

Cushing continued his slow progress towards Canada. In Montreal he worked as a cinema usher. He was asked to provide flags depicting the Japanese rising sun and the Nazi swastika to be used as special effects inserts in the Michael Powell and Emeric Pressburger film *49th Parallel*, starring Eric Portman and Laurence Olivier. Powell had said that he hoped the film would 'scare the pants off the Americans' and persuade the US to enter the war.

At his digs, the sight of the flags had caused the chambermaid to report him a spy. He was taken into custody by a couple of Mounties and questioned. When he was released he stepped out on to an icy road, slipped and suffered concussion.

By the middle of March 1942, he had reached Halifax and managed to hitch a ride on a Merchant Navy ship, the SS *Tilpala*. They set to sea in convoy, about fifty ships, mostly oil tankers. There was the ever present danger of attack by German U-boats while the battleship *Tirpitz* was known to be patrolling the North Atlantic. At night they sailed under blackout conditions and Cushing endured the wrath of one of the crew when he was found on deck with a lighted cigarette. At night he had to take his turn as lookout, climbing into the crow's nest, which terrified him. One night he was so overcome with cold that he had to be taken down in a chair to defrost.

On 27 March 1942 the ship docked in Liverpool.

In London, on his way to his brothers' farm in Reigate where his parents were living, he witnessed the devastation caused by the Blitz. He enjoyed the first bath he had had for some time, making sure not to exceed the five inches of water advised by the Government.

He made an appointment to see Henry Oscar, head of drama at ENSA which was based at the Theatre Royal, Drury Lane. The organisation had been set up in 1939 by Basil Dean and Leslie Henson to prove entertainment to British Armed Forces personnel and others.

The standard may not always have been high, but ENSA did a vast amount of work. One report in the *Musical Times* in 1941 notes:

> ENSA sends on its factory tours two groups of three performers, a fresh group visiting a centre weekly, and each group being on tour for a fortnight. (Leeds factory audiences were found to be highly appreciative, showing special enjoyment of Mozart, Schumann and Wagner.) One ENSA concert was given to interned women aliens in Holloway prison, and another for men interned at Pentonville. Six orchestral concerts were given in provincial centres (four by the London Philharmonic and two by the Hallé Orchestra). Numerous tours by small groups of singers and players have taken place in various parts of the country. The Old Vic Company has visited Lancashire towns with great success; and an extensive Northern tour was in prospect when the summary was written. A small company from Sadler's Wells has been popular in the North, and was reported to be enlarging its touring programme.

Oscar offered Cushing the leading role of Eliot in a production of Noel Coward's *Private Lives* which was touring all the Navy, Army and Air Forces stations in the British Isles. The actor who had been originally cast had been called up. This was where Cushing would meet his future wife Helen Beck, who had been cast as Amanda.

It was not an uneventful tour. One night, while entertaining the Navy in Dover, the Luftwaffe launched an attack on the harbour. The character of Sibyl (played by Yvonne Hills) has an argument with Eliot at the end of Act One. Eliot snaps at her: 'Don't quibble, Sibyl.'

Hills began to shake when the shells started to explode and her hands shook as she tried to drink a cocktail. 'Don't dribble, Sibyl,' called some wag in the audience.

Both Helen and Peter became ill during the run and were invalided out of ENSA. It was the end of Cushing's war.

On 29 December 1990, an elderly Peter Cushing did a radio play to mark the 50th anniversary of the Battle of Britain called *Human Conflict: the Strange Case of Hugh Dowding* in honour of Sir Hugh Dowding. Cushing played The Airman, with Alan Dobie as Dowding, Roland Fraser as Major Trafford Leigh-Mallory, Douglas Blackwell as Churchill, David Angus as Douglas Bader and Julie First as the reporter.

Dowding (1882–1970), who had been instrumental in the introduction of Hurricanes and Spitfires, was Air Officer Commanding RAF Fighter Command during the Battle of Britain. He made enemies due to disagreements over his strategy for defeating the Luftwaffe and ultimately Churchill asked him to step down.

There was another highlight in Cushing's career. *No White Peaks* was written by the lyricist and poet Peter Kayne in 1969. While taking a cabaret act on tour around England, Kayne came to a performance at the Mildenhall USAF base in Suffolk; there he saw the horrific effects of the Vietnam war on young servicemen. He was so moved that he wrote his anti-war poem *No White Peaks*. He has always sought to have the proceeds from this poem donated to charity.

In 1991 Peter Cushing recorded a reading of the poem which was released as a rap album. Kayne was not happy about this but Cushing, interviewed in *Terror Magazine,* politely said that 'I was worried that the marriage of an anti-war poem with the frivolity of a dance record would lose the overall message but I think it's worked out quite well.' Despite his frailty he did the recording in one perfect take at a recording studios in Canterbury, not far from his home.

An anti-war rap album. A very strange coda to Peter Cushing career, but somehow not totally unexpected.

* * *

Christopher Lee had what would be described as a 'good war', the active heroic war of a very young man. The question which inevitably arises is just how far his work in the special forces and intelligence services extended. 'I was attached to the SAS from time to time but we are forbidden – former, present, or future – to discuss any specific operations. Let's just say I was in Special Forces and leave it at that. People can read in to that what they like,' he said in 2011.

Gavin Mortimer, who published a history of the SAS in the Second World War, says this is nonsense and that wartime members of those special forces units are not – and never have been – prevented from discussing operations. In an article in *The Spectator* published just after Lee's death, he writes:

> According to some reports and obituaries in the days after his death, Lee served in the Special Air Service (SAS), Long Range Desert Group (LRDG) and Special Operations Executive (SOE). In reality he served in none. He was attached to the SAS and SOE as an RAF liaison officer at various times between 1943 and 1945, but he did not serve in them and never, as one paper stated, 'moved behind enemy lines, destroying Luftwaffe aircraft and fields'.

If it is now generally acknowledged that while he may have embellished his career somewhat, to emphasise the cloak and dagger aspects, there is no doubt that he saw very active service. What's more, he certainly mixed with the kind of people who are recruited by the intelligence services – ambassadors, politicians, European émigrés and exiles, public school Oxbridge people and the very rich. As already noted, he also spoke several languages.

His mother's second husband's sister was the mother of Ian Fleming, author of the James Bond novels. Lee and Fleming were friends and golfing companions. The extent of Fleming's involvement with British intelligence is also something of a mystery. He joined Reuters, and was sent to Russia in the 1930s before becoming a stockbroker. His war service found him working in naval intelligence in an unspecified capacity. Then, after the war, he returned to journalism and invented Bond. His biographer Nicholas Shakespeare describes his wartime activity as 'exciting operations that Ian was involved with and yet, in many cases, were never put into action ... ideas at the madder end of the spectrum'. The combination of discretion, vanity, the passage of time, the telling of a good anecdote and the paucity of surviving written records all play a part in colouring the accounts of lives well lived.

Denis Wheatley (1897–1977), the reactionary writer of occult thrillers, was a good friend of Lee who also flirted with the shadowy world of the intelligence services. He became a writer after his family's wine business went bust and during the war had dealings with military intelligence. His circle included Fleming, the bizarre clergyman and occultist Montague Summers, and the preposterous Aleister Crowley, who would claim that his public role in America during the First World War, as an anti-British propagandist, was a front and that he was in fact engaged on secret work for the British.

Lee loved to talk but sometimes he was picked up on tiny facts. Hardly surprising because he had lived a long, full life and his admirers are sticklers for detail. In an interview with Tim Walker, which was also published in *The Spectator*, the two men meet at the famous Mayfair restaurant Le Caprice. Lee sits down and says he has never been there before. Walker writes: '"Oh yes, you have," I replied. Aida Young, the Hammer Films producer, had taken him there in 1969 to persuade him to do *Taste the Blood of Dracula*. Lee is momentarily stunned into silence. The look on his face said the obvious: oh dear, a fan.'

Peter Jackson, producer of the *Lord of the Rings* films, describes how, in the scene where Saruman (Lee) is stabbed in the back by Grima Wormtongue, Lee said to him: 'Have you any idea what kind of noise happens when somebody's stabbed in the back? Because I do. See it's not, 'aah', like that. It's 'gasp' because the breath is driven out of your body.' Jackson was impressed and assumed that Christopher Lee knew best when it came to arcane knowledge of this kind.

The Second World War broke out when Christopher Lee was 17. He says he went to enlist and was sent to Finland with 'a few other recent schoolboys'. The Finns gave the boys some white uniforms (snow camouflage) and sent them somewhere perfectly safe. They all went home after a fortnight having not seen any other people, let alone any action.

He was working for a shipping company, United States Lines, in the City, but then took a job with Beecham's, an export company, based in Pall Mall. He was living at his mother's house next to Wentworth Golf Club and they prepared for the worst by sleeping on mattresses under the kitchen table. Beecham's moved out of London to Watford. Faced with an impossible journey to work, Lee took lodgings with a family called the Bowlers and joined the Home Guard.

His father died suddenly, at the age of 62, early in 1941. It felt momentous and Lee immediately volunteered for the RAF and was sent to the Uxbridge barracks where he became an AC2 (Aircraftman Second Class) and was sent to an Initial Training Wing at Paignton, with digs at the Tenbani Hotel, a seaside boarding house, followed by a period in Liverpool for examinations in navigation and Morse code, weapons, drill, Hurricane, Spitfires and Beaufighters. The would-be fighter pilots then set sail from west Kirby aboard the *Reina del Pacifico* for an uncomfortable six-week journey to Cape Town.

The Hillside train field was in Bulawayo in what is now Zimbabwe (then called Rhodesia). He enjoyed himself for a while, was 'adopted' by the wealthy Meilell family, who took him shooting and to glamorous parties in Bulawayo. He enjoyed the flying lessons, in Tiger Moths with open cockpits, and felt he was born to be a flyer.

He was nearing the end of his course but in one of his last sessions, at 5,000 ft, he was overcome by a brutal headache and a blurring of the vision in his left eye. His instructor took over the controls and they landed safely. Lee was diagnosed with a failure of the optic nerve and told that he would not be allowed to fly. It was a terrible blow.

The authorities then had him seconded to the Rhodesian Police Force and posted to Salisbury prison as a warder. Many of the prisoners were deserters. Promoted to leading aircraftman he was sent to Durban and then ordered to board the *New Amsterdam* which journeyed to Suez. He then travelled to Kasfarit, Egypt, a vast staging camp in the Canal Zone. It sounds a terrible place – windy, sandy and nothing to do.

On the Milton Keynes Heritage Association website there is a post from a former RAF man called Dick Croot, who was at Kasfarit at the same time as Lee and was the same age. He recalls:

> There was a Warrant Officer in charge who had got a touch of the sun and he used to have us digging holes in the sand one day and filling them in the next day, and then collecting stones and painting them white to put round his 'parade ground', which was only a square marked off in the sand. We heard later that he had been certified and sent home.

Lee himself wondered whether too many anti-malarial tablets were affecting the minds of the warrant officers. One, objecting to Lee's public school background, had him scouring a mountain of greasy pots with sand, using his bare hands before sending him off to empty the latrines.

He was relieved to be posted to the nearby city of Ismailia, on the west bank of the Suez Canal, for something that approximated to intelligence work, involving maps and collecting the fake pound notes made by the Germans. During the war thousands of forged £1 notes were dropped over North Africa with Arabic on the reverse. The aim was to tell the locals that the British Empire was in decline and that both empire and currency would fail. Each note had the same serial number: H86D 729630. If you find one, well done, they are worth a bit.

He was sent to the RAF hospital in Abbassia, Cairo, with a bout of malaria and on his discharge had a fight in a nightclub with a drunken Australian. Though he was not allowed to pilot a plane he was attached to 205 Group and flew out of Alexandria to drop propaganda leaflets over Benghazi suggesting that the Italians surrendered. He received orders to report to 260 Squadron as an intelligence officer and felt that at least he might have the real opportunity to contribute to the 'discomfort of the enemy' and do a real job.

Across Libya, through El Agheila, Homs and Tripoli, they averaged five missions a day. The P-40s fighter-bombers were used for strikes, cover or as artillery. Lee's job was to interrogate every member of the squadron as soon as they returned from a sortie and if they had hit the target, where were they and was there any anti-aircraft fire? Were any trucks or trains visible? What was the weather like? He forwarded the information to the senior intelligence officer of the wing who would pass it to HQ. He was called 'Spy' as a nickname or 'Duke'.

In Tunisia he was injured during a Messerschmitt attack on an airstrip. Grit from the blast caught him in the buttocks.

In July 1943 there were orders to move on to Pachino in Sicily to support the 8th Army and the American 5th Army. On his website, historian James Holland reproduces an interview with Lee. He is less gung-ho about his experiences than he is in his autobiography. In his capacity as an intelligence officer he drove from one strip to another while the pilots flew. Holland's post of Lee's account reads:

> So I could see the damage on the ground. We had awful experiences – we were shot up by the American air force in Italy near Vasto. We were shot up by JU88 bombers at night, which no one thought would ever happen, in Sicily. It was unexpected to say the least because we had air superiority. But going through these places, maybe the very next day, and seeing the appalling damage and of course all the bodies. We didn't want the pilots to see it. There was one occasion when one of our pilots took off from an airstrip in Italy. His port wing dipped & hit the strip and he catapulted off the strip into a kind of big dell where there was an Army Post Office [at San Angelo, the squadron's station for the assault on Monte Cassino in 1944].
>
> One of his bombs went off and we had to rush over there, myself and the doctor, and try to keep the pilots away. We had to get this chap out and there were dead bodies everywhere and a red hot

bomb still sizzling in the grass. I don't mention this in my book because it sounds like a crusade. Then there was a time in Italy when the American air force had been on bombing raids and ran out of fuel so they landed at our airstrip and all came crashing into each other. It was a terrible mess, and into some of our aircraft. I think the worst I've ever seen in my life was Cassino.

Lee entered Rome, the day after it fell, and went to look for his Italian relatives. He says that all through Italy he had to put up with jokes about his middle name of Carandini and how he was obviously a 'double agent'. It was a relief to meet his mother's cousin, Niccolò Carandini, and confirm that he was indeed a Resistance fighter.

Promoted to flight lieutenant, Lee had to part company with 260 in November 1944. The aftermath of the war seemed like something of an anticlimax and he says there was no sense of forward planning. Before returning to Britain for demobilisation he was assigned to Austria and the Central Registry of War Crimes and Security Suspects. His task was to round up the men and women wanted for interrogations, a duty which took him to several concentration camps. The war was over and he was barely 23 years old. He was not exactly unscathed. The old wound in his buttocks had not healed properly and required a penicillin drip. He had also suffered from seven bouts of malaria.

Back in demob Britain he found that his mother and sister were doing well. His sister Xandra had worked for Naval Intelligence at the Admiralty's Operational Intelligence Centre (where Ian Fleming was Lieutenant Commander). She was one of the 'Secret Ladies' who collated the intelligence coming via landlines or from teleprinters (operated by women known as 'teleprincesses') and handed it over to the 'watchkeepers' for further interpretation.

Like so many young men, Christopher Lee did not know what do next as his 'sole expertise was filling in the picture for crew of assault aircraft'. There was only one solution. He would have to become an actor.

* * *

Chapter Nine

Monsters

In 1894, an outbreak of polio in Vermont paralysed 130 children and killed eighteen. Until then polio been thought of as a serious but rare European disease. The Vermont epidemic brought it home to America. In 1916, a major outbreak hit New York, sweeping down the East Coast before turning towards the Mid-West. In this period 27,000 people were paralysed and 6,000 died. Cinemas were closed, public gatherings were cancelled and parents were told to keep children away from public places such as amusement parks and swimming pools.

Tragically, a vast number of the victims were hitherto healthy children who could be struck down overnight. Parents were only allowed to view them through glass windows. The cause of the disease was a mystery, with flies, dirt and cats being among the suspected culprits. In July, 70,000 cats were killed in New York City as a precaution. But there was no cure. Electrotherapy was a popular but useless treatment administered in the hope that atrophied muscles could be stimulated into action with an electrical current – just like Frankenstein's monster.

Roosevelt, who became president in 1932, had been paralysed with polio in 1921 (although now some medical analysts believe he had Guillain-Barré syndrome). Such was the public horror of the disease, known then as 'The Crippler', that he refused to be photographed in his wheelchair. In 1927, the iron lung was invented which helped patients to breathe. Like a coffin for the living, it was a terrifying symbol of the disease.

One of the awful effects of polio was the way it wasted muscles and deformed limbs. Various mechanical remedies were devised such as the Bradford Frame, a metal rectangle fitted with adjustable canvas straps to which patients were attached with legs and torso straight and their arms raised in an attempt to prevent the distortion of backs and legs.

Other appliances included 'artificial muscles' – heavy rubber bands or spiral steel springs – to correct the position of the feet. Iron callipers or leg braces became a publicity symbol for the National Foundation for Infantile Paralysis (NFIP) founded by Roosevelt in 1938.

James Whale's *Frankenstein* appeared in 1931 between the two major outbreaks of 1916 and 1934. The second epidemic began in Los Angeles while *The Bride of Frankenstein* (1935) was being filmed. At its height there were fifty new cases a day.

Many silent films of the 1920s, especially those starring Lon Chaney, had been intensely preoccupied with themes of amputation and disfigurement, turning people into monsters. It was the aftermath of the First World War which had seen mutilation of the human body on an unprecedented scale. Amputation was the most common operation performed by orthopaedic surgeons during the war. It has been estimated that in Germany there were 67,000 amputations, and in Britain there were 41,000. Facial disfigurement was also common, and masks were made of tin, enamel, or silver, carefully painted to resemble flesh tones. *The Hunchback of Notre Dame* (1923) and *The Phantom of the Opera* (1925) found Lon Chaney masked in one and deformed in the other. As Quasimodo in *Hunchback* he wore an outsize prosthetic jaw which made him unable to close his mouth. His heavy rubber hump was attached to a leather harness, connected to a breastplate which meant he was unable to stand upright. In *Alonzo the Armless* (1927), a film directed by Tod Browning who made *Freaks*, and Bela Lugosi's *Dracula*, Chaney plays an armless circus knife thrower who is in reality a fugitive from justice and wears his arms bound behind his back. His partner in the knife-throwing act Nanon (played by Joan Crawford) is comfortable with Alonzo because she cannot bear being touched by men. To win her love Alonzo has his arms amputated but then she gets over her phobia and falls for the circus strongman.

By the start of the 1930s, the slaughter in the trenches was receding into history and what is arguably the true preoccupation of the twentieth century – disease and contagion – was taking hold in American and European culture. The trauma of the Great War had itself been exacerbated by the Spanish flu pandemic of 1918 – the first time that a disease and its transmission had truly become a part of global consciousness.

Modernity was a kind of guiding principle in both the arts and sciences. But admiration of science, with its ability to eliminate disease through the benign application of technology was tempered by a fear that science and scientists could become an uncontrollable force for evil, a fear that found its apogee with the development of the atom bomb. Paradoxically, science's success in beating the killer diseases of the past made the fear of contagion and infection that much greater.

Disease created monsters either through its effect on the human face and body, or in making the body itself a source of death and infection. The monster is the *sine qua non* of the horror movie and must always be destroyed even if he, she, or it is coaxed back to life in a sequel.

One of the unanswerable questions about Mary Shelley's slim 1818 novel *Frankenstein, or The Modern Prometheus* is whether it would have the kudos it still has today had it not been for James Whale's 1931 film. Or would it be simply a forgotten footnote in Gothic literature like so many other books of that period?

In the book, the monster is intelligent (he reads *Paradise Lost*) but is ugly, misunderstood and shunned. In the film, it is the making of the monster in the laboratory (his accidental acquisition of a criminal brain is a plot addition) which dominates the narrative, along with the hubris of Frankenstein himself. In Christopher Fraying's 2018 book *Frankenstein: The First 200 Years*, he argues that Shelley's Frankenstein story replaced Adam and Eve as the modern creation myth but it was James Whale's film which made it into a 'mad scientist' story, giving us words like Franken-science and Franken-foods, and which we use whenever scientists seem about to overreach themselves.

What's more, it is Karloff's monster make-up and physicality which had such resonance for the audience in the 1930s and which continue to do so today. One compelling theory advanced by Dwight Code, an associate professor at the University of Connecticut, sees in the monster a response to that polio epidemic of the 1930s which would continue to haunt the public for two decades.[11]

It is well known that Jack Pierce's make-up regime at Universal Studios was brutal. Elsa Lanchester who starred as the monster's mate in *The Bride of Frankenstein* was no fan of his. Strangely, Pierce's make-up – as academic Dwight Code argues – also mimicked the effects of polio. Karloff had to wear a 5 lb brace on his spine and his boots weighed 12 lbs each. His face was distorted just as the facial muscles of polio sufferers can be – wire clamps were used to pull down Karloff's lips to make the mouth look more stiff. Mortician's wax was used to create the drooping eyelids. During the day it would often dry out and fall into Karloff's eyes causing great discomfort. The bolts, electrodes, in the neck 'suggest the fusion of organic and inorganic material', just like the braces for polio victims and the horror of the iron lung machine which required electricity to function. His unsteady gait was that of a creature learning to walk just as young polio victims had to relearn mobility.

During the filming of *Frankenstein*, Karloff had to arrive at 4 am at Dressing Room No 5 which had become known as 'The Bugaboudoir', where movie monsters had been created since the 1920s when Lon Chaney used it during filming of *The Hunchback of Notre Dame* and *The Phantom of the Opera*, and Bela Lugosi dressed for *Dracula*. The process would take four hours. It is said that once (though it is a story which has the ring of the publicity department) when he walked out on to the Universal lot in full rig he terrified a passing secretary who fainted. Carl Laemmle Sr. was so concerned that he might cause a miscarriage to any 'nice little secretaries' who were pregnant that he made Karloff wear a blue veil over this head if he stepped off the set.

As discussed earlier Karloff suffered long-term physical effects from the arduous filming schedule. Back and leg pain plagued him for the rest of his life and – a strange irony – he eventually had to wear the kind of leg braces that polio victims had worn when *Frankenstein* was made. There was no stunt double for the Monster and there is one scene where the Monster carries Henry Frankenstein (played by Colin Clive) up a hill to the old windmill. Karloff had to repeat this scene again and again until James Whale decided he had 'an acceptable take'. Karloff's suffering and long hours also contributed to his political activism on behalf of Hollywood performers. Even then the Academy of Motion and Picture Sciences stipulated that no actor work more than twelve hours at a time. Karloff was sometimes working eighteen hours without a break.

He was not invited to the premiere of the film – his 81st – which was held at the Mayfair Theatre in New York's Times Square on Friday, 4 December 1931. 'I was just an unimportant freelance actor', he would tell *The Saturday Evening Post* in 1962, 'the animation for the monster costume.'

In the opening credits the role of 'The Monster' is played by '?' And he is listed fourth among the characters. In the closing credits his name is revealed. The press release described Karloff as the successor to Lon Chaney, 'a truly great character actor' and 'a brilliant Englishman' who had enjoyed a 'long list of brilliant successes on the London and European stages'. This would have been news to Karloff!

Even if Universal did not realise the power of the monster they had created, the public and the critics did. As a result of the film's success, Karloff was put on contract by Universal and after a twenty-year career in acting he finally knew where the next meal was coming from. By now he was 44. In honour of its new signing, Universal set up a photoshoot with their two 'monster men'– Bela Lugosi and Karloff toasting each other with German beer steins and joking about which of them could scare the other to death.

Karloff's follow up to *Frankenstein* was *The Old Dark House* (1932), playing Morgan the butler, described as a 'brute' and a 'savage', his monstrousness finally redeemed in a wordless display of tenderness. As Universal's big star Karloff gets top billing, but the entire cast is superb in this high camp horror farce. It did poorly at the box office when word got out that Karloff's part was very low key.

Whereas Jack Pierce had contented himself with scarring and an angry looking eye for Morgan, he went to town on the make-up for Karloff's role in *The Mummy* (1932). It took eight hours to transform him into the mummified corpse of Imhotep, which comes to life. His ears were glued to the side of his head, his face covered with cotton strips, colloid and spirit gum. This was baked with a hairdryer before beauty clay was trowelled on to Karloff's hair. One hundred and fifty yards of linen were soaked in acid and heated, then wrapped around Karloff's naked body so that he was unable to move or speak. Grease paint covered his face and hands so it matched the tone of the bandages. Then he was covered in a layer of Fuller's earth. Imhotep had been buried alive. Karloff's shooting schedule was rather similar.

The Mummy! A Tale of the Twenty-Second Century is an 1827 three-volume science fiction novel by the 20-year-old Jane Webb about an Egyptian mummy brought back to life in the future. In many ways she was as precocious and visionary as Mary Shelley. Her interest in mummies – and that of the general public – had been inspired by Napoleon's invasion of Egypt in 1798. The discovery of the Rosetta Stone in 1801 made the study of ancient Egypt more accessible and it attracted amateur archaeologists and tourists the world over. In 1922 the discovery of Tutankhamen's tomb attracted a media frenzy known as Egyptomania. The idea of 'the mummy' was a new kind of monster inviting the audience into a rich new world of gods, curses, death cults, treasure and dark ancient places. Undisturbed, the dead of the Pharaonic age would sleep for eternity. But inevitably, the Western scientist with an obsessive quest of knowledge engages in clumsy, sacrilegious destruction of the sacred tomb, unleashing and reviving the mummy, who is essentially blameless.

Carl Laemmle Jr had assigned two Universal writers, Richard Schayer and Nina Wilcox Putnam, to write a treatment based on the Tutankhamen story. The result was called *Cagliostro* about an ancient Egyptian magician who prolongs his life with nitrate injections. It was then passed to John Balderston who had contributed to *Dracula* and *Frankenstein* scripts. He changed the action from San Francisco to Egypt and the title to *The King of the Dead*. *Im-Ho-Tep* was the third title (the mummy's name) and *The Mummy* was the fourth.

Karloff's mummified face stared out from New York's Mayfair Theatre across Times Square. 'There is a place for a national bogeyman in the scheme of things', wrote the critic in *The New York Times*. The popular monster had arrived – revolting but inviting compassion.

In mythology, monsters represent pure evil. In the twentieth century, monsters become more complex, representing both dark aspects of ourselves and creatures who have become othered, outlawed and tormented. They are victims too. The word 'monster' comes from the Latin verb 'monere' which means 'to warn'. Monsters in films are always a warning – what we may become, what we may create, what may do us harm.

The Bride of Frankenstein (1935) opens with a fairly lengthy section explaining how – contrary to what the audience might have thought – both Henry Frankenstein and the Monster have survived what seemed to be their violent deaths at the end of *Frankenstein*. Having got that awkward plot detail out of the way the evil Dr Pretorius (Ernest Thesiger) toasts what he calls 'a new world of gods and monsters'. *Gods and Monsters* was also the name given to the 1998 film about the last days of the director James Whale (played by Ian McKellen).

The Black Cat (1934) teamed Karloff and his 'rival' Bela Lugosi and its success prompted Universal to pair them together again in *The Raven* (1935), based on two of Edgar Allan Poe's stories. Lugosi plays the mad scientist monster who builds the torture chamber described in Poe's *The Pit and the Pendulum*, and gets Karloff (as bank robber on the run Edmond Bateman) to do his bidding. This was the last film featuring Karloff and Lugosi in which Lugosi gets top billing.

The sinister power of unseen but deadly radioactivity to cause monstrous mutations was to become a staple of sci-fi horror. In *The Invisible Ray* (1936), Boris Karloff (billed as simply 'Karloff' again, with co-star Bela Lugosi in second place in smaller type) plays Dr Janos Rukh who comes into contact with a meteorite composed of 'Radium X'. He begins to glow in the dark, his touch becomes deadly and he gradually loses his mind. In *The Walking Dead* (1936) made for Warner Brothers, Karloff plays a man who is wrongly executed and brought back to life. He is monstrous only in the sense that he is an aberration, the result of a scientific experiment to reanimate the dead. *Black Friday* (1940) is another gangster horror movie written by Curt Siodmak starring Karloff and Lugosi, again involving our old friend the transplanted brain (always very popular with Siodmak).

In *Son of Frankenstein* (1939), directed by Rowland Lee, Karloff gets second billing to Basil Rathbone, with Bela Lugosi coming in third. Rathbone plays Baron Wolf von Frankenstein who returns to the ruin of the family castle and discovers the remains of the Monster, which he proposes to resurrect in order to restore the family's honour. His late father's tomb bears the inscription 'Heinrich von Frankenstein', with 'Maker of Monsters' added in chalk. Wolf scratches out the word 'Monsters' and writes 'Men'.

But it felt to Karloff as though the Frankenstein brand was running out of steam and that the Monster was becoming an 'oafish prop'. Notwithstanding Karloff's misgivings, *Son of Frankenstein* – premiered on 13 January 1939 – was an immediate box office hit.

One of Karloff's more extraordinary outings as a mad scientist was *The Ape* (1940), which returns to the theme of polio. He plays mild-mannered doctor Dr Bernard Adrian in smalltown America trying to help Frances, a young woman in a wheelchair (played by Maris Wrixon). We are led to believe that Dr Adrian's wife and daughter both succumbed to the disease years earlier. The Doctor's cure involves tapping spinal fluid and to get what he needs he disguises himself as an ape (using the skin of a vicious circus ape that he kills when it breaks into his lab) and kills various townspeople so that he can harvest enough serum to help Frances walk again.

The film was made by Monogram, known as one of the 'poverty row studios' which made very low-budget B movies between the 1920s and 1950s. It is not a very good film but it is extremely interesting as a social document, highlighting the preoccupations of the time.

The Man They Could Not Hang (1939) and *The Man with Nine Lives* (1940) are both Karloff vehicles directed by Nick Grinde, loosely based on the case of Dr Robert Cornish, a University of California professor, who announced that he had brought back to life a dog named Lazarus, killed under laboratory conditions for the purpose of this experiment. Cornish (1903–1963) had been a child prodigy who received a doctorate when he was 22. After his claim that he had successfully brought a couple of dogs back to life he hoped to expand his research by reanimating a prisoner on San Quentin's Death Row.

Fortunately the request of this real-life mad scientist was refused, but the public was fascinated by the story.

More mad scientist movies were to follow. In *The Climax* (1944), the first film he made in Technicolor, Karloff plays a Viennese doctor who murders his opera singer fiancée in a fit of jealousy and (ten years later) becomes obsessed with another singer who reminds him of the dead woman.

House of Frankenstein (1944) covered all bases with a cast that included Karloff, Lon Chaney Jr. and John Carradine and brought in a full roster of monsters – Frankenstein's monster, the Wolf Man and Count Dracula. Karloff referred to the film as the 'monster clambake'. *The New York Herald Tribune*'s reviewer said the 'plot stumbles along endlessly in its top-heavy attempt to carry on its shoulders too many of yesterday's nightmares'.

Making movies where horror and comedy balance each other is a fine art and nobody was better at it than Roger Corman, whose films *The Raven* (1963) and *The Terror* (1963) do exactly that. *The Raven*, scripted by Richard Matheson, is a send-up from start to finish starring Karloff, Peter Lorre, Jack Nicholson and smouldering scream-queen Hazel Court. *The Terror* offers more of the same and was made back-to-back with the first film, using the same sets and some location work on the beach at Monterey.

Karloff's final monster role was voicing the Grinch in Chuck Jones's animated version of Ted Geisel's *Dr Seuss* story *How The Grinch Stole Christmas!* made in 1966. *The Hollywood Reporter* accurately predicted that the twenty-six-minute special would 'find a perennial berth on the holiday schedule'. He was 79 at the time and suffering badly from emphysema, but the role won him a Grammy award. Geisel and Jones chose Karloff because of his 'beautiful, rhythmic, caring' voice. CBS repeated it annually over Christmas until 1988.

Karloff's monsters were very modern in that they were conflicted, capable of redemption, in some sense victims. Monstrous criminals are often described as 'dead behind the eyes', but Karloff's eyes were always windows into his soul. Modern monsters inflict suffering, but they also suffer grievously. Apart from Frankenstein's monster Karloff played scores of ordinary men – often scientists or doctors – who meant well but became monsters out of professional vanity and an inability to resist playing God.

From the late nineteenth century the discovery of the causes of killer diseases such cholera, TB, typhoid and diphtheria was not merely of interest in medical journals, but front-page news, and of immense interest to ordinary people. Breakthroughs in treatment added to the growing prestige of medics while the lack of truly effective treatment for some diseases (such as polio) exacerbated the fear they engendered, a fear of contagion and a fear of other people which finds its way into horror films again and again. And as so many of Karloff's films demonstrate, the figure of the well-respected doctor can quickly become reviled and monstrous.

It was not until the end of the nineteenth century that 'germ theory' had become the orthodox scientific theory for the genesis and transmission of diseases – the belief that they are caused by microorganisms. Until then miasma theory held sway, and the (literally) airy belief that infectious disease were the result of toxic vapours.

The victory of germ theory in the twentieth century was rational and correct, yet susceptible to metaphoric and symbolic interpretation in popular Western culture – particularly in films and specifically in horror films. Germs cannot be seen with the naked eye. They are invasive, the enemy in our midst. They engage in unlawful, secret entry. They can wipe out humanity. We can be infected without knowing it. They can be manipulated by conspiratorial scientists who want to destroy us or mutate us. They can turn us into monsters. In 1961 an American virologist and Nobel Laureate Wendell Stanley wrote an important scientific text called *Viruses and the Nature of Life* in which he reaches for a host of colourful metaphors. A virus is only identifiable 'once the damage is done', he writes; it will 'lose completely its own identity', 'tricking the cell' like an 'espionage agent' and extracting information from it. The way these images of disease clash with Cold War imagery reminds us how horror embraced sci-fi with its stories of radioactive rays and infiltration by aliens.

* * *

In an interview published in *ABC Film Review* in November 1964, Peter Cushing said gently: 'People look at me as if I were some sort of monster, but I can't think why. In my macabre pictures, I have either been a monster-maker or a monster-destroyer, but never a monster. Actually, I'm a gentle fellow. Never harmed a fly.'

He was kind to children too. The former child actor Janina Faye – who appeared in *Dracula* in the role of Janine when she was only 8 years old – remembers how concerned he was about her feelings especially when they were filming in the graveyard. He returned to her after every shot to make sure she had not been frightened in any way.

Watch any film starring Cushing and there is no doubt that he is a serious, highly emotional actor. Yet he never seemed to have any problem with the public's perception of him as a horror star and the general critical view that horror films were second rate. As we can see from the above quote, he played along with it happily when he was interviewed later in his career – insisting that he was a mild-mannered chap (which he was) but hamming his horror credentials up at the same time.

While the concept of 'the monster' is one that taps into modern anxieties, there was also a need to neutralise it, to make monsters funny and even cuddly. There was the novelty pop song *Monster Mash*, sung by Bobby Pickett and released in 1962. The lyrics introduce us to a mad scientist whose monster creation rises up to perform a new dance inspired by the Mashed Potato (a popular dance at the time). Recently Bob Dylan gave us his own Monster Mash with his macabre song *My Own Version of You* on the 2020 *Rough and Rowdy Ways* album. In the song, he is in planning a Frankenstein-ian project of his own in order to recreate a loved one. He has been searching for body parts and knows that "one strike of lightning" is all he needs to jump-start his creation.

In 1958, the year after *The Curse of Frankenstein* was released, the American editor and sci-fi writer Forrest J Ackerman (1916–2008) founded the magazine *Famous Monsters of Filmland*, which has continued in various forms and formats to the present day. Jokey, blokey and good humoured, it is aimed at horror fans who relish their image as lowbrow yahoos. They have a sense of proprietorship about the movies that are sometimes in the 'so bad they're good' category. They like the fact that they are in a club to which a lot of people do not want to belong. For as the horror fiction writer Stephen King said, there is a feeling among some 'that the taste for horror is abnormal'.

The magazine spawned the Famous Monsters Conventions, held in New York in 1974 and 1975. Cushing was guest of honour at the second convention and took part in a late-night TV chat on *The Tomorrow Show* hosted by Tom Snyder for NBC. The other guests were Ackerman and Leonard Wolf, a writer known at the time for his authoritative annotated editions of horror classics such as *Frankenstein, Dracula* and *The Strange Case of Dr Jekyll and Mr Hyde*. He also taught a course called 'Monsters' at San Francisco State University. No surprise that the theme of their discussion was 'Monsters in the Movies' and it was well and truly camped up. Ackerman was wearing one of Bela Lugosi's capes. 'You look scary,' Snyder tells Cushing, who smiles demurely. 'Look at those eyes, the high cheekbones.'

Cushing is in great form, cutting in to some rather tedious story about Vlad the Impaler with a joke and the observation that 'we're all comics at heart'. At one point Snyder hands Cushing an outsize stake. 'Where are you Chris?' quips Cushing, before musing on how such a big stake might get an inappropriate laugh which is why Van Helsing usually dispatches Lee with a more compact tool.

The appropriation of horror monsters as cuddly buddies continued with TV shows such as *The Munsters* and *The Addams Family* (based on Charles Addams's *New Yorker* cartoons) which were both launched in 1964. Each series satirised suburban life and were firmly on the side of the macabre families – the Munsters and the Addams – who are always innocently puzzled when they provoke terror in others.

The Munsters came about because in the early 1960s Universal sold the rights to their monsters – Dracula, Frankenstein's monster and the rest. CBS wanted a new programme about movie monsters that would rival ABC's *The Addams Family*. Fred Gwynne, who was 6ft 5in, played Herman Munster, a dead ringer for Frankenstein's monster, with Al Lewis as a Lugosi-ish grandpa, Yvonne de Carlo as vampire mom Lily, and Butch Patrick as Eddie the little boy werewolf. Beverley Owen was Marilyn Munster, the unfortunate niece who looks 'normal'. It was one of those innocent TV comedies beloved by children and adults alike. The fondness that children have for movie monsters is now reflected in the plastic tat-fest that Halloween has become since the 1970s.

The big question about horror films is whether you show the monster in its full, repulsive glory or keep it under wraps, teasing the audience with a glimpse of a slimy claw here or a flash of coal-black eyes there. Your budget, as much as your artistic convictions, may have some bearing on the final decision.

When Cushing starred in *The Abominable Snowman* (1957) directed for Hammer by Val Guest and written by Nigel Kneale, the writer and director were at loggerheads over how much of the Yeti should be seen. Kneale wanted it to be seen and Guest (who prevailed) only wanted a glimpse of the creature's eyes. Cushing plays Dr John Rollason, who joins an American expedition led by the gung-ho Tom Friend (Forrest Tucker), attempting to track down the Yeti in the snowy wastes of the Himalayas. But who is the real monster here? asks the film. The Yeti or the crasser members of the expedition? As Cushing's character Rollason says to Friend: 'It isn't what's out there that's dangerous, as much as what's in us.' In the climax of the film, Rollason finally gazes into the Yeti's face. 'The face? There was nothing ape-like about it, nothing human either. But I felt it had a sadness and it was probably only a surface resemblance to wisdom.'

In *The Curse of Frankenstein* (1957), Cushing is the true monster. In the role of Baron Frankenstein his slide into hubris and villainy is chilling. Universal banned Hammer from either using the word 'monster', or recreating Boris Karloff's iconic make-up. And Christopher Lee's lurching car-crash of a creature plays second fiddle to Cushing's icy malevolence. From the start, screenwriter Jimmy Sangster wanted to shift the emphasis of Hammer's version, saying, 'I was as more interested in Baron Frankenstein than the monster. The monster couldn't help doing monstrous things … On the other hand, everything monstrous that the Baron did was well thought out. Done for a reason. A much more interesting character.'

Corruption (1968) took Cushing back into mad-scientist territory. He plays Sir John Rowan, an eminent and attractive surgeon who is in love with a model, Lynn (played by Sue Lloyd). Persuaded to go to a swinging Sixties party that is not really his scene ('dolly birds' in crochet dresses and people who say 'freak out baby'), Rowan gets into a fight with an obnoxious photographer (Tony Booth) and in the struggle a photographer's light falls on Lynn and scars her face. Rowan becomes obsessed with restoring her beauty and his first attempt (using a pituitary gland from a post mortem) seems successful. But soon the scarring reappears and he has to seek out fresh pituitary glands by becoming a serial killer of young women. In this film Cushing is the monster – the theme is almost Frankenstein-ian – but still we empathise with his awful predicament, not least his discomfort among all the kaftan-clad trendies. A poster campaign for the film – accompanied by an image of a room full of dead women, screams: '*Corruption* is not a woman's picture! Therefore: no woman will be admitted alone to see this super-shock film.' Different times.

Frankenstein and the Monster from Hell (1974) was the last of Hammer's Frankenstein films with Dave Prowse as the monster but Peter Cushing is as pedantically chilling as ever. This time round, Frankenstein – now using the alias Dr Carl Victor – has taken up residence in an insane asylum where he continues to pursue his scientific experiments.

Sometimes Cushing keeps you guessing as to whether he is a force for good or evil in a film. In *The Ghoul* (1975), directed by Freddie Francis, he plays Dr Lawrence welcoming some spoilt young people (their car has broken down) to his remote moorland home. Is he being genuinely kind or merely preparing his guests for some unspeakable horror?

* * *

Frankenstein's monster is not sexy. In *The Bride of Frankenstein*, Elsa Lanchester takes one look at her shambling fiancé and screams the house down. King Kong is not sexy either, nor are werewolves, nor is the creature in the black lagoon, nor is Godzilla, nor is the Abominable

Snowman, nor are Mummies, nor are any of the blobs, the slithery abominations and the bug-eyed humanoid aliens that infest horror films.

The great exception to this rule is Dracula, as played by Christopher Lee in the Hammer films. Though Bela Lugosi was a very attractive man he looks heavy and ponderous in the 1931 *Dracula*. Odd, because Carol Borland, who starred with him in MGM's *Mark of the Vampire* (1935) said that Lugosi was 'the most sexually attractive male I have ever known in my life'. And Max Schreck is not exactly love's young dream in F.W. Murnau's *Nosferatu* (1922). Neither is Klaus Kinski in Werner Herzog's 1979 *Nosferatu the Vampire*.

Hammer films were all about sex. Hammer boss Anthony Hinds told *Fangoria* magazine: 'I wanted the Hammer horror shows to be rich-looking, slow, deliberately paced, bursting with unstated sex but with nothing overt.'

Lee himself says that as far as his career was concerned it was playing Dracula that made the difference. He made a point of not watching the Lugosi film but instead read Bram Stoker's novel twice. There were aspects of Dracula with which he could identify – his stillness and the contrasting explosions of bouts of manic energy, his quality of being both doomed but undead; and the fact that he was an embarrassing member of an aristocratic family.

All this is evident in Lee's performance, particularly the manic energy, but it is director Terence Fisher who brings out Lee's sexual charisma. His women victims simultaneously fear him and long for him. Invariably he pauses before gorging on their blood as though he might be about to kiss them but is compelled by the forces of darkness to do what a vampire must do.

Dracula came out in the late 1950s when the Western world was on the cusp of the sexual revolution. Hammer films reflect swinging Britain with an emphasis on nudity, breasts, see-thru nighties, available temptresses and innocence debauched. Long before the Aids epidemic of the 1980s, Hammer vampire films also refer obliquely to the societal fascination for, and fear of, the dark consequences of sexual liberation – disease and death.

There is a theory that it was not only the contraceptive pill which ushered in the sexual revolution, but the post-war use of penicillin – which was a far more effective treatment for sexually transmitted diseases such as gonorrhoea and syphilis than anything that had been available before. Nevertheless, the fear of VD (venereal disease) as it was then known, persisted with the suspicion that female promiscuity was encouraged by effective contraception and increased the spread of VD, and that foreigners (particularly from ethnic minorities) would bring infection with them.

Dracula is always the foreigner, the outsider who must (according to vampire lore) be invited over the threshold. He is utterly ruthless and promiscuous in his quest for blood. Blood is both life-giving and a symbol of death, a sacrament and a blasphemy. His infected victims will spread the contagion of vampirism unless he, the source of the tainted blood, can be destroyed by a stake or a silver bullet through the heart. He is also a threat to men because his victims (both male and female) are visibly brought to orgasm as he drains their blood. Nobody does it better than Count Dracula.

This was the monster that Lee played until he became utterly sick of it, a monster whose true evil flows through his tainted blood, a monster who brings death and disease but also pleasure and liberation from conventional society. Once infected, his female victims become voluptuous, sexually predatory, knowing,

After Christopher Lee, the sexiness of Dracula became an option for anyone who played him. Hot Draculas include Claes Bang, Gary Oldman, Frank Langella. Pin-ups of their day, Tom Cruise and Brad Pitt starred in the 1994 film of Ann Rice's book *Interview with a Vampire*. The teen vampire *Twilight Saga* called on the pale-but-interesting actor Robert Pattinson.

Unlike Cushing, Lee was never comfortable with his association with horror and though he was a graduate of the Rank Charm School he never fulfilled his potential as romantic leading man. Both Cushing and Lee tended to get gruff and embarrassed when talking about sex. For instance, in that Tom Snyder TV interview Cushing looks appalled when it is suggested to him that the penetration of the stake into

Dracula's body is a metaphor for the sexual act, though he is willing to concede that there is a certain sexiness in the scenes with the Count's female victims.

Lee was the same. He always maintained that he had no idea that Jess Franco's 1970 film *Eugenie* was soft porn, and that the sex scenes were shot separately from the scenes he appeared in. He thought he was appearing in a biopic about the Marquis de Sade and flew out to Spain for one day's work as the narrator, required to wear a crimson jacket. The people behind him in the shot all had their clothes on, he insisted. Later, a friend asked if he knew he was in a film showing in one of the cinemas in Old Compton Street that showed soft porn, traditionally enjoyed by the 'dirty mac' brigade. Appalled, Lee crept along to the cinema wearing dark glasses and a scarf as disguise. He was furious at what he saw.

What does one make of his apparent naivety, or the idea that he went to Soho in disguise? That's the strange disconnect in Hammer films – the obvious sexiness mingled with stuffy suburban prudishness.

It could be that both men were of a generation that found it difficult to embrace the permissive society, insisting that horror films were simply innocent 'entertainment'.

In Hammer's *Dracula AD 1972* (made in 1972, as you may imagine) Cushing and Lee team up for the very first time since the 1958 original, which would have been a cinematic event if the film had been a bit better.

Cushing plays Professor Van Helsing's descendent, Abraham Van Helsing, an expert in the occult, who lives with his granddaughter Jessica (Stephanie Beacham). Cushing is very good in the strict-but-loving grandfatherly role and their scenes together are among the best in the film.

The film opens at a party where Jessica and her bohemian hippy friends are outraging the other guests, who are all pompous squares. A girl in hot pants dances on a piano, a signal of youthful depravity if ever there was one. Characters say things like 'weird man' and 'way out'. They drive around Chelsea and go to a bar called The Cavern. One of their fast set, a whey-faced boy called Johnny Alucard (Christopher

Neame), whose name is Dracula spelt backwards, summons the Count in a noisy satanic ritual carried out in a deconsecrated church.

Unfortunately it is a wasted opportunity for Lee, as he is never allowed to step outside the ruined church and grapple with the modern world of Jessica and her chums, which could have made for an interesting storyline. A parallel there, one feels, with the real-life actor. He doesn't look much more at ease in *The Wicker Man* (1973), rather too ostentatiously cool about the naked girls leaping around his estate on the sexually liberated Isle of Summerisle.

Lee gets second billing to Cushing in *The Mummy* (1959), scripted by Jimmy Sangster and directed by Terence Fisher. He is rather dismissive of the film, but the scenes where he, the mummified remains of the High Priest Kharis, locks eyes with Yvonne Furnaux, recognising in her the reincarnation of the Princess Ananka, are truly affecting.

After Ananka's death, Kharis had been punished by being buried alive as a punishment for trying to bring her back from the dead. Their tomb had been sealed for 4,000 years until the team of English archaeologists arrives. The arrogant archaeologist who has no respect for the Egyptian burial site he is desecrating (and pays the consequences as a result) is a variant on the mad scientist who plays God. Both awaken monsters.

Again it falls to Cushing – in the role of sensitive archaeologist John Banning – to raise the question of whether it is modern rational man who is the true monster. Lee, wrapped in bandages and dunked in a muddy swamp, is both physically impressive and emotionally touching in his role, especially as his bandages become ever tattier each time someone takes a shot at him. There are some marvellous lines from Sangster too. 'The best part of my life has been spent among the dead,' says Cushing. Never was a truer word spoken.

Lee played one of history's real life monsters, Rasputin, in *Rasputin, The Mad Monk* (1966) directed by Don Sharp and filmed at Bray Studios. He believed it was one of his best pieces of work. There were legal difficulties because Prince Yusopov, implicated in Rasputin's assassination, was still alive at the time of filming. Lee felt a strong sense of connection with the film because he had met Yusopov when he was a child. He met Rasputin's daughter Maria in 1976, who told

Lee that he had caught her father's 'expression' in the film. Born in 1899 she had worked as a lion tamer with the Hagenbeck-Wallace Circus in the 1930s, often sharing the arena with two lions, two tigers, three bears, two leopards and two pumas. After she retired from the circus she later found work as a riveter in a California shipyard during the Second World War. She died in 1977.

Lee's Rasputin is of the 'treat 'em mean, keep 'em keen' school of dating, favouring hypnotism over conversation and with a sexual magnetism that turns every woman into a willing doormat. He seduces one of the Tsarina's ladies-in-waiting (played by Barbara Shelley) so that she will introduce him to the Tsarina (played by Renée Asherson). It could have been that in playing a monster who is simply a man, Lee might have tried to show Rasputin as morally complex. But rather boldly, he makes him irredeemably evil, intent on using his weird powers for his own gratification. Like Cushing, Lee is skilled enough to never overthink his roles. He goes, you might say, straight for the jugular.

In the classical world and in fairy tales, monsters and other supernatural creatures are an accepted part of the universe. For example, a giant in a fairy story may be destroyed or outwitted but there is no sense that all giants must be destroyed, or that the presence of a giant is in any way surprising. The American film academic Noel Carroll brilliantly observes that whereas in fairy tales the monster is an ordinary character in an extraordinary world, in horror films the monster is an extraordinary character in an ordinary world.

In modern horror – fiction and films – the monster is an anomaly, a contradiction, both dead and alive, sometimes both organic and mechanical, both repellent and attractive. The monster threatens to disrupt, corrupt, destroy and infect the world of reassuring normality whose foundation is rational, science-based and free of superstition. The monster can be a six-foot tall man wrapped in bandages who has been dead for 4,000 years, which challenges our belief that 'such things cannot happen'. Or it can be a microscopic contagion.

The Covid-19 pandemic of 2020 is still at the forefront of our minds and was alarming because it brought to an abrupt end the confident belief, fostered by the scientific developments of the twentieth century, that humanity had – if not completely conquered disease – at least assembled the tools to do so. Smallpox had been eliminated, as had common childhood illnesses thanks to vaccination. Improvements in sanitation, hygiene and nutrition added to our perception that the old diseases, such as TB and cholera, had been overcome in the developed world.

Yet in the 1980s and 1990s, Aids, a disease associated with blood and sex and carrying a stigma that is only now beginning to lift, presented the possibility that there could be new, mysterious diseases coming down the line. It is easy to forget the moral panic it created thirty years ago, as it is easy to forget the terror of polio which only began to recede with the introduction of Jonas Salk's vaccine in 1955.

Horror films and fiction tailor the monsters they create to the times we live in. Disease in an age which *almost* conquered disease is our greatest fear, and its ability to upend our normal, ordinary lives. We look to science to save us yet fear its potential. Boris Karloff, Peter Cushing and Christopher Lee embodied our fears and yet made them entertaining at the same time.

* * *

Chapter Ten

Downtime

Christopher Lee would say 'No you haven't' to fans who came up to him gushing that they had seen all his films. He made more than 350 films and even he had not seen them all. He never stopped working. Neither did Boris Karloff nor Peter Cushing. Actors tend to be like that. In a notoriously insecure profession you never want to turn down any job that comes your way.

The surprising thing is that all three managed to find time for an impressive array of extra-curricular activities.

Cricket was Boris Karloff's great love. At Uppingham he was not academically gifted but he was a good athlete and all-rounder with a love of cricket, rugby, hockey and tennis. He was involved with the cricketing Overseas Club in Hollywood from 1919. In 1931, by now newly contracted to Universal and earning decent money, he and fellow actor Charles Aubrey Smith (1863–1948) went to the University of California in Los Angeles (UCLA) and negotiated the use of their cricket ground at weekends with the proviso (according to Boris Karloff) that we 'try to pull in a few students'. Apparently Karloff was a very good coach.

Smith had been a Sussex county cricketer and played in one test match against South Africa in 1889, taking five wickets for nineteen runs in his first innings. He was known as 'Round the Corner Smith' because of his curved bowling run-up. After a decent career on the London stage he went to Hollywood, where he played English gents and officers and was a sort of unofficial leader of the expat film community. Others included David Niven, Ronald Colman, Rex Harrison, Leslie Howard and Basil Rathbone.

Smith (never seen without his boater, white flannels and striped blazer) showed his officer-like qualities by overseeing the construction of a field and pavilion at Griffith Park, near the film studios in Burbank, using grass seed imported from England. In 1932 he launched the Hollywood Cricket Club with Karloff as a keen member. PG Wodehouse, then one of Hollywood's most successful screenwriters, was a vice-president and took the minutes at the first meetings.

Woe betide any useful cricketers who did not sign up and attend nets regularly. When Laurence Olivier arrived in Hollywood in 1936 he checked into the Chateau Marmont and found a note from Smith. 'There will be net practice tomorrow at 4 pm. I trust I shall see you there.' Olivier did as he was told, wearing cricket boots borrowed from Boris Karloff.

Fixtures were sometimes arranged with visiting Royal Navy battleships such as the HMS *Delhi*. A side from Australia arrived and enjoyed a visit to the set of *The Mask of Fu Manchu* in which Karloff starred and Smith also had a role. These visiting teams must have been suitably impressed by the glamorous ladies who appeared to watch the matches and help serve tea – among them Olivia de Havilland, Joan Fontaine, Elsa Lanchester and Merle Oberon.

Karloff always followed English cricket and when he visited Britain it was a great joy to him to attend matches, both test matches and small local matches, once umpiring a charity match at Hitchin in Hertfordshire. He was a Lord's Taverner and belonged to Middlesex and Surrey Cricket clubs.

He was a voracious reader and put together a couple of anthologies of horror stories. In 1943 *Tales of Terror* was published with a long introductory essay. Three years later a new compilation was published called *And The Darkness Falls*, featuring works by – among others – Turgenev, Guy de Maupassant, Ambrose Bierce, Arthur Conan Doyle, Edgar Allan Poe, Jonathan Swift, Yeats, Gogol and – always a favourite of Karloff's – Joseph Conrad. Karloff wrote potted biographies of the authors and added his own thoughts about horror fiction.

He was also a very keen gardener. In the 1930s, living in Cherokee Lane, he worked obsessively on his estate of 2½ acres, which he called 'the farm'. There was a lawn which needed constant attention in the California climate. Sometimes he would water it wearing swimming trunks and a top hat. Another favourite gardening outfit was an old pair of dungarees.

He had a large fruit orchard. With so much space, he and his wife Dorothy could acquire more pets. Their Scotties, Whisky and Soda, were joined by two Bedlingon terriers Agnus Dei and Silly Bitch, a tortoise called Lightning Bill, a parrot, some ducks, chickens, turkeys, a cow and a pig called Violet. Violet would sometimes wear a knitted vest. After the gruelling shoot for *The Bride of Frankenstein* in 1935 he would find solace and true relaxation in his garden, a pattern he would repeat whenever he had a break between pictures.

In the last decade of his life – from 1959 – he and his then wife Evie lived in a delightful cottage in the village of Bramshott in Hampshire, where Boris added to his small, typically English cottage garden by renting some land where there were a few apple trees.

He played the piano too but regretted that he had not done enough practising when he was at school.

Although he was very much at home in Hollywood, he still relished the opportunity to return to England and enjoy what it had to offer, especially since he had become a world-famous movie star. His off-screen persona was always that of the mildly erudite and refined Englishman, an image which was adored by America. But he was also being true to himself. Many who had left the UK to find a better life in the waves of immigration that occurred in the early part of the twentieth century never had the opportunity to return to the mother country. Karloff did, and he made the most of it. It was his rest and relaxation.

* * *

As a boy Peter Cushing had become a collector of model soldiers. The big name then (and still revered today) is W. Britain, a firm started by William Britain at a time when imports from Germany dominated the toy market. In the early 1890s, Britain's son (also William) perfected the technique of hollow casting in lead. This process gave them a light model with considerable strength, along with large savings in the amount of lead used. It gave the company the competitive edge it needed. Gamages department store in Holborn was also instrumental in the success of the company, stocking the new line and selling model soldiers at a reduced cost.

From the start, the soldiers were standardised on a scale equivalent to the most popular size of toy train at that time. This meant producing soldiers that were 54mm (2.25 inches) tall. This measure is still known as the standard scale. Great care was taken to ensure that the uniform details were correct.

Rather surprisingly perhaps, sales of military toys dropped during the First World War. So, in 1921, Britain launched the Model Home Farm collection consisting of thirty farm figures and animals which were introduced along with the first farm vehicle, the '4F' Tumbrel Cart. But it was Cushing's love of model soldiers particularly that stayed with him throughout his life.

As an adult he also commissioned figures by the model maker Frederick Ping, who had started in the 1930s and worked in what was known as the 'French style' by building each figure from layers of lead. Cushing also made his own exquisite models from compressed drawing paper, complete with detachable swords and helmets.

He was a member of the British Model Soldiers' Society, set up in 1935 which had branches all over the country and now has members worldwide. In the 1950s he would go to the meetings held once a month in a pub in Regent Street.

Friends and colleagues were happy to add to his collection. He recalls that one day while he was on tour in Australia with Laurence Olivier's Old Vic Company, Olivier's then wife Vivien Leigh caught Cushing staring longingly into a shop window at a boxed set of The 11th Hussars. It duly appeared on his birthday, beautifully wrapped and left on his dressing-room with a note from Vivien and Larry.

Before he became known as a horror star, Cushing was better known for his TV work. In the early 1950s he also appeared in a couple of opulent Technicolor historical films full of swords and soldiering. One was *The Black Knight* (1954), an Arthurian yarn with Cushing in black wig and drop earrings as the villainous Saracen knight Sir Palamides, filmed at Pinewood and on location in Spain. Alan Ladd takes the title role in one of the films he was obliged to make outside the US for tax reasons. Another was *Alexander The Great* (1956) starring Richard Burton and Claire Bloom, in which Cushing played his military adversary, Memnon. There are some spectacular massed battle scenes.

Cushing, with his love of historical battlefields and model soldiers, was a gift for the publicists for these kinds of epics. In a 1956 Pathé newsreel he is filmed in his house in Hillsleigh Road, Kensington, in the room where he kept his 5,000-strong collection, his painting equipment and his books. We see him getting down on the floor to play, as the commentary has it, 'solemnly and conscientiously'.

He also had an impressive model trainset and, as a lifelong smoker, he had a collection of 40,000 cigarette cards. He collected coins, toys, *The Strand Magazine* and stamps, and made both miniature theatre sets and dolls' houses. He is known to have designed and made bracelets for actresses, Joanna Lumley and Ingrid Pitt.

He and Helen loved nothing more than playing board games in the evenings and would invite friends to parties where out would come Monopoly, Totopoly, Buccaneer and Careers. The board game manufacturer Waddington used to send the couple new games to try out with their friends. Among their celebrity chums who could face such an evening were the artist Edward Seago, Ellen and Stanley Baker, Billie Whitelaw and her husband Peter Vaughan, Richard Pasco, and Gordon Jackson and his wife Rona Anderson.

After their silver wedding anniversary, Peter and Helen moved out of London to live permanently in their second home in Whitstable. It was hoped that this would be beneficial for Helen's fragile health. With less space, Peter had to sell many of his model soldiers which went under the hammer at Phillips auction house in 1969. When Helen died his hobbies became of even less interest to him and all these delicate artefacts were stored in the loft studio. After his death, these too were put up for auction in 1994.

One of his hobbies for painting silk almost became a career when he was frequently out of work in the 1940s. To mark the movie premiere of Olivier's *Hamlet* (1948), in which Cushing plays Osric, he designed a scarf adorned with characters from the play, along with quotations.

Printed on filament rayon crepe it was produced in twelve colours by Blond Brothers, a company that had supplied military uniforms during the war. It also produced scarves and made underwear for Marks and Spencer. Gaumont British and Odeon cinemas were provided with stocks of the scarves to be sold in their theatres while Jean Simmons, who played Ophelia, was photographed modelling one of them.

He designed a hand-painted silk headscarf for Queen Elizabeth II's coronation. It is believed that the late Queen herself owned one of Cushing's scarves and he was thrilled when he met the Queen Mother in 1956 and saw that she too was wearing one of his creations.

In an auction of Cushing memorabilia in 2023, one hand-painted silk scarf made for Helen (estimate £600–£800) sold for £1,150.

Whitstable, on the Kent coast, is still very much a town where Peter Cushing's memory is honoured and where he loved to spend what free time he had. He had first visited the town (which he always referred to as a 'village') in the 1940s. Their house was 3, Seaway Cottages. A local beauty spot, near the bottom of High Street, has been named 'Cushing's View', with a memorial seat. The Oxford Cinema, so called because it was on Whitstable's Oxford Street, is now (since 2011) a Wetherspoon pub called The Peter Cushing, and a museum of memorabilia. The Whitstable Museum itself, also on Oxford Street, has a small collection devoted to his memory. In his later years Cushing visited the Tudor Tea Rooms on Harbour Street almost every day which has photographs, letters and notes from him on the wall.

In Whitstable he could indulge his love of painting in watercolours and he was tutored and encouraged by his and Helen's friend, the British painter Edward (Ted) Seago (1910–1974). Seago had had an interesting war. Commissioned as a Second Lieutenant in the Royal Engineers he had developed camouflage techniques for Field Marshal Auchinleck. In his autobiography Cushing recalls an evening at Seago's house in Ludham, Norfolk. Claude Auchinleck was one of the guests and they played a parlour game called 'Have you anything to declare?', in which the great man took the part of a customs officer. All the other guests drew slips of paper out of a hat on which were written the various items people bring back from trips abroad. Auchinleck would then question them before asking for the imaginary bags to be opened.

Cushing tactfully describes another guest – Peter Seymour – as Seago's secretary, whereas in fact they were in a long relationship and Seymour was a painter in his own right.

The Queen Mother was a great admirer of Seago's Post-Impressionist work, though the sheer popularity of this self-taught artist meant that he did not gain the critical approval of the art world that he deserved. The Queen Mother bought so many of his paintings that eventually he gave her two paintings every year, on her birthday and at Christmas. Prince Philip invited him on a tour of the Antarctic in 1956 and the resulting paintings hang in Balmoral. He was also commissioned to paint a portrait of Queen Elizabeth in her dress uniform as Colonel-in-Chief of the Coldstream guards.

Cushing and Helen were staying at Seago's house when one of the Queen's aides phoned to say that Her Majesty and her mother would like to come over from Sandringham to see how the portrait was progressing. It was arranged that they would come for lunch and that Helen and Cushing would join the party.

Cushing recalled how the Queen's initial scrutiny of the couple gave way to the famous smile. He felt as though he was was sitting down with old friends. The royal mother and daughter put the Cushings entirely at their ease at this informal lunch. The Queen Mother told Cushing that he was a great favourite at 'Buck house'.

In 1958 Cushing was interviewed on BBC television and some of his watercolours were shown. The following day he had a call from The Fine Art Society in Bond Street who wanted to mount an exhibition of his work. It was called *Here and There* and opened on 3 December. The Royal Academician Sir William Russell Flint and Ted Seago were among the first visitors to the exhibition and he was thrilled when both of them bought his paintings.

There was no end to Cushing's enthusiasms and interests. He was a man of precise and somewhat eccentric habits who wore white gloves to prevent his fingers being stained by nicotine. He was also fussy about his teeth and had a collection of some thirty toothbrushes. He never used toothpaste, believing that shaving soap was better.

He was a member of the Royal Society for the Protection of Birds. In 1973 he contributed an article to an RSPB book called *The Birds From Your Window*. Other celebrity contributors included Humphrey Lyttelton, Joyce Grenfell, and Robert Dougall. Cushing wrote:

> My beloved wife Helen and I spent so many happy times observing the birds from our kitchen. The sill was their meal-table, and one particular male blackbird would tap on the pane with his beak if we were late in putting out some tit-bit or other. As birdwatchers we were extremely fortunate: the rear windows of our house face the garden and the front overlooks a vast bay and estuary. Thus we could enjoy the best of two 'bird worlds' – those that inhabit trees, shrubs and lawns – and the glorious waders along the shoreline. During that dreadful winter of 1962/3 when the sea froze in undulating waves, the birds had a terrible time finding food. Helen made a wondrous mixture from stale bread, bacon-rinds and tins of pilchards, and I would walk along the beach scattering it from a plastic bucket, rather like a Victorian seed-sower, the birds in my wake as those that follow the plough, fear of man completely – if, alas, only temporarily – forgotten in this emergency. We really had no especially favourite birds: all are so delightful and interesting in their own particular ways. The bold and beautiful little robin stole Helen's heart. A pair dominated our garden for some years, and nested regularly in the boxes we hopefully erected. Some blue tits also took up permanent residence amongst a grape-vine growing on a walled terrace where we would take tea on warm and sunny days.
>
> A list of birds seen and loved would be tedious perhaps, but worthy of note was the appearance of a very rare snowy owl on the beach, being harassed by a pair of black-headed gulls; and a black-throated diver, unfortunately covered with crude oil. Amongst the many and varied calls, the curlew's lonely – yet somehow soul-soothing – cry of solitude always thrilled us. But

the humble and 'simple' sounds were those that filled our hearts with gladness and peace, the the world not lacking in wonder but sometimes for wonderment.

(Reproduced with the kind permission of the RSPB)

Cushing's friend, the comic Eric Morecambe, along with his wife Joan also did a lot of work for the RSPB. In 1971 Eric and Peter appeared in the BBC's *Nature* programme. On another occasion, Christmas 1972, Cushing presented a *BBC Wildlife Spectacular* with Dr David Bellamy (a big star at the time).

He was also, as one might expect, a voracious reader. He liked biographies, histories of the First World War, novels, books about birds and reference books in general. His favourite book, according to his devoted secretary Joyce Broughton, was the *Oxford Dictionary of Quotations*.

Cushing was always thrilled that his fans were often as interested in his hobbies – birdwatching and model-making – as they were in hearing him talk about *Frankenstein*. And there is no doubt that if his career as an actor had not taken him to such great heights he would have become an accomplished and successful artist and designer.

* * *

Golf was Christopher Lee's escape from the demands of playing the undead. After all, he had spent his earliest years wandering the links of Sunningdale golf course because his family had owned and built a number of houses in the vicinity. His parents lived in the White Cottage, off the second tee of the Old Course. After they went their separate ways, his mother lived in Crowood on the Ladies' Course. As a small child Lee would often stray off until the police were called and he would usually be found in the rough and brought home.

He cannot have had much time for golf as an adult because he claimed his longest stretch between acting projects was four weeks. On the other hand, he does seem to have played an awful lot of golf.

He associated many of the films he made with the courses he played on his free days. For him, *The Private Life of Sherlock Holmes* (1970) would aways bring back memories of Nairn Golf Club in Scotland. While filming *Nothing But The Night* (1973) near Dartmoor, he played at the scenic Thurlstone Golf Club while co-star Peter Cushing carried his clubs and pointed out the birdlife. On *The Man with the Golden Gun* (1974) he nearly stepped on a cobra at the newly-built Navatanee golf club in Bangkok.

He was a good golfer, with a handicap of one. He achieved a hole in one when he was 50. He played countless pro-am tournaments across the world and was a regular on BBC2's *Pro-Celebrity Golf* and *Around with Allis*. In 1965 he and English golfer Peter Oosterhuis beat Tom Weiskolf and Telly Savalas (Lee's co-star in *Horror Express*). His golf clubs were given to him by Arnold Palmer, who had had them made specially for Lee's great height at his factory in Chattanooga, Tennessee.

There are more than forty golf clubs within striking distance of Bray Studios but Lee was a member of Muirfield in East Lothian and came to love golf in the Californian sunshine. He was a member of Bel-Air Country Club in Los Angeles, founded 1927, whose members included James Garner, Fred Astaire, Jack Nicholson, Ronald Reagan, Bing Crosby, Richard Nixon, Humphrey Bogart, Clark Gable, James Stewart, Spencer Tracy, Clint Eastwood and Tom Cruise. Lee's golfing companions included Jack Lemmon and Burt Lancaster.

Designed by George Thomas Jr (1873–1932) it included two grassy mounds (now removed) in front of the 12th green which earned it the nickname 'Mae West'. Johnny Weissmuller had filmed scenes for one of the Tarzan movies in a hidden cave above the fourth hole. Howard Hughes landed his plane there when he was late for a golf date with Katharine Hepburn. After the club towed the plane away and handed him the bill, he paid up but resigned his membership.

Lee's other extra-curricular passion was singing. He always said that one of the greatest regrets of his life was that he had not become an opera singer. The first opera he saw was during the war in the Teatro San Carlo in Naples. It was *The Barber of Seville* with Titto Gobi and Guilio Neri. Interviewed in *Gramophone* just before he died, he said that this was the opera that anyone who has never seen an opera should go to because of the catchy tunes and marvellous characters.

His mother was a great singer, as was his great grandfather, Girolamo Carandini, 10th Marquis of Sarzano, who sang at the Modena Opera House. Carandini eventually settled in Tasmania where he married the country's finest soprano.

Lee's meeting in Stockholm with the tenor Jussi Björling, who praised his singing voice, was a 'sliding doors' moment. Lee knew that while his acting career could continue until his death, the career of a professional singer is never as long. He said in 2015: 'I'm too old to perform as a singer, but I can still sing. That's what's so extraordinary: it's because I haven't sung opera for three hours or whatever a day that I can still sing.'

Heavy metal fans will know that while Lee never became a name in opera, he did release a symphonic metal concept album, called *Charlemagne: By the Sword and the Cross* in 2010. As he was keen to tell anyone who would listen, he could trace his ancestry to Charlemagne, the first Holy Roman Emperor. A follow-up album called *Charlemagne: The Omens of Death* was released in 2013. His daughter Christina provided the narration.

Lee had become a fan of heavy metal in the 1970s when he first heard Black Sabbath. He very much admired the guitarist Tony Iommi. According to an article in *Rolling Stone* magazine in 2015, Lee told Iommi: 'You are the father of metal', to which the guitarist replied: 'But *you're* the one that started it, really, because we used to go watch *Dracula* and the horror films you did and that's what influenced us.'

In 2005 Christopher Lee provided the spoken narration on Rhapsody of Fire's single *The Magic of the Wizard's Dream*. In 2006 he released an operatic pop album *Revelation with Toreador March (Metal Mix)*, a take on the song from *Carmen*. In 2010 he recited a spoken word passage on Manowar's re-recording of the 1982 album *Battle Hymns*, as *Battle Hymns MMXI*. Naturally, in keeping with his metal credentials, he had also golfed with Alice Cooper and said: 'Of course, [Alice] had all that incredible stuff going on live – hanging himself and so on …

When I go to see a good concert from a metal band, it's exhilarating. Like nothing you've ever heard before!'

The metal magazine *Metal Hammer* honoured him with a Spirit Of Metal award at the 2010 Golden Gods.

The Omens Of Death would be his final album. He released three metal EPs – *A Heavy Metal Christmas*, *A Heavy Metal Christmas Too* and *Metal Knight* – the last of which came out barely a year before his death.

Chapter Eleven

Afterlife

Boris Karloff died on 2 February 1969 in the King Edward VII Hospital, Midhurst, in Sussex. Always a heavy smoker he was suffering from bronchitis and pneumonia. He was 81.

Peter Cushing died on 11 August, 1994, also aged 81. In 1982 he had been diagnosed with prostate cancer and rushed to hospital. His left eye had swollen to three times its normal size, one of the effects of the cancer, and it was not expected that he would live long. But in fact he was to live another twelve years and continued working.

Sir Christopher Lee died on 7 June 2015, aged 93, in the Chelsea and Westminster Hospital, suffering from respiratory problems and heart failure.

* * *

Boris Karloff was awarded two stars on the Hollywood Walk of Fame. In 1997 he was featured on stamps issued by the US Postal Service as both Frankenstein's Monster and the Mummy in its series 'Classic Monster Movie Stamps'. A street in Rochester, Kent, called Karloff Way is named in his honour.

In 1989 his widow Evie endowed the church of St Mary in Bramshott, Hampshire (where Karloff lived for the last decade of his life), with new bells. The inscription reads: 'The Bells of Bramshott were rehung in 1989 & rededicated on 16th July in memory of Boris Karloff actor who lived and died within the sound of the bells.'

He was never nominated for an Oscar. Horror films did not win awards when Karloff was making films. The first horror film to be nominated for Best Picture (as well as nine other Academy Awards) was *The Exorcist* (1973). It won Best Adapted Screenplay. Karloff won a Grammy Award for the *The Grinch that Stole Christmas* and a Tony on Broadway way for *The Lark*.

His daughter Sara Jane Karloff keeps his memory alive on The Official Boris Karloff Website which says it is 'Maintained by the Descendants of the Master of Horror'. Fans can buy tumblers, models, masks, statues, the Boris Karloff Master of Horror Coffee Blend, books and clothing. She posts tribute letters, videos, artworks, articles, interviews and cute pictures of her first great-grandson in a green romper suit adorned with the faces of Frankenstein's monster. Now in her late eighties she continues to attend the many conventions, screenings and festivals that celebrate the actor and the iconic roles he played, especially Frankenstein's Monster.

As Sara Jane says, his voice is still recognisable today. A quick search on the internet reveals that there are hundreds of podcasts devoted to all things Karloff. Horror fan conventions and film seasons occur worldwide – the Mad Monster Party Carolina, the Vampire Fan Weekend, Bizarre World Miami, the Monster-Mania Con, Days of the Dead Las Vegas, Spooky Empire, the Living Dead Weekend: Monroeville, the Nashville Horror Con, the Houston Horror Film fest. In the UK, the For the Love of Horror expands ever year. HorrorConUk has been running since 2015. There is a Leeds Horror fest, the ScareFest Weekend at Alton Towers and so many others.

Obviously other monsters get a look in – zombies, vampires, things from outer space, werewolves and ghouls. But Frankenstein's monster is always a staple ingredient. He is the horror daddy of them all.

Peter Cushing enjoys an afterlife which even the maddest of the scientists he played could never have imagined. In the 2016 movie *Rogue One: A Star Wars Story*, he returns to play the Imperial Grand Moff Tarkin – which was remarkable because he died in 1994. The technical wizardry involved (rather old hat now, one imagines) is known as 'digital resurrection', developed by Industrial Light and Magic (ILM), the special effects studio founded by George Lucas. Using a 3D model of Cushing's face made for his appearance in the 1984 comedy *Top Secret!*, the whole process took eighteen months to perfect. The estate and its representative – Cushing's former secretary Joyce Broughton – gave the go-ahead. The movie includes a cameo of the young Princess Leia also created with CGI. The actress Carrie Fisher saw and approved it, but died suddenly on 27 December 2016 while *Rogue One* was on release, adding a poignant, if slightly tasteless note as far as viewers were concerned. In *USA Today* the reviewer Kelly Lawler noted: 'The Leia cameo is so jarring as to take the audience completely out of the film at its most emotional moment. Leia's appearance was meant to help the film end on a hopeful note (quite literally, as 'hope' is her line), but instead it ends on a weird and unsettling one.'

There is a fine irony that Peter Cushing, who spent his life making movies about things being brought back to life, should be reanimated in this way. Indeed, the American film critic Roger Ebert once wrote, 'His dialogue runs along the lines of, "But good heavens, man! The person you saw has been dead for more than two centuries!"'

Of course the digital Cushing is in a sense an *homage* to a great actor. But Cushing was also a jobbing actor who took almost every part that was offered to him. He understood, through bitter experience, what it was like to be out of work. Would he have been happy to see himself brought back to life at the expense of some living, breathing actor? Guy Henry, the actor whose face was replaced by the digital Cushing mask in *Rogue One* found it an unnerving experience. He had to wear a headcam device which he found claustrophobic, unwieldy and frightening.

He hoped the technique would not become commonplace.

Unfortunately, the signs are that this technique *will* become a commonplace thing. We are beginning to realise what a threat Artificial Intelligence (AI) poses to just about every area of human creativity. Actors can also be de-aged as Robert De Niro, Al Pacino and Joe Pesci were in Martin Scorsese's *The Irishman* (2019), to portray younger versions of mobsters Frank Sheeran, Jimmy Hoffa and Russell Bufalino, respectively. Harrison Ford got the treatment in *Indiana Jones and the Dial of Destiny* (2023).

Even as long ago as 2005, Lucasfilm had wanted to bring Tarkin back for a cameo in 2005's *Star Wars: Episode III – Revenge of the Sith*. A digital mock-up of a younger Cushing was considered but instead they cast another actor, Wayne Pygram, and used facial prosthetics to make him look more like Cushing. Technology has moved on apace since then. No doubt modern AI techniques could whistle up a convincing Peter Cushing in a minute.

The Cushing one sees in *Rogue One* is uncanny, both uncannily like him but also uncanny in the sense that it has that not-quite-human look of all AI bots. When Cushing was first cast, the point of his character was to present a human visage which would offset the faceless Darth Vader. Cushing's veteran status and his very familiar face provide that counterpoint. But that is somehow swept away by his eerie presence in *Rogue One*.

I have no way of knowing, but somehow I think Cushing would have disapproved of his digital resurrection. He was an actor who always showed deep concern for the wellbeing of those he worked with and he also cared deeply about the craft of acting. Neither the community of actors nor the business of acting are served by computer games of this kind. It is akin to grave-robbing.

'Normally as an actor, you are you pretending to be another person,' said Guy Henry. 'Here, I was me pretending to be Peter Cushing, pretending to be Tarkin.'

Technology does of course make it possible to honour much-loved screen actors in more benign ways. In the 1980s a range of funny TV adverts for Holsten Pils used footage of old movie stars spliced with Griff Rhys Jones. In one, a scene is used featuring Peter Cushing in the role of the urbane and sinister Doctor Peter Von Brecht in *The Man Who Finally Died* (1963).

The Peter Cushing Appreciation Society and The Peter Cushing Association (created in 1994 by Joyce Broughton and Brian Holland) are full of stories, videos and fun facts about the great man. The Sherlock Holmes Society of London often celebrates his portrayal of the great detective in its programme of events. Christopher Lee also took on the role in *Sherlock Holmes and the Deadly Necklace* (1962), and in the TV movie *Sherlock Holmes and the Leading Lady* (1991). He played Mycroft Holmes in the 1970 film *The Private Life of Sherlock Holmes*.

Like Karloff, Cushing has appeared on a postal stamp – in 2008 to mark the 50th anniversary of the release of Hammer's *Dracula*. In 2013 the Royal Mail issued a set of ten first class stamps celebrating 'Great Britons'. Joining Cushing were the actress Vivien Leigh, football manager Bill Shankly, former prime minister David Lloyd George, John Archer (the first mayor of African-Caribbean descent to head a London Metropolitan Borough Council), cookery writer Elizabeth David, composer Benjamin Britten, society photographer Norman Parkinson, broadcaster and journalist Richard Dimbleby, and archaeologist Mary Leakey.

Actors survive after death when their films – originally viewed as disposable dross – become considered 'cult', appealing to a specialised, knowing audience who reclaim the film, reevaluate it, appreciate its merits which may not have been immediately apparent to its initial audience, and champion its distinctiveness. Acquiring cult status turns the low-brow into high-brow and turns low-budget into art movie.

The concept of the cult film has diminished somewhat as its vigorousness depends upon it being viewed in a collective way, by a like-minded community, at a midnight screening in an independent cinema, or at a film festival or honoured in some way by the British Film Institute. Cult films are traditionally 'so bad, they're good', challenging the accepted form and content of mainstream cinema.

People will go and see a cult film over and over again because being part of the audience who share your taste is a crucial part of the pleasurable experience. Now that the number of independent cinemas has dwindled and, increasingly, we stream films on the likes of Netflix or Amazon Prime, it feels as though the idea of the cult film and the camaraderie that accompanies it is disappearing. Partly this is because the idea of the counterculture no longer has any meaning. True, Hammer retains its cult following and the affection of fans. But films or directors who were once considered 'cult' slip off the radar, either because their cult credentials were weak or because the 'cult' of cult is itself on the wane.

For instance, Cushing appeared in a sci-fi version of *Biggles* (1986) playing Colonel Raymond, a survivor from the Royal Flying Corps of

1914–1918. The film received a royal premiere at the Empire Theatre, Leicester Square, attended by Prince Charles and Princess Diana but it received lacklustre reviews. It was directed by John Hough, an interesting figure in British films and TV. He directed episodes of the 1968 season of TV's *The Avengers* and made *Twins of Evil* (1971) for Hammer. He then went to Hollywood where he made the 1974 road movie *Dirty Mary, Crazy Larry* starring Peter Fonda and Susan George. On the back of the success of this film – which has a sort of cult status – he made *Escape to Witch Mountain* (1975) and the horror film *Watcher in the Woods* (1980) starring Bette Davis, Carroll Baker and David McCallum. This too accrued a following. It has been said that his *Biggles* movie has a cult status through its weird sci-fi take on the W.E. Johns stories and the casting of the (by now) veteran star Peter Cushing. It is often listed among films that have been overlooked, undervalued or considered obscure.

Cushing was awarded an OBE in 1989 though many felt he deserved a knighthood. Christopher Lee said that it was 'too little, too late'. Recipients of OBEs and MBEs must be nominated and it was Ian Scoones, who created special effects for Hammer Films, who put Cushing's name forward. In the past Cushing, always kind and considerate to fellow workers, had helped Ian, who died in 2010, to get a job at Bray Studios.

When he accepted the OBE, Peter Cushing said:

> I suppose I am an incurable romantic because I would like to have slain a dragon or saved the Queen's life or done some other brave deed which would make me feel I really deserved this honour. But I love this country of ours and its people so very much indeed and am deeply proud of the recognition.

On 13 January 1995, a few months after his death, a memorial service was held at the actors' church of St Paul's, Covent Garden. Among the many who attended were Richard Briers and Paul Eddington, both from the sitcom *The Good Life*, Joanna Lumley, Donald Sinden – and of course, his great friend Christopher Lee.

Another friend, producer Kevin Francis told the congregation: 'In his later years he would talk about death, he wasn't upset by it. He asked if anybody would come to his memorial service. I told him: "It's free. You know these theatricals, if you're giving it away they'll always come."'

The horror writer Stephen Volk wrote a book called *Whitstable*, published in 2013, exactly a century after the birth of Cushing. It is set in 1971 just after his wife Helen died. As a distraction from his grief Cushing becomes a real-life vampire hunter for a little boy who thinks his mother's boyfriend is one of the undead. It is a rather touching tribute from a lifelong fan.

* * *

Interviewed outside the Palace when he received his knighthood for services to drama and charity in 2009 (he had received a CBE in 2001), Sir Christopher Lee was still complaining about the Dracula movies. 'They made too many of the films,' he said, but admitted that as a result he was 'now known to every generation. And that's what it's all about – survival.'

The interviewer pushes her luck by telling him that he has been honoured by (the then) Prince Charles on the 'eve of Halloween'. 'Is it? I had no idea,' he says crisply. He received the BAFTA Fellowship in 2011 and the BFI Fellowship in 2013.

He did charity work for UNICEF and for Cinema for Peace which was founded in 2002 to 'promote peace and international understanding through the medium of film'. In 2014 he was guest of honour at a Cinema for Peace Gala held during the Berlin Film Festival.

Out of these three great film actors, Christopher Lee was always the one least comfortable with his career – he was almost ashamed of it. The film he wanted everyone to see was *Jinnah* (1998), a Pakistani-British biopic of the founder of Pakistan Muhammad Ali Jinnah, but unfortunately it is a film which very few people have had any interest in seeing. Lee also received death threats because of his history as a star of horror films though not, apparently, because he was a European playing an Asian role.

He seems to have felt the need to talk up his other achievements and denigrate his Hammer and horror credentials. In a Thames TV interview just after his autobiography *Tall, Dark and Gruesome* was published, he is asked by the presenter (very unfairly) if he had written the book or if it was ghosted. Lee asserts that he wrote every word. But he didn't. It was written by the late journalist Alex Hamilton.

In an interview with the journalist Ann McFerran in 2002, his niece Dame Harriet Walter speaks of him with great affection – as he does her – saying that he brought 'great dignity' to the Hammer films in which he appeared. She also wonders if he felt a 'twinge of envy' for her success in classical theatre.[12]

Lee mentions in this interview that he is a Conservative, while his niece is a Labour supporter. We live in an age when stating your identity and political allegiance is almost mandatory and it is one of the aspects which distinguishes Karloff, Cushing and Lee from modern actors. They never felt any pressing need to say how they voted or tell others how to conduct themselves. They were too modest and perhaps didn't feel it was their role for they were, after all, merely jobbing actors.

And while they never made any great claims for their films, it is the very fact that they were mostly low key and low budget which makes them so attractive to a modern audience. Films in all genres now have to carry a message, take a side, make a point. They are experiential, immersive, self-important. The films that our three old actors starred in had slighter aims. They wanted to entertain and tell a story. That was all. The master of horror fiction Stephen King says in his book *Danse Macabre*: 'What the good horror film does above else is to knock the adult props from under us and tumble us back down the slide to childhood.' The horror films made by Karloff, Cushing and Lee all tell stories, appealing to that childhood sense of anticipation which we surely all remember when someone sat us down and said: 'Once upon a time'.

Of the three, Karloff – who died in 1969 and whose last role in *Targets* saw him playing an old-style horror film star who believes his time has passed – would be the most astonished at how the horror genre, frequently written off and never taken seriously, has not only survived, but flourished in the films of M. Night Shyamalan, Jordan Peele, Julia Ducournau, Nia DaCosta, Ari Aster and Issa López. From the studio lots of Hollywood and the damp fields of Bray the horror movie has expanded with fantastic films coming out of Japan, Scandinavia, Korea and Italy, to name but a few. Today horror films are taken seriously. In the modern world we are never short of monsters that must be destroyed … .

Chapter Twelve

The Films

Some longer pieces on my favourite films, not necessarily the best known but all of great interest. Almost all are available on YouTube or other sites.

Frankenstein   1931

The film opens in an eerie, mangled graveyard with crosses askew, a rotting skeleton in a military helmet and blighted trees somehow evoking a First World War battle landscape. Henry Frankenstein (Colin Clive) and his assistant Fritz steal a freshly buried corpse but reject a hanged man because his neck is broken and his brain would have been no use. Fritz steals a brain from a laboratory but it is a criminal's brain. Meanwhile, Henry's fiancée Elizabeth (Mae Clarke) cannot understand why Henry has become so obsessed with his scientific work that he shows no interest in their wedding.

The use of the criminal brain is one of the bigger departures from Mary Shelley's original story and one that seems to have been forgotten during the filming, because Boris Karloff's performance gives no indication of the brain's criminal tendencies. He plays the Monster as though he is a clumsy child, unused to his body and the world but essentially innocent. Though his fingernails are blackened, his hands are fine, elegant hands, raised to the light that Henry lets into the laboratory. His soulful gaze is heart-breaking. At first he responds well to Frankenstein. It is only when Fritz torments him – whipping him and terrifying him with a burning torch – that the Monster turns violent.

The most controversial scene in the film is when the Monster, having escaped from Henry Frankenstein, meets a little girl, Maria, in the countryside. Unafraid, she asks him to play with her and they throw petals in a lake. Intending Maria no harm, he picks her up and throws her in the lake where she drowns. Censors took exception to this scene and on many prints it was cut. It was partly as a result of this scene that the British Board of Film Censors introduced the H certificate, which was replaced in 1956 with the X certificate.

Later in the film, Maria's grieving father carries her lifeless body through the streets where the villagers are celebrating in preparation for the delayed wedding between Elizabeth and Henry Frankenstein. As he makes his progress, we see how the villagers respond, breaking off from eating, drinking, dancing, playing as they catch sight of the dead child. A reminder of director James Whale's brilliance.

* * *

The Old Dark House 1932

The film is based on a J.B. Priestley novel called *Benighted*, published in 1928, a harshly satirical take on post-war British society. Mercifully, director James Whale strips the film of any political pretensions and invents the old dark house horror movie, of which, subsequently, there were many. It is the dark and stormy night (the horror genre loves a dark and stormy night) somewhere in Wales and five travellers (Gloria Stewart, Charles Laughton, Melvyn Douglas, Raymond Massey and Lilian Bond) are forced to take refuge in a creepy house where monstrous shadows flicker against the walls and curtains billow in the wind. Karloff is Morgan, the butler with a hideously scarred face and a bad drinking habit. Their unwilling hosts are Horace Femm and his sister Rebecca (Ernest Thesiger and Eva Moore). Their centenarian father Sir Roderick Femm lies upstairs in bed (played by Elspeth Dudgeon as Whale couldn't find a male actor who looked old enough).

'Can you conceive of anyone living in a house like this if they didn't have to?' demands Horace, posing the question that underlies every haunted house film. Don't go in there! And why does Gloria Stewart feel the need to change into a satin evening dress (apart from the fact that she looks wonderful in it?). 'You think of nothing but your long straight legs and your white body and how to please your man,' hisses Rebecca.

It is hilarious, surreal and dry as a martini. And Brember Wills, as the evil brother Saul, is one of Hollywood's finest homicidal maniacs.

* * *

The Mummy 1932

The camera lingers on the Egyptian mummy, propped up in its case, the bandages rotting. Pause. Then a single eye, behind half closed lids, lights up. The body shifts. The young archaeologist who has made the mistake of reading the Scroll of Thoth which wakes the dead goes mad and (we are told) will die laughing. Ten years later the revived mummy, a high priest called Imhotep, reappears in the guise of Ardeth Bey (played by Boris Karloff). Buried alive because he himself had committed sacrilege by trying to wake the Princess Ankh-es-en-Amon, he is still intent on rekindling their love of thirty-seven centuries. The Princess, now reincarnated as the half-Egyptian Helen Grosvenor (played by Zita Johann), is drawn to sinister Ardeth Bey but her modern self loves archaeologist Frank Whemple. He is played by David Manners who is Jonathan Harker in Tod Browning's *Dracula* starring Bela Lugosi.

'My love has lasted longer than the temples of our gods,' says Karloff mournfully. Desiccated and impassive, he still manages to engage our sympathy.

Directed by Karl Freund and released by Universal Studios, the film benefits from location filming in the Mojave desert.

* * *

The Black Cat 1934

Possibly one of the weirdest films ever made. Boris Karloff plays Hjalmar Poelzig, an Austrian architect living in a modernist art deco house on the ruins of a First World War battlefield. Thunder rolls and the rain lashes down with the arrival of his former war comrade

Dr Vitus Werdegast (Bela Lugosi), accompanied by a couple of dopey American honeymooners, Peter and Joan Alison, who have had the misfortune to share a train carriage with him and have been involved in a bus accident. After eighteen years in a Siberian jail Dr Werdegast is seeking revenge for Poelzig's part in the death of his wife and daughter (both called Karen). Little does he know that Poelzig has kept wife Karen's body in a state of suspended animation and married the daughter Karen. A black cat stalks the premises, cosily described as a 'living embodiment of evil'.

It's no use even thinking of phoning for help as the phone is dead. 'Do you hear that, Vitus?' purrs Karloff, 'The phone is dead. *Even* the phone is dead.'

Necrophilia, narcotics and satanism add to the mix. Dr Werdegast's final revenge is to flay Poelzig alive. It is directed by Edgar G. Ulmer who had been apprenticed to F.W. Murnau, director of *Nosferatu* (1922). With its continuous musical soundtrack the film has a surreal, nightmarish feel putting it firmly in the tradition of German Expressionist cinema.

* * *

The Black Room 1935

'Mr Boris Karloff has been allowed to act at last,' wrote Graham Greene, reviewing the film for *The Spectator*. He plays dual roles, Anton and his evil twin Gregor, born to the aristocratic de Berghmann family. The birth of twins raises the spectre of the family curse and the sealing up of the 'black room'. The only feature that distinguishes the twins is Anton's paralysed arm. After a long spell away from the baronial home, Anton returns at Gregor's behest. But soon Gregor's depraved behaviour manifests itself.

Karloff has fun playing the raffish Gregor – leg thrown carelessly over a chair arm as he taunts the villagers who object to his serial killing of the local women – and the goody-goody Anton.

One of Karloff's less well-known films but very enjoyable.

* * *

The Bride of Frankenstein 1935

This time Karloff is merely billed as 'Karloff', an indication of his star power by the mid-1930s. The sequel to the original *Frankenstein* is generally held to be the superior movie with a splendid performance by Ernest Thesiger as the evil and irredeemably camp Dr Pretorius, who persuades the weak-willed Henry Frankenstein to return to his scientific meddling by constructing a woman who is pieced together from a suitably youthful cadaver and assorted body parts. Elsa Lanchester plays both the Bride and (in the opening scene where she begins telling her tale of 'what happened next' to Byron and Shelley) Mary Shelley.

The film has a number of brilliant scenes, particularly the moving section where the Monster finds a friend in the blind cottager and the spectacular laboratory scene where the Bride is animated by galvanic forces.

* * *

The Invisible Ray 1936

The 'Foreword' to the film reads: 'Every scientific fact accepted today once burned as a fantastic fire in the mind of someone called mad.'

This film contains so many tropes of the mad-scientist movie that it is occasionally unintentionally comic, but directed with great flair by Lambert Hillyer. It opens at night (dark and stormy, as ever) at a castle-cum-laboratory atop the Carpathian mountains. 'Who would expect to find a place like this on top of the Carpathian mountains,' asks one character, disingenuously.

Dr Rukh (Boris Karloff) has been harvesting rays from the Andromeda nebula and gives a demonstration to sceptical scientist Dr Benet (Bela Lugosi) and his friends. Ruek's blind mother worries that 'there are some secrets that we are not meant to probe'.

Rukh then accompanies the scientist led by Dr Benet (Lugosi) on an African expedition where he discovers the meteor which he predicted had come from the nebula millions of years ago.

Inadvertently, he infects himself with Radium X which issues from the meteor, begins to glow in the dark and finds that his touch can kill. Benet manages to limit the damage but Rukh starts to lose his sanity and takes his sadistic revenge on Benet's group.

The scenes in Africa featuring the black 'boys' who accompany the expedition are difficult to watch with modern eyes.

* * *

The Walking Dead 1936

Karloff was loaned out to Warner Brothers for this crime horror directed by the demanding and prolific Michael Curtiz (1886–1962) who had made stars of Errol Flynn, Olivia de Havilland and Bette Davis. He directed film classics such as *Casablanca* (1942), *Mildred Pierce* (1945) and *White Christmas* (1954).

Karloff plays John Ellman, a beaten, gentle musician who has been wrongly jailed. The judge who sent him down is killed by a group of racketeers and Ellman is framed for the murder. Even his defence attorney is part of the criminal gang and Ellman is dispatched to the electric chair just as a couple of witnesses who saw the judge's body being planted in his car desperately try to contact the DA. He is brought back to life by the use of an artificial heart (known as the Lindbergh Heart, an actual device invented by the famous aviator) which the two young witnesses (both scientists) had been instrumental in developing.

After he is reanimated Ellman develops a supernatural sense of the gangsters who framed him and they get their comeuppance.

The film has the typical hard edge of a Warner Brothers' film and Karloff's performance is outstanding. Playing Arthur Rubinstein's *Kammenoi Ostrow* at a recital for a group that incudes the men who framed him, we see his eyes change from sad and gentle to implacable hatred.

* * *

Corridor of Mirrors 1948

This film marked the directorial debut of the ever-versatile Terence Young, who would go on to direct three Bond films, *Dr No* (1962), *From Russia with Love* (1963) and *Thunderball* (1965). It is a strange feverish confection, Cocteau-esque art film and Gothic horror, with music by Georges Auric (a musician who was a member of Les Six, a group that included Jean Cocteau and Erik Satie). Eric Portman plays a reclusive artist who meets a beautiful woman (Edana Romney) in a nightclub and becomes convinced they were once lovers in Renaissance Italy. It all goes horribly wrong. Cue the wonderful line: 'I should have known that four centuries can't change a woman's soul.' Adapted from a novel by Chris Massie it was scripted by Romney and Rudolph Cartier who would produce Orwell's *Nineteen Eighty-Four* for TV in 1954, starring Peter Cushing.

Lee plays a good-looking young man in the nightclub. It's a case of blink and you miss him. But it is pleasing to note that his very first appearance is in a kind of horror film.

* * *

The Curse of Frankenstein 1956

Folding a head tenderly in a piece of white cloth as though it is a baby, Baron Frankenstein wipes his bloody hand on the lapel of his frock coat. The stain remains throughout the film as Victor Frankenstein's moral collapse is mirrored in his increasing dishevelled appearance. This is Peter Cushing's first outing as the Baron with Hazel Court as his cousin Elizabeth and Robert Urquhart as Paul Krempe.

Krempe arrives at the household years earlier, answering an advertisement for a tutor to the precocious Victor Frankenstein, witnessing with increasing dismay his transformation from brilliant young scientist to ruthless madman. In real life Urquhart was also said to be disgusted by the gore and violence in the film, walked out of the premiere and never appeared in another Hammer film. On a happier note he adopted the puppy who is brought back to life in Frankenstein's laboratory.

Cushing dominates this film. His sensitive features harden when his plans to create life from a jumble of human organs are threatened. His callous affair with the chambermaid Justine (played by Valerie Gaunt) confirms that he is irredeemably damned. Christopher Lee's turn as the mute, brain-damaged Creature cannot compete with Karloff's iconic Monster but there is still a certain pathos in his performance.

Hazel Court, a graduate of the Rank Organisation 'charm school' would become a horror film stalwart, though in this film she has a fairly thankless role as the prissy, teacup-tinkling Elizabeth. The red ribbon around her neck in her penultimate scene signals her vulnerability as Frankenstein's resolve hardens. Valerie Gaunt has a livelier role as Justine, finally discarding her chambermaid uniform for that garment bestowed on so many Hammer ladies – the transparent white nightdress.

* * *

Time Without Pity   1957

One of the last films that Peter Cushing would make before he became forever associated with Hammer horror. It is a feverish film noir, directed by Joseph Losey and based on a 1953 play *Someone Waiting* by Emlyn Williams.

Michael Redgrave plays David Graham, a drunk and a failed writer, attempting to secure a last-minute reprieve for his son Alec (Alec McCowen) who is due to hang for the murder of his girlfriend. Alec, more or less abandoned by his father, has been mentored and financially helped by the wealthy Stanfords. It is they who have paid for the lawyer Jeremy Clayton (Peter Cushing) who helps Graham in his frantic quest. Leo McKern plays the loud and abrasive Robert Stanford, whose business is racing cars, with Ann Todd as his wife Honor. From the opening scene of the film we know that he is the real murderer.

This was the first film that Joseph Losey directed in Britain after he was blacklisted in the McCarthy era. Cinematographer is Freddie Francis who would go on to direct many films for Hammer.

It is a tense, agitated film full of ticking clocks and trembling hands, with Redgrave's character at the end of his tether as he flounders around seedy London trying to save his son from the end of a rope. He goes to visit a Fleet Street newspaper editor who he was at Cambridge with, hoping to enlist his help. The editor does nothing but savagely throw darts at a board on the back of his office door.

The terrific cast also includes Lois Maxwell, Joan Plowright (as a chorus girl) and Renée Houston as a drunken hysteric.

* * *

Violent Playground 1958

The social menace of the 'juvenile delinquent' was on everyone's mind in the 1950s and this Liverpool-set film (though mostly filmed at Pinewood Studios) was the British film industry's answer to American films such as *Rebel Without a Cause* (1955).

Stanley Baker plays a hard-boiled cop in an urban jungle swarming with feral kids. Peter Cushing, in wire-framed glasses, plays the parish priest Father Laidlaw who can mediate between the children and the authorities when there is a spate of arson attacks. David McCallum, moody and good-looking, plays the troubled Johnny, the one with the gun. It was directed by Basil Dearden whose name became synonymous with the output of Ealing Studios.

The danger to social order presented by the explosion of jive and rock music echoes through the film and is particularly enjoyable in the title track, *Play Rough*, sung by Johnny Luck and released on the Fontana label.

* * *

Dracula   1958

In Hammer's first excursion into vampire territory, Jonathan Harker (played by John Van Essen) arrives as the Count's new librarian. But he does precious little indexing, for his true mission is to rid the world of the monstrous Count, with Jimmy Sangster's script moving the story on at a cracking pace – with some forgivable shuffling of characters and elisions of plot and location.

In the earlier film *The Curse of Frankenstein*, the true chemistry of the Christopher Lee and Peter Cushing combo was diluted by the obliterating make-up of Lee's monster. But in *Dracula*, for the first time, you get a sense of their devastating screen power when they appeared together. Lee is suave, urbane and sexy. Cushing, as vampire hunter Dr Van Helsing, is cerebral and intense. But what both actors have is a purposeful energy which takes your breath away and, under Terence Fisher's assured but ungimmicky direction, propels the film to its all-action ending. The dank, dreamy languor of the horror films of the 1930s gets an injection of modern energy.

Yet even as Dracula succumbs to Van Helsing and crumbles to dust, a look mingling profound sadness and disgust passes across Van Helsing's face. It's one of those terrific moments of cinema. If anyone needs proof of Cushing's genius, it is right there.

* * *

Corridors of Blood   1958

Originally called *The Doctor from Seven Dials*, it stars Boris Karloff as a nineteenth-century doctor who experiments with opium on himself in order to further his researches into anaesthesia. As his addiction inevitably takes hold his ability to perform amputations and other surgery at lightning speed deserts him with terrible consequences.

Christopher Lee plays Resurrection Joe, a body snatcher, with Adrienne Corri as his girlfriend. The Victorian squalor depicted on the film is done with relish and the lower classes in the local tavern are always ready to burst into a song and a jig.

The film was not released until the mid-1960s, by which time Lee's fame had increased and he gets equal billing with Karloff, though his role is much smaller.

* * *

The Hound of the Baskervilles   1959

The film opens with a flashback to the days of depraved Sir Hugo Baskerville, carousing with a mob of braying toffs in red jackets, torturing peasants and killing innocent village girls for pleasure.

He gets his comeuppance in the jaws of the supernatural hound that haunts Grimpen Mire. Fast forward to Sherlock Holmes's study in Baker Street where Holmes (Cushing) and Watson (André Morell) are invited to investigate the mysterious death of Sir Charles Baskerville. His heir Sir Henry Baskerville has just arrived from South Africa to take up his inheritance. Christopher Lee plays handsome Sir Henry in a succession of extremely fine tweed suits. It is one of the few occasions when he gets to play something approaching a romantic lead.

Cushing's Holmes is vigorous and capricious. He has some terrific lines delivered with absolute confidence ... 'The power of evil can take many forms' ... 'There is more evil around us here than I have ever encountered before' ... 'Some revolting sacrificial rite has been performed'.

This was the first adaptation of a Sherlock Holmes story to be filmed in colour and the trademark Hammer red glimmers through the swirling murk of Dartmoor.

* * *

The Flesh and The Fiends   1960

A lot of cadavers flop around in this sombre retelling of the Burke and Hare story, with Peter Cushing as Robert Knox, the morally compromised Edinburgh surgeon who turns a blind eye to the activities of the two unsavoury characters who bring him fresh corpses for his medical research. One wonders whether the drooping eye that Cushing adopts for the role (Knox did have a bad eye following childhood smallpox) reflects this very metaphor.

Billie Whitelaw plays Mary Patterson, a lively prostitute who distracts medical student Chris Jackson (played by John Cairney) from his exam revision.

Directed by John Gilling, who would make a number of horror films for Hammer.

* * *

The Devil's Agent 1962

Peter Cushing claimed to have no memory of appearing in this Cold War thriller (a British, West German, Irish co-production). But legend has it that he did, and the passed-out drunk slumped next to Billie Whitelaw in a nightclub certainly looks like him.

Set in 1950, the German actor Peter van Eyck plays George Drost, a Viennese wine merchant whose reunion with an old friend Baron Von Straub (Christopher Lee), who lives in the Soviet Zone, results in him becoming a spy playing both East and West off against each other in an increasingly dangerous game. Lee has a small role appearing at the beginning and the end of the film, but it's an indication of the aristocratic Euro-menace that he would use to full effect in his Hammer films.

* * *

Dr Terror's House of Horrors 1964

The first Amicus film to star both Lee and Cushing finds the passengers in a train compartment hurtling towards their doom as Dr Schrek (Cushing) shuffles his pack of tarot cards and proceeds to tell the fortunes of his fellow passengers – none of which is cheerful.

Lee plays a self-important art critic whose savage reviews have driven an artist to take his own life and is then haunted by the man's disembodied hand. Also starring are Alan Freeman (death by a plant), Donald Sutherland (vampire trouble), Roy Castle and Kenny Lynch (happy-go-lucky musicians who infringe voodoo religion.)

This was screenwriter Milton Subotsky's attempt to repeat the successful formula of Ealing Studios' *Dead of Night* (1945) which he considered to be the 'greatest horror film ever'. Filming began on 25 May 1964 and ended on 3 July. A model of efficiency.

* * *

The Skull 1965

An Amicus film adapted by Milton Subotsky from a story by Robert Bloch with Christopher Lee billed as guest star. Peter Cushing gives a typical intense performance as Christopher Maitland, noted expert on the occult, who occasionally buys items from a sleazy dealer Anthony Marco (sweatily played by Patrick Wymark) and is very unpopular with Mrs Maitland, played by Jill Bennett. She was a close friend of the Cushings.

When the skull of the Marquis de Sade comes up for sale, Maitland is surprised that Marco offers to drop the price and Lee (playing his urbane friend Sir Matthew Phillips) warns him against acquiring the object. This of course whets Maitland's interest in the creepy relic.

The acting honours belong to Cushing, first in a surreal dream sequence which looks as though it could have come out of an episode of *The Avengers*, followed by a prolonged final scene in which he battles against the forces of evil as the Skull becomes ever more powerful and urges him to go on a killing spree. It was the first time that Peter Cushing appeared in a horror film in modern clothing.

* * *

Dracula, Prince of Darkness 1966

Where is Van Helsing when you need him? The film opens with a reprise of Dracula's destruction at the hands of Peter Cushing in Hammer's original *Dracula*. But after that there is no more Cushing. The role of vampire slayer goes to Andrew Keir playing Father Sandor. 'What, may I ask, are four charming English people doing in the Carpathians?' he asks when he encounters them in a local tavern. What indeed? Francis Matthews, Barbara Shelley, Susan Farmer and Charles Tingwell play the four idiots. Don't go to the castle, says Sandor. So obviously they head straight there and move in with their luggage.

The Count had been destroyed ten years earlier by Van Helsing but he is brought back to rude health when his sinister manservant Klove (Philip Latham) mixes the blood of one of the tourists with his ashes. Lee has no lines in this film and without Cushing's presence it is oddly unengaging. Worth seeing though because it underlines how very crucial Cushing was.

* * *

The Sorcerers 1967

'How long do you think this can last?' asks Ian Ogilvy's languid character Mike, surveying the scene at Blaise's nightclub, where the gilded youth of the Swinging Sixties is dancing the night away.

But this sci-fi horror (directed by Michael Reeves who also made the cult film *Witchfinder General*) turns the tables on that era's disapproving attitude towards the young. Boris Karloff and Catherine Lacey play Marcus and Estelle, a batty old couple who have perfected a hypnosis machine which enables them to control and experience the sensations of their chosen victims.

Mike, bored and looking for new experiences, is zapped by the psychedelic gizmo machine and, under the control of the increasingly maniacal Estelle, embarks on a spree of stealing, speeding and murdering. Estelle's penchant for evil increasingly horrifies Marcus, who had hoped (as is the way with all mad scientists) to use this new power for the good of mankind.

The film is also notable for its London locations. Blaise's nightclub (named after the character Modesty Blaise) was in the basement of the Imperial Hotel in Kensington. On any night you might see The Byrds, Martha and the Vandellas, Wilson Pickett, Brian Auger or Jimi Hendrix. Alcoholic drinks were three shillings and the A La Carte menu was £1.

* * *

The Night of the Big Heat 1967

It is winter on the island of Farra but the temperature is soaring into the 90s and beyond. This sci-fi horror directed by Terence Fisher finds Christopher Lee, Patrick Allen and Peter Cushing battling the blobby aliens who have brought about climate change by tapping into radar stations or TV signals ... or something.

Christopher Lee is the enigmatic scientist who works it all out, Peter Cushing is the island's suave doctor and Patrick Allen is the hunky novelist whose mistress Angela (played by Jane Merrow) arrives in an open-top sports car pretending to be his secretary and threatening his marriage to Frankie (played by Sarah Lawson).

Everyone has shiny faces because of the damned heat and the men's shirts become sweatier with every scene. The question is, how many of them are going to die screaming when the funny noise starts? Laughable but very watchable.

In reality the weather was very cold and the cast were sprayed in glycerine at the start of each shot so they would look convincingly sweaty.

* * *

Theatre of Death 1967

Christopher Lee plays Philippe Darvas, the sinister, silk-shirt wearing director of a *grand guignol* Parisian theatre – Le Theatre de la Mort

– which stages inventive productions featuring voodoo, vampirism, witchcraft, cannibalism and decapitation. Julian Glover plays a police surgeon, whose girlfriend, Dani Gireaux (Lelia Goldoni), is one of Darvas' troupe.

She tries to warn her flatmate Nicole Chappelle (Jenny Till) against getting involved with Darvas, whose foolproof seduction technique includes hypnosis. He is altogether less attentive to the emotionally fragile Dani, telling her she is 'unattractive both as a woman and an actress' and criticising her eye make-up. These days she would be straight off to HR to raise a complaint.

The final showdown cuts repeatedly to a gratuitously erotic voodoo dancing scene performed by Lita Scott, possibly because the main action is a little on the dull side.

Filmed at Elstree Studios and produced by London Independent Producers, founded in 1951 by Sydney Box (previously head of Gainsborough Pictures) and William MacQuitty (who produced the 1958 Titanic disaster film, *A Night to Remember*).

* * *

The Curse of the Crimson Altar 1968

A British film made by Tigon Films and produced by Tony Tenser. Clearly in poor health, this was Boris Karloff's final appearance in a British movie.

He plays an occult expert, Professor Marsh who collects instruments of torture. Mark Eden (who was the villainous Alan Bradley in *Coronation Street*) is antiques dealer Robert Manning investigating the disappearance of his brother who winds up at the home of Mr Morley (Christopher Lee), sleeps with his niece and is troubled by satanists, led by the wonderful Barbara Steele in green body make-up.

The Morley house is creepy, says the observant Manning, adding that you expect that 'Boris Karloff is going to pop up at any minute'.

* * *

Targets   1968

This was Boris Karloff's last film and director Peter Bogdanovich's first feature. Karloff's daughter Sara Jane says that of all his movies this one is her favourite. Karloff plays Byron Orlock, an elderly horror movie star who has decided that he wants to retire.

Bogdanovich, like John Carpenter and Steven Spielberg, was of that generation of directors who were movie-mad kids so the film is full of homages to old movies, including a clip from Howard Hawks' *The Criminal Code* and a long sequence from Roger Corman's *The Terror*, which stars Karloff/Orlock. The movie is being shown at a Los Angeles drive-in movie theatre where Orlock is making a final personal appearance.

But the gentle camp of classic horror movies contrasts with the truly evil character of Bobby Thompson (played by Tim O'Kelly), a nondescript suburbanite and gun nut who has slaughtered his family and arrives at the drive-in to take pot shots at total strangers. The film is an eloquent cry of dismay at American gun culture and a kind of elegy for old Los Angeles and old Hollywood. Meanwhile, the new Hollywood is portrayed in this film as a soulless wasteland of freeways and little grey homes.

* * *

The Devil Rides Out   1968

Christopher Lee and Charles Gray star in this terrific adaptation of Lee's old mate Denis Wheatley's 1934 novel scripted by Richard Matheson and directed by Terence Fisher. Lee plays the Duc de Richleau investigating the alarming occult interests of the son of his late friend (played by Patrick Mower). Gray plays Mocata, the head of the devil worshippers, with admirable and convincing seriousness. As far as Lee was concerned this was one of the few films he made which he believed carried an important message about the perils of meddling with the occult.

* * *

Frankenstein Must Be Destroyed 1969

An action-packed opening involves a severed head in a bucket, a corpse in a tank and Peter Cushing in a fright mask. In this outing as Baron Frankenstein he is in the brain transplant business and forces a young doctor (played by Simon Ward) to become his unwilling accomplice. His former colleague, Dr Brandt, has been confined to a lunatic asylum. Frankenstein plans to kidnap him and cure his madness with a bit of brain surgery so that they can continue their work which will (as is always the way) benefit mankind by harvesting the brains of geniuses.

Brandt suffers a heart attack so his brain, once cured, must also be transplanted into another body. Freddie Jones is terrific as the asylum administrator who becomes the recipient of Brandt's brain. Cushing's energy drives the film relentlessly.

Cushing was deeply disturbed by the scene in which he rapes Veronica Carlson, written in because it was felt the movie needed 'sexing up'. He discussed it with her at length before the filming but found it distressing in the extreme.

* * *

The House That Dripped Blood 1971

There is no blood at all in this film, written by Robert Bloch (author of *Psycho*). The BBFC gave it an 'A' certificate, but according to Amicus producer Milton Subotsky the distributors refused to handle it unless it was given an 'X', which would make the audiences anticipate something suitably shocking. It was always the conundrum with horror films once the X certification was introduced. An 'A' certificate would in theory guarantee a bigger box-office, but would it put off diehard horror fans? Subotsky once said: 'I'd love to make a U horror film that children could go and see. I've got stacks of horror anthologies for children but I don't think the distributors would go for it.'

One of the best performances in this enjoyable anthology film (full of genuinely surprising twists) is that of 8-year-old Chloe Franks, a beautiful child who became something of a veteran of horror films. She plays Jane, whose father (Christopher Lee) takes her to live in the remote house and hires a private tutor (Nyrée Dawn Porter). Why doesn't he want the little girl to mix with other children, why won't he let her have a doll, why does he get in a panic when the candles go missing? For once Lee turns out (spoiler alert) to be the victim.

Other unlucky tenants in the house include Peter Cushing, Denholm Elliott, Jon Pertwee, Joss Ackland and Ingrid Pitt. Pertwee plays a horror film star in the final segment and admitted that he based his performance on his friend Christopher Lee. And in a film full of verbal and visual in-jokes for the horror fan, there is a scene where Pertwee's character says he prefers 'Bela Lugosi's Dracula to the man who plays him nowadays'.

* * *

Twins of Evil 1971

So often Peter Cushing is so much better than the films in which he appeared. So it is in this Hammer production based on a story by Sheridan le Fanu. He plays Gustav, a pious witchfinder devoted to God's work which involves hunting down pretty young women and burning them at the stake.

The arrival of his pretty twin nieces Frieda and Maria (played by twin sisters Madeleine and Mary Collinson who were *Playboy* models) creates havoc. Up in the castle the evil Count Karnstein (Damien Thomas) amuses himself with satanic practices and gradually lures the nubile twins into his evil schemes.

This was one of the projects that Cushing threw himself into after the death of his wife. His despair is so palpable that we can never believe him entirely villainous. He acts more in sorrow than in anger.

* * *

Horror Express   1972

A highly enjoyable film starring Peter Cushing and Christopher Lee (both good guys for a change) speeding through the icy wastes on the Trans-Siberian Express in 1906, with some sort of humanoid fossil defrosting in a wooden crate in the baggage compartment. There is a Rasputin-esque mad monk on board (effectively played by Argentine actor Alberto de Mendoza) and Telly Savalas gives a wonderful performance as a psychotic Cossack.

The alien in the fossil can transfer itself to anyone who catches a glimpse of its evil red eye, so pretty soon the passengers have no idea who it is. 'Which one of you is the monster?' asks a character of Lee and Cushing. 'We're British,' says Cushing, by way of refuting such a ridiculous idea. Directed by Eugenio Martin.

* * *

Asylum   1972

An anthology film made by Amicus Productions, also titled *House of Crazies* for its US release. Scripted by the ever reliable Robert Bloch and directed by Roy Ward Baker, it features four short stories explaining why four characters end up in a home for the incurably insane.

First off is the story which should have made any 1970s housewife rethink her craving for a chest freezer. Walter (Richard Todd) buys his wife Ruth (Sylvia Sims) one of these desirable appliances, before dismembering her and putting her in it. Barbara Parkins – star of the 1960s TV series *Peyton Place* – plays his mistress Bonnie, who gets her well-deserved comeuppance.

Peter Cushing's story is up next. He plays a sinister sort who commissions a traditional tailor to make a suit for his son, adding some peculiar stipulations. The story had previously been adapted as an episode of the Boris Karloff TV series *Thriller*.

Charlotte Rampling is in the next story, insisting she is not insane, with Britt Ekland as her friend Lucy. Herbert Lom stars in the final story and Robert Powell plays the psychiatrist who links the segments.

* * *

The Wicker Man   1973

Christopher Lee said this was the 'best scripted film I ever took part in', and he was so enthusiastic about the low-budget project, written by Anthony Shaffer and directed by Robin Hardy, that he (by now one of the UK's top-earning actors) waived his modest fee entirely.

Edward Woodward plays the God-fearing policeman Sergeant Howie, who travels to the remote Scottish island of Summerisle to investigate the disappearance of a child. Here he finds a sex-mad society of Celtic pagans led by the charismatic Lord Summerisle (Lee), who thwart him at every turn.

Lee, part kilted laird and part swinger, presides over his private fiefdom where naked girls jump over bonfires, topiary tends towards the phallic and nobody needs encouragement to launch into a suggestive folk ditty. The cast includes Diane Cilento (who met Shaffer during the film's production and would go on to marry him in 1985), horror It Girl Ingrid Pitt, and Britt Ekland as the innkeeper's sexually liberated daughter whose erotic dance routine is one of the film's most famous sequences. Spoiler alert: her voice was dubbed by the Scottish singer Annie Ross, and they used a body double for the shots of her bottom.

Filmed on location in Scotland, the weather was cold, the finances were precarious and it wasn't a very happy shoot. It was released as part of a double-bill with *Don't Look Now* and has become one of the so-called Unholy Trinity of 'folk horror' films along with Michael Reeves' *Witchfinder General* (1968) and Piers Haggard's *The Blood on Satan's Claw* (1971).

All three films rely on a theme that gained a lot of traction in the late 1960s and early 1970s – namely, that even in modern Britain the old pagan ways were still practised in remote parts of the country. It fitted the mood of that era, which saw the beginnings of the environmental movement and a rejection of all that was modern and scientific. Like many horror films concerned with ancient practices it includes a scene where one character (in this case, Howie) reads up on the custom of human sacrifice to appease the sun god and the goddess of the orchards. Most of this entertaining hokum, presented as authoritative, derives from Sir James George Frazer's study of magic, comparative religion and fertility cults – *The Golden Bough* – first published in 1890 and now almost entirely discredited.

The Wicker Man was remade in 2006 starring Nicolas Cage but is not a patch on the original. Now more than fifty years old, the 1973 cult film has lasted well. Films such as *Wake Wood* (2011), *The Ritual* (2017) and *Midsommar* (2019) show how influential it has been. Christopher Lee was right.

* * *

The Creeping Flesh 1973

Peter Cushing plays Professor Emmanuel Hildern in this Tigon production, home from his travels to New Guinea with the giant skeleton of an ancient hominid. He is a loving but over-protective father to Penelope (played by Lorna Heilbron), terrified that she will inherit the madness of her wayward mother Marguerite who has just died in an asylum for the criminally insane run by Hildern's half-brother James Hildern (Christopher Lee). Following the actual death of his wife Helen in 1971, Cushing is again acting – and painfully revisiting – the role of the bereaved husband.

Attempting to clean the skeleton, Hildern is intrigued when one of the finger bones grows flesh following contact with water. In some nicely devised laboratory scenes (Cushing always makes these science bits so convincing) Hildern tests the blood cells of the throbbing finger and finds that they provide evidence of essential evil.

Victorian taverns, mental asylums, laboratories and a couple of nice subplots (Heilbron is terrific as she goes off the rails) makes this a thoroughly enjoyable movie with a delicious twist at the end. Again, Cushing's character is essentially a good man whose professional vanity lures him into evil.

* * *

Nothing But the Night   1973

A number of wealthy trustees of an orphanage on the remote Scottish island of Bala meet mysterious and violent deaths. One of the children in its care – Mary – suffers a psychotic reaction following a coach crash which kills the driver.

Peter Cushing plays Sir Mark Ashley, a senior doctor at the hospital where the child is taken, and Christopher Lee is his friend and police inspector Colonel Charles Bingham. A fabulously blowsy Diana Dors plays Mary's real mother who reappears after a spell in Broadmoor, and Georgia Brown is a hardboiled tabloid journalist. Gwyneth Strong, a child actor who would find fame in *Only Fools and Horses*, makes a wonderful debut as the problematic Mary.

This is also the only movie to be made by Christopher Lee's production company Charlemagne Films. Directed by Peter Sasdy.

* * *

From Beyond the Grave   1973

As horror aficionado Mark Gatiss says, this anthology film from Amicus 'exudes a dark, queasy, very British atmosphere all of its own'. Based on stories by the Isleworth-born gothic writer Ronald Chetwynd-Hayes, it stars Peter Cushing (sporting a duffel coat, flat cap and a northern accent) as the proprietor of a down-at-heel antiques shop. In all but one of the four stories, a customer tries to swindle him and pays with his life in some fabulously awful manner.

David Warner is the would-be man about town with a hideous regency bedsit 'off the Edgware Road' who buys an antique mirror containing an evil spirit demanding blood. Warner's character sets off on a murder spree which turns his pad into an abattoir. In the second tale, Ian Bannen plays a former military type (turned low-paid clerk) who attempts to impress an ex-serviceman (Donald Pleasence) selling matches on the street by stealing a medal from Cushing's shop. The match seller takes Bannen home to meet his weird daughter (Angela

Pleasence) who provides a diversion from Bannen's desperate marriage to Mabel (Diana Dors).

In the third story Ian Carmichael plays a character who swindles the antiques dealer over a silver snuff box. 'Hope you enjoy snuffing it,' says Cushing as the miscreant leaves the shop.

In the fourth story Ian Ogilvy plays the one decent chap who buys an antique door to jazz up his stationery cupboard in the trendy home he shares with Lesley-Anne Down.

* * *

The Ghoul   1975

It's the 1920s and at a party of bright young things Billy and Daphne decide to race Geoffrey and Angela to the coast. Billy and Daphne's car runs out of petrol and Daphne seeks help at the big house on the fog-bound moor. Here, John Hurt is the demented gardener/handyman with Peter Cushing as Dr Lawrence and Gwen Watford as Ayah.

Veronica Carlson plays Daphne and Alexandra Bastedo is Angela, both in sparkly flapper dresses. Cushing used a photograph of his recently deceased wife Helen in the film, and his character tells Daphne that it is his dead wife. Carlson said that director Freddie Francis made Cushing do many takes of this scene in which he talks of his love for his dead wife, reducing the actor and the crew to tears.

A slightly dull gore fest redeemed by Cushing's ethereal melancholy.

* * *

Glorious 39   2009

Beautifully costumed but rather languid political conspiracy thriller written and directed by Stephen Poliakoff set in the run-up to the start of the Second World War and in the present day. Anne Keyes, elder daughter of an attractive aristocratic family, uncovers secret recordings revealing the extent of the appeasement movement. Christopher Lee plays one of the family, Walter, in the modern scenes. Said Poliakoff at the time of the film's release:

> It is truly thrilling to be making it with such a tremendous cast which combines some of the most exciting young talent in the country including Romola Garai, Eddie Redmayne, Juno Temple, Charlie Cox and David Tennant with such great names of the British film industry as Bill Nighy, Julie Christie and Christopher Lee.

* * *

Notes

1. Ezard, J. 'Historic moment when trumpets sounded to turn relief into spontaneous celebration', *Guardian*, 16/05/24
2. Jacobs, Stephen, *Saskatchewan History*, Spring 2007, Number 1
3. Jacobs, Stephen https://www.karloff.com/wordpress/ The Official Boris Karloff Web Site
4. Gullo, Christopher, In All Sincerity, Peter Cushing, p.118
5. Barnett, David 'Re-vamped: British horror film-makers Hammer and Amicus are back from the dead', *Guardian*, 29/10/2023
6. Clark, Nick 'Simon Oakes: It's a welcome return. We've managed to fire people's imaginations' *The Independent*, 20/02/2012
7. Gullo, Christopher In All Sincerity, Peter Cushing, p.115
8. Fisher, Terence *Films and Filming* July 1964
9. Nollen, Scott Allen Boris Karloff - A Gentleman's Life, Chapter 11
10. Doreen Hawkins' obituary, *The Telegraph*, 28/06/2013
11. Codr, Dwight, 'Arresting Monstrosity: Polio, Frankenstein, and the Horror Film' (PMLA, vol. 129, no. 2, 2014, pp.171–87)
12. McFerran, Ann *The Sunday Times*, Relative Values 05/05/2002

Further Reading

Bell, James, ed. *Gothic: The Dark Heart of Film* (BFI, 2013)
Bolton, Ferrell, *The Need for Moving Picture Theatres for Children* (Peabody Journal of Education, vol. 8, no. 2, 1930, pp.75–78)
Brosnan, John, *The Horror People* (The Book Service, 1976)
Charlton-Stevens, Uther, *Anglo-India and the End of Empire* (Oxford Academic, 2022, online edition)
Clarens, Carlos, *An Illustrated History of the Horror Film* (Putnam, 1967)
Cochrane, Claire, *Twentieth-Century British Theatre : Industry, Art and Empire* (Cambridge University Press, 2011)
Codr, Dwight, *Arresting Monstrosity: Polio, 'Frankenstein', and the Horror Film* (PMLA, vol. 129, no. 2, 2014, pp.171–87)
Curtis, James, *James Whale: A New World of Gods and Monsters* (University of Minnesota Press, 2003)
Cushing, Peter, *An Autobiography and Past Forgetting* (Midnight Marquee Press, Inc.,1986)
Del Vecchio, Deborah; Johnston, Tom, *Peter Cushing: The Gentle Man of Horror and His 91 Films* (McFarland and Co, 2009)
Feinholtz, Noam, *Death on Live TV: Cinema's Struggle Against Television* (Quarterly Review of Films and Video, 2020 Vol 37, No 3 pp 248–274)
Gullo, Christopher, *In All Sincerity: Peter Cushing* (Xlibris, 2004)
Harling, Philip, *Assisted Emigration and the Moral Dilemmas of the Mid-Victorian Imperial State* (The Historical Journal, vol. 59, no. 4, 2016, pp.1027–49)
Holmes, Sean P., *The Hollywood Star System and the Regulation of Actors' Labour, 1916–1934* (Film History, vol. 12, no. 1, 2000, pp.97–114)
Jacobs, Stephen, *Boris Karloff: More Than a Monster* (Tomahawk Press, 2010)
James, Robert, *Popular Film-Going in Britain in the Early 1930s* (Journal of Contemporary History, vol. 46, no. 2, 2011, pp.271–87
Jancovich, Mark, *Two Ways of Looking': The Critical Reception of 1940s Horror* (Cinema Journal, vol. 49, no. 3, 2010, pp.45–66)
King, Stephen, *Danse Macabre* (Everest House, 1981)
Lawrence, Jon, *Forging a Peaceable Kingdom: War, Violence, and Fear of Brutalization in Post–First World War Britain* (The Journal of Modern History, vol. 75, no. 3, 2003, pp.557–89)
Lee, Christopher, *Tall Dark and Gruesome* (Midnight Marquee Press, Inc. 1999)
Lucas, Tim, *The Arm of God.* (Film Comment, vol. 30, no. 6, 1994, pp.86–88)

Nemerov, Alexander, *Icons of Grief* (University of California Press, 2005)
Nollen, Scott Allen, *Boris Karloff: A Gentleman's Life* (BearManor Media 2018)
Nowell, Richard, ed., *Merchants of Menace : The Business of Horror* Cinema (Bloomsbury Academic & Professional, 2014)
Pirie, David, *A New Heritage of Horror: The English Gothic Cinema* (I.B. Taurus and Co, 2007)
Pointer, Michael, *Playing Sherlock Holmes: Interviews with John Wood, Robert Stephens and Christopher Lee,* Andrews UK Ltd., 2017
Porter, Bernard, *The Absent-Minded Imperialists : Empire, Society, and Culture in Britain* (Oxford University Press, 2006)
Priestley, J.B, *An English Journey* (1934)
Rigby Jonathan, *English Gothic: A Century of Horror Cinema* (Reynolds & Hearn, 2000)
Roper, Michael, *Between Manliness and Masculinity: The 'War Generation' and the Psychology of Fear in Britain, 1914–1950* (Journal of British Studies, vol. 44, no. 2, 2005, pp.343–62)
Sargeant, Alexi, *The Undeath of Cinema* (The New Atlantis, no. 53 (2017): pp.17–32)
Sedgwick, John, and Michael Pokorny, *The Film Business in the United States and Britain during the 1930s* (The Economic History Review, vol. 58, no. 1, 2005, pp.79–112)
Sweet, Matthew, *Shepperton Babylon: The Lost Worlds of British Cinema* (Faber, 2006)
Underwood, Peter, *Karloff: The Life of Boris Karloff* (Drake Publishers, 1972)
Wohl, Robert, *The Generation Of 1914* (Harvard University Press, 1979)

Dear Reader,

We hope you have enjoyed this book, but why not share your views on social media? You can also follow our pages to see more about our other products: facebook.com/penandswordbooks or follow us on X @penswordbooks

You can also view our products at www.pen-and-sword.co.uk (UK and ROW) or www.penandswordbooks.com (North America).

To keep up to date with our latest releases and online catalogues, please sign up to our newsletter at: www.pen-and-sword.co.uk/newsletter

If you would like a printed catalogue with our latest books, then please email: enquiries@pen-and-sword.co.uk or telephone: 01226 734555 (UK and ROW) or email: uspen-and-sword@casematepublishers.com or telephone: (610) 853-9131 (North America).

We respect your privacy and we will only use personal information to send you information about our products.

Thank you!